MINI

ENCYCLOPEDIA

SCIENCE

SCIENCE

Miles
KeLLy

First published as *Science* in 2010 by Miles Kelly Publishing Ltd
Harding's Barn, Bardfield End Green, Thaxted, Essex, CM6 3PX, UK

Copyright © Miles Kelly Publishing Ltd 2011

This edition printed 2014

2 4 6 8 10 9 7 5 3 1

Publishing Director Belinda Gallagher

Creative Director Jo Cowan

Cover Designer Jo Cowan

Series Designer Helen Bracey

Volume Designer Martin Lampon (Tiger Media Ltd)

Junior Designer Kayleigh Allen

Image Manager Liberty Newton

Indexer Jane Parker

Production Manager Elizabeth Collins

Reprographics Stephan Davis, Jennifer Cozens, Anthony Cambray

Assets Lorraine King

Contributers John Farndon, Steve Parker, Clint Twist

ISBN 978-1-78209-448-7

Printed in China

British Library Cataloguing-in-Publication Data
A catalogue record for this book is available from the British Library

Made with paper from a sustainable forest

www.mileskelly.net
info@mileskelly.net

Contents

Energy, force and motion

Electricity, magnetism and radiation

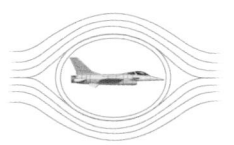
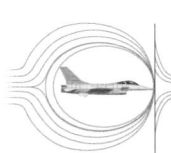
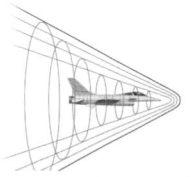

Frontiers of science

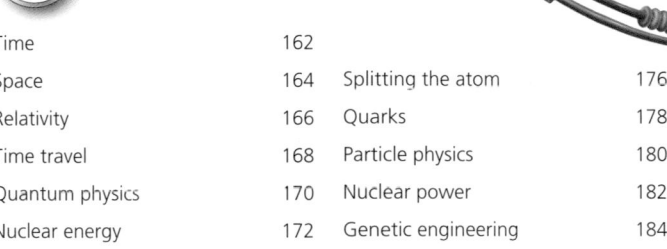

Technology

Planet Earth

Plants

Animals

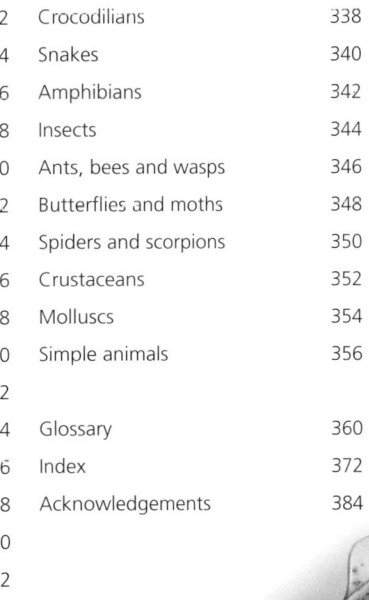

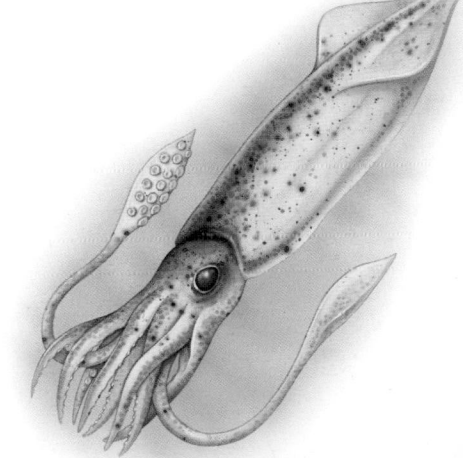

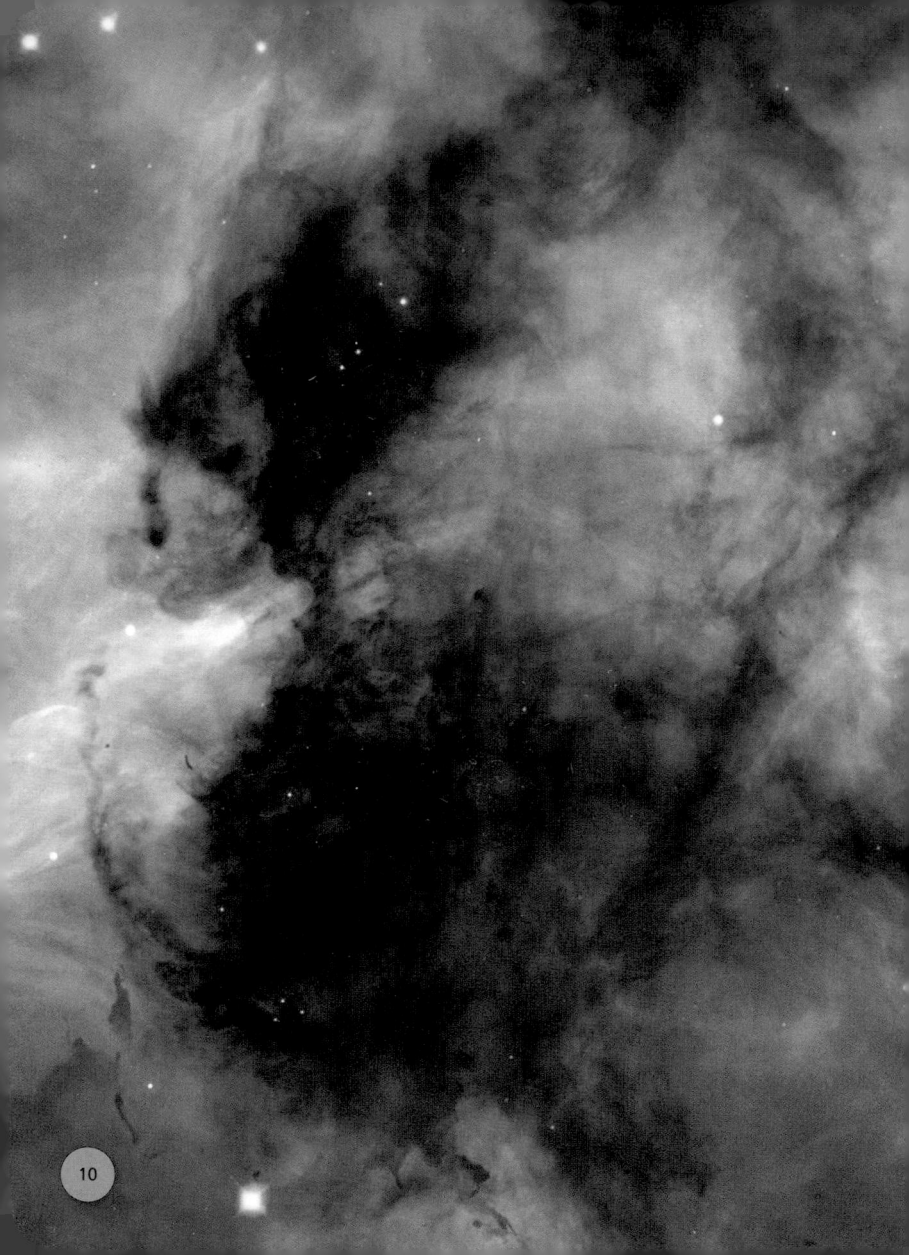

Matter

11

Atoms

⚙ **Atoms are the tiny particles** that make up every substance. An atom is the tiniest part of any basic substance.

⚙ **You could fit** two billion atoms on the full stop at the end of this sentence. The approximate number of atoms in the Universe would be expressed as 10 followed by 80 zeros.

⚙ **Atoms are mostly empty space**, dotted with a few even tinier particles, called subatomic particles.

⚙ **Every atom** has a dense core (nucleus) made up of two kinds of particle: protons and neutrons. Protons have a positive electrical charge, and neutrons have none.

⚙ **If an atom** were the size of a sports arena, its nucleus would be the size of a pea.

⚙ **Smaller, negatively charged** particles called electrons whizz around the nucleus.

⚙ **Protons and neutrons** are made from different combinations of even smaller particles, called quarks.

⚙ **Atoms can be split**, but are usually held together by the electrical attraction between positive protons and negative electrons, and the forces that hold the nucleus together.

⚙ **All the atoms** that make up an element are identical, so all atoms inside a particular element have the same number of protons. For example, an iron atom has 26 protons, while a gold atom has 79. The number of protons an atom has is known as its atomic number.

⚙ **Typically**, an atom has an equal number of protons and neutrons. An atom that has an unequal number of protons and neutrons is called an isotope.

▼ *Inside every atom, electrons (green) whizz around a dense nucleus built up from protons (red) and neutrons (yellow).*

Molecules

⚙ **A molecule** is two or more atoms that are bonded (held) together. It is usually the smallest particle of a substance that can exist independently.

▼ *Molecules of carbon dioxide gas are made from two atoms of oxygen (red) and one carbon (black).*

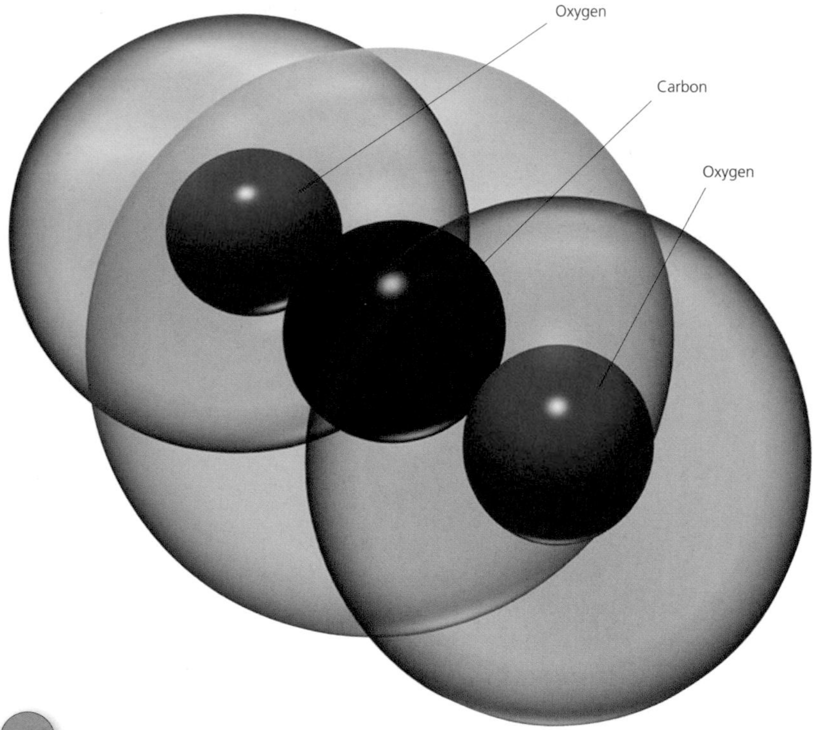

Oxygen

Carbon

Oxygen

- **The atoms** of the element hydrogen can exist only in pairs, or joined with atoms of other elements. A linked pair of hydrogen atoms is known as a hydrogen molecule.

- **The atoms in a molecule** are held together by chemical bonds (forces of attraction).

- **The structure** (shape) of a molecule depends on the arrangement of bonds that holds its atoms together.

- **Molecules made from atoms** of different elements are called compounds. Most molecules like this are made of just two or three kinds of atom.

- **The smallest part** of a compound that can exist independently is the molecule.

- **If the atoms** in the molecule of a compound were separated, the compound would cease to exist.

- **Chemical formulas** show the make-up of a molecule or compound. For example, the formula for ammonia is NH_3. This tells you that an ammonia molecule consists of one nitrogen atom and three hydrogen atoms.

- **The molecular mass** is the sum of the atomic weights of all atoms making up a molecule.

Electrons

- **Electrons are by far** the smallest of the three main, stable parts of every atom (the other two parts are protons and neutrons). In a normal atom there are the same number of electrons as protons.

- **Electrons were discovered** by English physicist J J Thomson in 1897. He realized that the glowing rays made by electricity inside a glass tube called a cathode ray tube were streams of tiny particles. Until then, an atom was thought to be a solid ball.

- **Electrons are much smaller** than protons. They are more than 1800 times lighter.

- **Electrons are** packets of energy travelling around the nuclei of atoms. It is impossible to pinpoint the exact location of an electron. An electron does not circle a nucleus as a planet circles the Sun. Instead it is more accurate to think of an electron wrapping around a nucleus like a cloud.

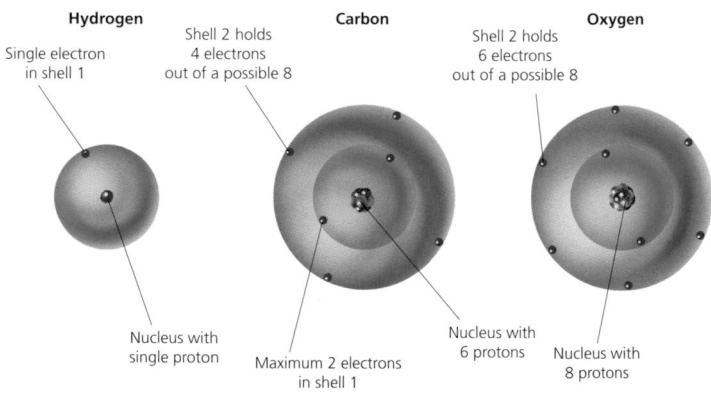

Hydrogen
Single electron in shell 1

Shell 2 holds 4 electrons out of a possible 8
Carbon

Shell 2 holds 6 electrons out of a possible 8
Oxygen

Nucleus with single proton

Maximum 2 electrons in shell 1

Nucleus with 6 protons

Nucleus with 8 protons

⚙ **Electrons have a tiny** negative electrical charge. This means they are attracted to positive electrical charges and pushed away by negative charges.

⚙ **Electrons remain close to the nucleus** because the protons in the nucleus have a positive charge that equals the negative charge of the electrons.

⚙ **Electrons circle the nucleus** in layers. The distance between the electron and nucleus depends on the energy level of the electrons in that layer. The greater an electron's energy, the farther it will be from the nucleus. Two electrons cannot occupy the same energy level. This is known as the exclusion principle.

⚙ **Electrons are arranged** in shells at different distances around the nucleus. Each shell can hold a particular number of electrons: the first shell can hold up to 2, the second up to 8, the third up to 18, the fourth up to 32, the fifth about 50, and the sixth about 72.

Sodium

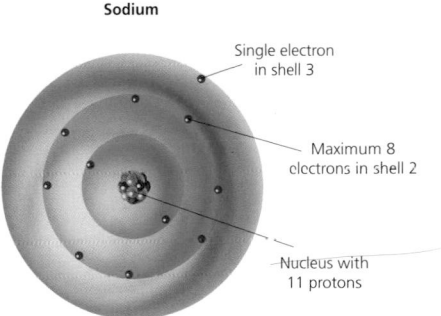

Single electron in shell 3

Maximum 8 electrons in shell 2

Nucleus with 11 protons

◀ *Every type of atom has a different number of electrons. An atom's chemical character depends on the number of electrons in its outer shell. The electron shell structures of four common atoms are shown here.*

Elements

⚙ **Elements are** the Universe's basic chemicals. Each element is made from atoms with a particular number of protons (the atomic number).

⚙ **Nearly 120 elements** have so far been recognized.

⚙ **Chemists have organized** the elements into a table called the Periodic Table.

⚙ **Of the most recently** identified elements, at least 20 were created by scientists and do not exist in nature.

⚙ **The most** recently discovered elements all have large, heavy atoms.

⚙ **Hydrogen is** the lightest element. It has an atomic number of 1.

▶ *Iron and other heavy elements were created when smaller atoms were forced together in giant supernova explosions in space.*

🔩 **The heaviest** element that occurs naturally is osmium, with an atomic number of 76.

🔩 **When elements combine** with other elements they form chemical compounds.

🔩 **New elements** are given temporary names based on their atomic number. For example, the new element with atomic number 116 is called ununhexium because *un* is Latin for 'one' and *hex* is Latin for 'six'.

DID YOU KNOW?

Scientists fired calcium atoms at californium atoms to create the element ununoctium, which has an atomic number of 118 and the heaviest-ever atoms.

Chemical bonds

▼ *To make the ionic bond in a sodium chloride (table salt) molecule, a sodium atom donates an electron to a chlorine atom.*

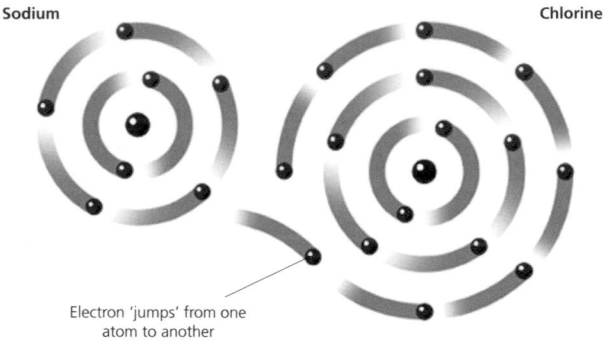

Sodium

Chlorine

Electron 'jumps' from one atom to another

⚙ **Chemical bonds** link atoms together to form molecules.

⚙ **Atoms bond** in different ways using the electrons in their outer shells.

⚙ **In ionic bonds**, one atom 'donates' one or more electrons to another.

⚙ **Ionic bonds occur** when atoms with just a few electrons in their outer shell 'donate' them to others with just a few missing from their outer shells.

⚙ **The atom** that loses electrons becomes positively charged and the atom that gains electrons becomes negatively charged. The two atoms are then drawn together by the electrical attraction of opposites.

⚙ **When sodium** forms an ionic bond with chlorine to create the sodium chloride (table salt) molecule, an electron is transferred from the sodium atom to the chlorine atom.

⚙ **Covalent bonds** occur when atoms share electrons.

⚙ **The shared electrons** are negatively charged, so they are all equally drawn to the positive nuclei of both atoms. The atoms are held together by the attraction between each nucleus and the shared electrons.

⚙ **Metals form giant structures** in which electrons in the outer shells of their atoms move freely. The atoms are held together by the attraction between the electrons and the positive nuclei.

▶ In this carbon dioxide molecule the carbon is held to two oxygen atoms by covalent bonds.

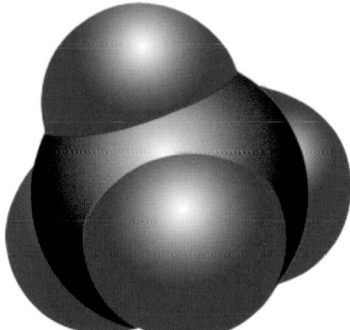

◀ Each of the four hydrogen atoms in methane (CH_4) shares its electron with the central carbon atom to create strong covalent bonds.

Chemical compounds

⚙ **Compounds** are substances that are made when the atoms of two or more different elements join together.

⚙ **The properties** of a compound are usually very different from the properties of the elements from which the compound is made.

⚙ **Atoms in a compound** are joined chemically, and can only be separated by a chemical reaction.

⚙ **All molecules** in a compound have identical combinations of atoms.

⚙ **A compound's scientific name** is usually a combination of the names of the elements that make it up, although it might have a different common name.

⚙ **In the chemical compound** sodium chloride (table salt), each molecule has one sodium and one chlorine atom.

⚙ **The chemical formula** tells you which and how many atoms a molecule contains. The chemical formula for water is H_2O because every water molecule has two hydrogen (H) atoms and one oxygen (O) atom.

⚙ **There are only** about 100 elements but they combine in different ways to form many millions of compounds.

▶ *Robot space probes landing on Mars have confirmed that it gets its red colour from rust – the chemical compound made when iron combines with the oxygen in water.*

⚙ **Combinations of the same elements**, such as carbon and hydrogen, can form many different compounds.

⚙ **Compounds** are either organic, which means they contain carbon atoms, or inorganic.

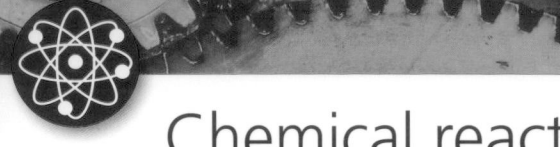

Chemical reactions

- **A chemical reaction** is when two or more elements or compounds interact chemically, breaking old bonds between atoms and making new ones.

- **The chemicals** in a chemical reaction are called the reactants. The results are called the products.

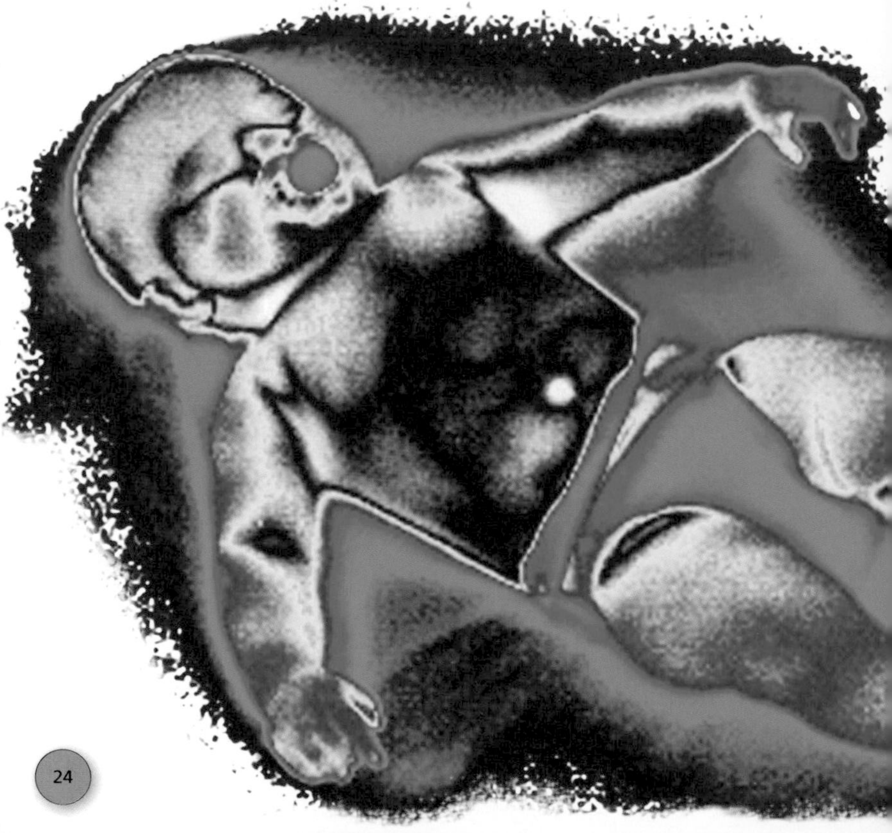

🔧 **The products** of a chemical reaction contain the same atoms as the reactants but in different combinations.

🔧 **The products** of the reaction will have the same total mass as the reactants.

🔧 **Most reactions** cannot be reversed – the products cannot be changed back into the reactants. For example, toasting bread causes an irreversible chemical reaction.

🔧 **In a chemical reaction**, elements may join to form compounds, while the elements making up compounds may be separated, or find partners in other compounds.

🔧 **A catalyst** is a substance that speeds up or enables a chemical reaction to happen.

🔧 **Nearly all reactions** involve energy. Some involve light or electricity, but most involve heat. Reactions that give out heat are called exothermic. Those that draw in heat are called endothermic.

🔧 **Oxidation is a reaction** in which oxygen combines with a substance. Burning is oxidation – as the fuel burns it combines with oxygen in the air. Reduction is a reaction in which a substance loses oxygen.

◄ *The heat of the human body, shown clearly in this thermal image, is maintained by chemical reactions involving fats and carbohydrates.*

Solutions

🔩 **A solution** is a liquid that has a solid dissolved within it. Tap water is a solution because it usually contains a number of dissolved solids, such as minerals.

🔩 **When a solid dissolves**, its molecules separate and mix completely with the molecules of the liquid it is in.

🔩 **The liquid** in a solution is called the solvent.

🔩 **The solid** dissolved in a solution is the solute.

🔩 **As a solute dissolves**, the solution becomes more concentrated (stronger) until at last it is saturated. This means that no more solute will dissolve – there is literally no more room in the solvent.

🔩 **If a saturated solution** is heated the solute will expand, making room for more solute to dissolve.

◀ A cup of tea is made up of the solvent, water and a number of solutes: the tea, milk and perhaps sugar.

▲ Stalagmites form when water containing dissolved calcium carbonate evaporates, leaving solid calcium carbonate behind.

⚙ **If a saturated** solution cools or is left to evaporate (the process in which a liquid turns into a vapour) there is less room for the solute. This will cause the solute to precipitate (come out of the solution).

⚙ **Precipitated solute** molecules often link together to form solid crystals.

Mixtures

⚙ **Mixtures are substances** that contain two or more different ingredients (elements or compounds).

⚙ **Many common substances** are mixtures, including air (a mix of oxygen, nitrogen and other gases), milk and oil.

⚙ **The properties of a mixture** are often a combination of the properties of its ingredients. For example, a mixture of sugar and water is both sweet-tasting and wet.

⚙ **Mixtures can often** be separated into their ingredients. This is usually done by making use of a property that is present in one ingredient but is in none of the others.

⚙ **Gold prospectors** can separate a mixture of gold and sand by swilling the mixture in water. Gold is denser than sand, so it is left behind as the sand is washed out.

⚙ **Metal is extracted** from ores in the ground by smelting (heating), which causes it to melt and drain out.

◀ *Air is already a mixture of gases, and pollution adds new substances to the mix.*

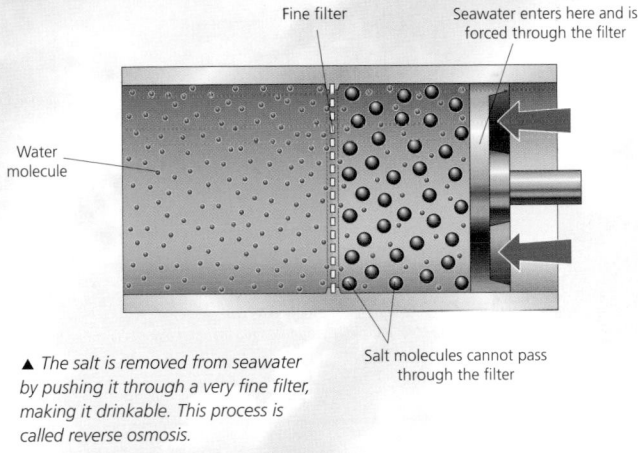

Fine filter

Seawater enters here and is forced through the filter

Water molecule

Salt molecules cannot pass through the filter

▲ *The salt is removed from seawater by pushing it through a very fine filter, making it drinkable. This process is called reverse osmosis.*

✿ **Mixtures of liquids** can be separated using a process called distillation, in which the mixture is heated, and the drops of vapour are collected as they condense.

✿ **This separates** the mixture because the different ingredients will evaporate and condense (change from a gas or vapour to a liquid) at different temperatures.

✿ **Crude oil is separated into petrol** and various other substances by distillation.

✿ **Solutions are a type of mixture** in two or more substances that are so thoroughly mixed that their molecules separate and combine.

Acids and alkalis

⚙ **Acids are solutions** that are made when certain substances containing hydrogen dissolve in water.

⚙ **Hydrogen atoms** have a single electron. When acid-making substances dissolve in water, the hydrogen atoms lose their electron, becoming positively charged ions (an ion is an atom that has gained or lost electrons).

⚙ **The strength** of an acid depends on how many hydrogen ions form. Mild acids, such as acetic acid (found in vinegar), have a sharp or sour taste. Strong acids, such as sulphuric acid, are highly corrosive (they dissolve metals).

⚙ **A base** is the opposite of an acid. Weak bases such as baking powder taste bitter and feel soapy. Strong bases such as caustic soda are corrosive.

⚙ **A base that dissolves** in water is called an alkali. Alkalis contain negatively charged ions – typically ions of hydrogen and oxygen, called hydroxide ions.

◄ *Citrus fruits such as oranges, lemons and limes have a tart taste because they contain a mild acid, called citric acid. It has a pH of 3.*

Hydrochloric acid   Vinegar

0   1   2   3   4   5   6   7

⚙ **When you add an acid** to an alkali, both substances are neutralized (they cancel each other out). The acid and alkali react together forming water and a salt.

⚙ **The strength of an acid** can be measured on the pH scale. The strongest acid has a pH of 1. The strongest alkali has a pH of 14. Pure water has a pH of about 7. It is neutral – neither acid nor alkali.

⚙ **Chemists use indicators** to test for acidity. An indicator is a substance such as litmus paper that changes colour depending on the pH of a solution.

> DID YOU KNOW?
> Hydrochloric acid in the stomach is essential for digestion. It has a pH of between 1 and 2.

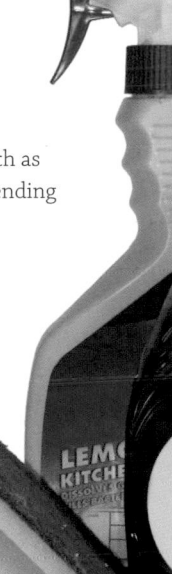

▶ *Household cleaners often contain alkalis to help them break down grease and fat. Some cleaners have a pH of 10.*

▼ *Universal indicator on the pH scale reveals acidity or alkalinity.*

Household cleaner

10   11   12   13   14

31

Soaps and salts

- **Soaps and detergents** are salts that can remove grease and dirt. Soaps are natural while detergents are synthetic. They are known as surfactants.

- **Surfactants have special molecules** that cling to dirt particles on surfaces and lift them away.

- **Surfactant molecules** are comprised of two parts. One part is hydrophilic (attracted to water), while the other is hydrophobic (repelled by water).

- **The hydrophobic tail** of a surfactant molecule digs its way into the dirt, while the hydrophilic head is drawn to the water.

- **Surfactants increase** water's ability to make things wet by reducing the water's surface tension.

▼ *Soap nuts are berries of the soapberry tree. They contain a natural, soapy chemical that can be used to wash clothes.*

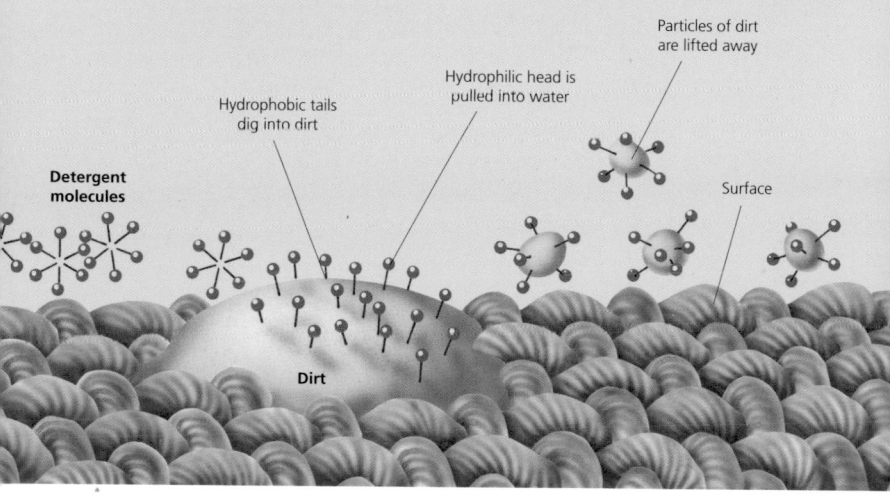

▲ Surfactant molecules on soap penetrate dirt with their water-hating tails, and so help lift the dirt off surfaces.

⚙ **Soap is made from** natural substances such as animal fats or vegetable oil combined with alkalis, such as sodium or potassium hydroxide. Most also include perfumes, colours and germicides (germ-killers) as well as a surfactant.

⚙ **Enzymes are molecules** that speed up chemical reactions. Certain enzymes can be added to detergents to help break down stains from natural substances such as blood, grease and starch.

⚙ **Biosurfactants are natural** surfactants. Some bacteria and yeast produce biosurfactants that may be used to clean up oil spillages in the future.

Solids, liquids, gases

⚙ **Most substances** can exist in three states – solid, liquid and gas. These are known as the three states of matter. Substances change from one state to another as temperature and pressure change.

⚙ **As temperatures rise**, solids melt to become liquids. As they rise further, liquids evaporate to become vapours or gases. The temperature at which a solid melts is known as its melting point. The melting point of ice is normally 0°C, but increased pressure will lower the melting point.

⚙ **The boiling point** is the maximum temperature a liquid can reach before it turns to gas, although liquids can partially evaporate at well below the boiling point.

⚙ **The kinetic theory of matter** explains the changes from solid to liquid to gas in terms of the movement of the molecules. The movement of molecules depends on their energy. The more a substance is heated, the more energetic its molecules are.

⚙ **Solids have a definite shape** because their molecules are bonded in a rigid structure, so they can only vibrate.

⚙ **A liquid** flows and takes up the shape of any container into which it is poured. This is because its molecules are bonded loosely enough to move over each other.

⚙ **A gas**, such as air, does not have any definite shape or fixed volume. This is because its molecules are barely bound together at all, and are free to move around.

⚙ **When a gas cools,** its molecules slow down until bonds form between them to create drops of liquid. This process is called condensation.

⚙ **There are two** other states of matter – plasmas and Bose-Einstein condensates. Plasmas are special types of gas in which all the particles are electrically charged. Lightning bolts turn air into a plasma. Bose-Einstein condensates were created by scientists in 1995. They form when temperatures are so low that all the atoms almost stop moving.

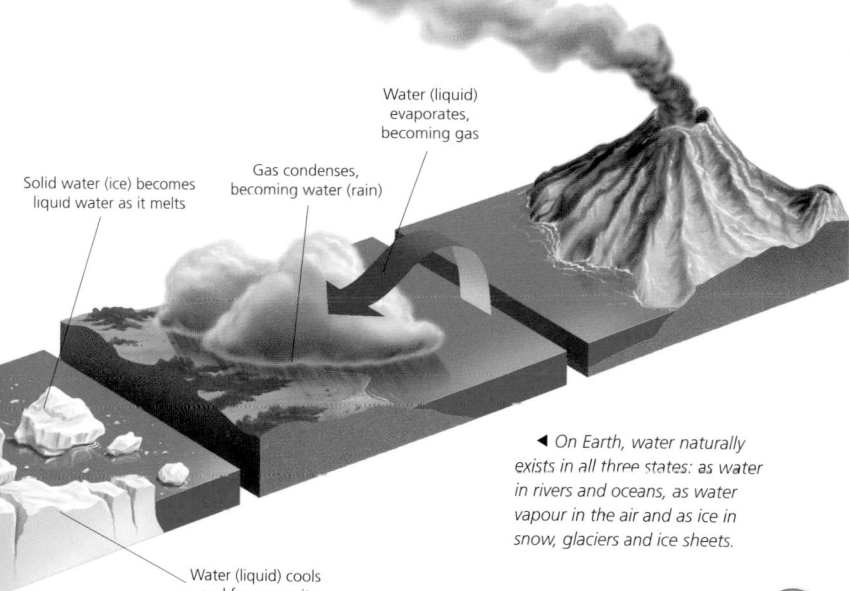

Water (liquid) evaporates, becoming gas

Gas condenses, becoming water (rain)

Solid water (ice) becomes liquid water as it melts

◄ On Earth, water naturally exists in all three states: as water in rivers and oceans, as water vapour in the air and as ice in snow, glaciers and ice sheets.

Water (liquid) cools and freezes as it becomes ice (solid)

Moving particles

⚙ **Molecules are constantly moving.** The speed at which they move depends on temperature. Heat gives molecules extra energy, making them move faster.

⚙ **In 1827**, Scottish botanist Robert Brown examined microscopic pollen grains in water and saw that they were moving. They were being knocked by moving molecules too small to be seen. This is called Brownian motion.

▼ *The movement of molecules increases dramatically as substances change from solid to liquid to gas to plasma.*

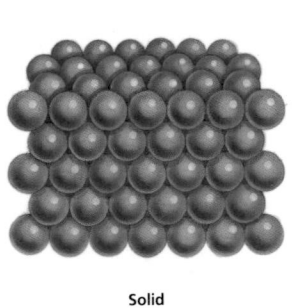

Solid

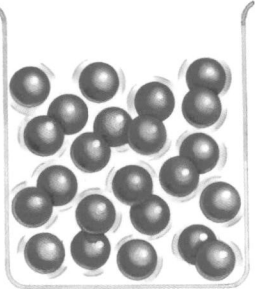

Liquid

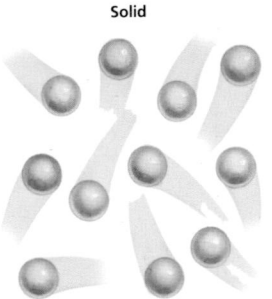

Gas

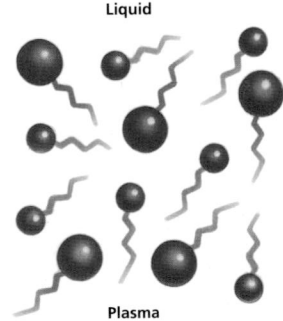

Plasma

- **In a solid**, molecules can't move around. This means that you can pick up solids, whereas liquids just slip through your hands.

- **Liquid molecules** can slide past each other, so they can flow to take the shape of whatever is holding them.

- **Without the movement of liquid molecules**, materials would not move in and out of the cells in our bodies.

- **The atoms** in a gas are so far apart that they zoom about freely in all directions.

DID YOU KNOW?

The Sun's heat causes air molecules at the edge of the atmosphere to move so fast that many escape Earth's gravity and zoom off into space.

▶ In a plasma globe, electricity turns gases into a glowing, charged plasma filled with beams of light that move when a hand touches the globe's surface.

Crystals

- **Crystals are particular kinds** of solid that are made from a regular arrangement, or lattice, of atoms. Most rocks and metals are crystals, as are snowflakes and salt.

- **Most crystals** have regular, geometrical shapes with smooth faces and sharp corners. They grow in dense masses, such as metals. Some crystals grow separately, like grains of sugar.

- **Crystals were named** after chunks of quartz that the ancient Greeks called krystallos, which they believed were unmeltable ice.

- **Crystallization is the process** in which crystals form. It occurs when liquid evaporates or molten solids cool, and the chemicals dissolved in them solidify.

- **Crystals that grow** as atoms attach themselves to the lattice, just as icicles grow when water freezes onto them.

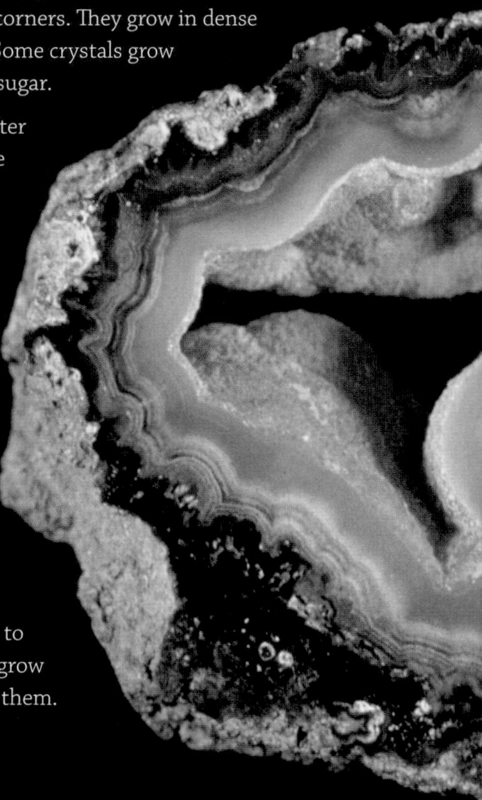

⚙ **The smallest crystals** are microscopic, but occasionally crystals of a mineral such as beryl may grow to the size of telegraph poles.

⚙ **A liquid crystal** is a crystal that can flow, like a liquid, but has a regular pattern of atoms, like a solid.

⚙ **A liquid crystal** may change colour or go dark when the alignment of its atoms is disrupted by electricity or heat. Liquid crystal displays (LCDs) use a tiny electric current to make the crystals twist light passing through them.

⚙ **X-ray crystallography** uses X-rays to study the structure of atoms in crystals. It is also used to study biological molecules, and it is how we know the structure of many important life substances such as DNA.

◄ Crystals often form from mineral-rich liquids on the lining of cavities in rocks called geodes.

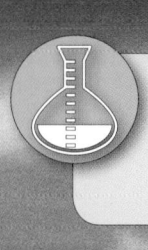

Materials and chemicals

The Periodic Table

⚙ **There are 118** known elements. Of these, 92 are known to occur naturally on Earth, while the rest were created by scientists. Two of these, plutonium and neptunium, are now known to occur naturally.

⚙ **In the table**, all the elements are ordered by atomic number (the number of protons in an atom of a particular element). The atomic number is shown in the top left corner of every element entry.

⚙ **The atomic mass** is shown in the bottom left of every entry. If you subtract an element's atomic number from its mass, the result (rounded to the nearest whole number) is a guide for how many neutrons there are in that element's atoms. For example, calcium's atomic number is 20 and its mass is 40, so it has 20 neutrons.

⚙ **The vertical columns** in the table are called groups. The horizontal rows are called periods. As you move across the table from left to right, the number of electrons increases.

⚙ **Each group** is made up of elements with a certain number of electrons in their outer shell. This is what largely determines the element's character. All the elements in each group have similar properties.

⚙ **Each period starts** on the left with a highly reactive alkali metal of group 1. Each atom of elements in group 1 has a single electron in its outer shell. Every period ends on the right with a stable 'noble' gas of group 18. These elements have the full number of electrons in their outer shell and so they are unreactive.

▶ *The Periodic Table arranges all the chemical elements in columns and rows according to their atomic number, showing clearly how they are related.*

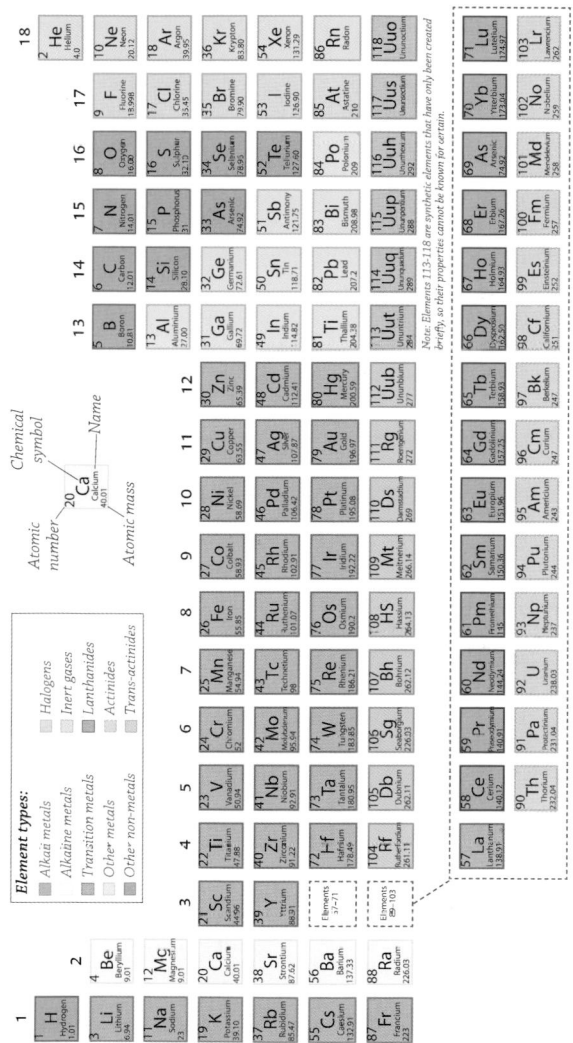

Element types:

- Alkali metals
- Alkaline metals
- Transition metals
- Other metals
- Other non-metals
- Halogens
- Inert gases
- Lanthanides
- Actinides
- Trans-actinides

Atomic number → 20 ← Chemical symbol
Ca
Calcium
40.01 ← Atomic mass
Name

| 1 | 2 | 3 | 4 | 5 | 6 | 7 | 8 | 9 | 10 | 11 | 12 | 13 | 14 | 15 | 16 | 17 | 18 |

1
H
Hydrogen
1.01

3 Li Lithium 6.94 — 4 Be Beryllium 9.01

11 Na Sodium 23 — 12 Mg Magnesium 24.31

19 K Potassium 39.10 — 20 Ca Calcium 40.01 — 21 Sc Scandium 44.96 — 22 Ti Titanium 47.88 — 23 V Vanadium 50.94 — 24 Cr Chromium 52 — 25 Mn Manganese 54.94 — 26 Fe Iron 55.85 — 27 Co Cobalt 58.93 — 28 Ni Nickel 58.69 — 29 Cu Copper 63.55 — 30 Zn Zinc 65.39

37 Rb Rubidium 85.47 — 38 Sr Strontium 87.62 — 39 Y Yttrium 88.91 — 40 Zr Zirconium 91.22 — 41 Nb Niobium 92.91 — 42 Mo Molybdenum 95.94 — 43 Tc Technetium 98 — 44 Ru Ruthenium 101.07 — 45 Rh Rhodium 102.91 — 46 Pd Palladium 106.42 — 47 Ag Silver 107.87 — 48 Cd Cadmium 112.41

55 Cs Caesium 132.91 — 56 Ba Barium 137.33 — Elements 57–71 — 72 Hf Hafnium 178.49 — 73 Ta Tantalum 180.95 — 74 W Tungsten 183.85 — 75 Re Rhenium 186.21 — 76 Os Osmium 190.2 — 77 Ir Iridium 192.22 — 78 Pt Platinum 195.08 — 79 Au Gold 196.97 — 80 Hg Mercury 200.59

87 Fr Francium 223 — 88 Ra Radium 226.03 — Elements 89–103 — 104 Rf Rutherfordium 261.11 — 105 Db Dubnium 262.11 — 106 Sg Seaborgium 266.03 — 107 Bh Bohrium 262.12 — 108 Hs Hassium 264.13 — 109 Mt Meitnerium 266.14 — 110 Ds Darmstadtium 269 — 111 Rg Roentgenium 272 — 112 Uub Ununbium 277

13 B Boron 10.81 — 14 C Carbon 12.01 — 15 N Nitrogen 14.01 — 16 O Oxygen 16.00 — 17 F Fluorine 18.998 — 18 He Helium 4.0

13 Al Aluminium 27.00 — 14 Si Silicon 28.09 — 15 P Phosphorus 31 — 16 S Sulphur 32.13 — 17 Cl Chlorine 35.45 — 18 Ar Argon 39.95

31 Ga Gallium 69.72 — 32 Ge Germanium 72.61 — 33 As Arsenic 74.92 — 34 Se Selenium 78.95 — 35 Br Bromine 79.90 — 36 Kr Krypton 83.80

49 In Indium 114.82 — 50 Sn Tin 118.71 — 51 Sb Antimony 121.75 — 52 Te Tellurium 127.60 — 53 I Iodine 126.90 — 54 Xe Xenon 131.29

81 Tl Thallium 204.38 — 82 Pb Lead 207.2 — 83 Bi Bismuth 208.98 — 84 Po Polonium 209 — 85 At Astatine 210 — 86 Rn Radon 222

113 Uut Ununtrium 284 — 114 Uuq Ununquadium 289 — 115 Uup Ununpentium 288 — 116 Uuh Ununhexium 292 — 117 Uus Ununseptium 294 — 118 Uuo Ununoctium —

Lanthanides:
57 La Lanthanum 138.91 — 58 Ce Cerium 140.12 — 59 Pr Praseodymium 140.91 — 60 Nd Neodymium 144.24 — 61 Pm Promethium 145 — 62 Sm Samarium 150.36 — 63 Eu Europium 151.96 — 64 Gd Gadolinium 157.25 — 65 Tb Terbium 158.93 — 66 Dy Dysprosium 162.50 — 67 Ho Holmium 164.93 — 68 Er Erbium 167.26 — 69 Tm Thulium 168.93 — 70 Yb Ytterbium 173.04 — 71 Lu Lutetium 174.97

Actinides:
90 Th Thorium 232.04 — 91 Pa Protactinium 231.04 — 92 U Uranium 238.03 — 93 Np Neptunium 237 — 94 Pu Plutonium 244 — 95 Am Americium 243 — 96 Cm Curium 247 — 97 Bk Berkelium 247 — 98 Cf Californium 251 — 99 Es Einsteinium 252 — 100 Fm Fermium 257 — 101 Md Mendelevium 258 — 102 No Nobelium 259 — 103 Lr Lawrencium 262

Note: Elements 113–118 are synthetic elements that have only been created briefly, so their properties cannot be known for certain.

Metals

⚙ **Most of all known elements** – in fact 75 percent of them – are metals.

⚙ **Typical metals** are hard but also malleable, which means they can be hammered into thin sheets without breaking.

⚙ **Metals are usually shiny**, strong, and conduct (transmit) heat and electricity well.

⚙ **Instead of forming** separate molecules, metal atoms 'knit' together with metallic bonds to form lattice structures (regular three-dimensional arrangements).

⚙ **All metals** have electron shells that are less than half-full. In chemical reactions, metals give up their electrons to non-metals.

◀ Molten gold is poured into moulds at a smelting plant. When the bullion cools, it forms bars that are about 99.99 percent pure.

⚙ **Most metals** occur naturally in the ground in rocks called ores. Gold, copper, mercury, platinum, silver and a few other rare metals occur naturally in their pure form.

⚙ **Mercury** is the only metal that is liquid at normal temperatures. It melts at −38.87°C.

⚙ **When the element ununquadium** (atomic number 114) was created in 1999, it was thought to be a new metal, but now scientists think it may be more like a gas.

▶ *The strength of steel is an essential component in skyscrapers such as the Petronas towers in Kuala Lumpur, Malaysia.*

Alloys

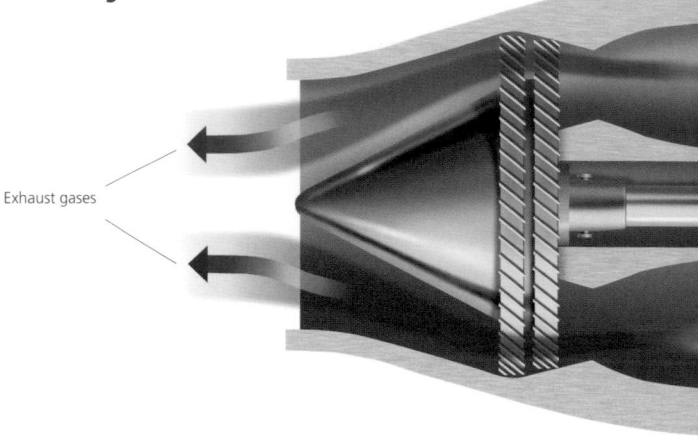

Exhaust gases

- **An alloy** is a man-made combination of metals, in which one metal is added to another to combine their properties.

- **Bronze is an alloy** of copper and tin. Copper is a soft metal, and combining it with tin makes it stronger. People discovered how to make bronze around 6000 years ago. Prior to this, tools and weapons were made from stone or copper.

- **Brass is an alloy** made from copper combined with zinc.

- **Pewter is an alloy** made from tin with a little copper and antimony to harden it. It was widely used for tableware in the Middle Ages.

- **Steel is a strong alloy** made of iron with traces of carbon and other metals such as tungsten added. It is used in a variety of products from engineering materials to kitchen equipment.

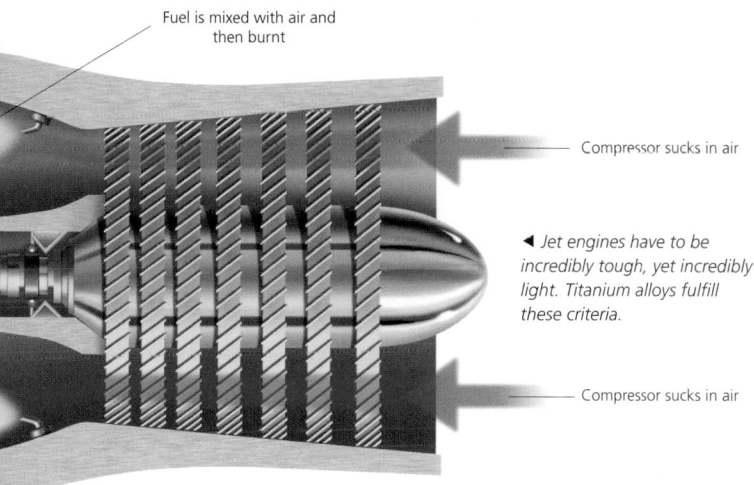

Fuel is mixed with air and then burnt

Compressor sucks in air

◀ Jet engines have to be incredibly tough, yet incredibly light. Titanium alloys fulfill these criteria.

Compressor sucks in air

- ✿ **Spacecraft** incorporate incredibly light, tough alloys such as aluminium and lithium.

- ✿ **Titanium alloys** are among the strongest, lightest and most heat- and corrosion-resistant of all elements, which is why they are used in aircraft and spaceships.

- ✿ **Data is stored** on the grooves on the surface of CDs and DVDs. These grooves are made of an alloy called GST, made from tellurium, antimony and germanium. GST may in future be used in computer memories.

- ✿ **In 2008**, scientists created an alloy of boron, aluminium and magnesium with titanium boride that is almost as tough as diamond and as slippery as Teflon®, so it can be used to protect mechanical parts from wear and tear.

Aluminium

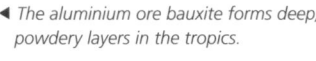

◄ The aluminium ore bauxite forms deep, powdery layers in the tropics.

🔩 **Aluminium is by far** the most common metal on Earth's surface, making up 8 percent of Earth's crust.

🔩 **Aluminium** never occurs naturally in its pure form – it is typically found combined with other chemicals in minerals in ore rocks.

🔩 **The major source** of aluminium is layers of the soft ore rock bauxite, which is mostly aluminium hydroxide.

🔩 **Alum powders** made from aluminium compounds are used in the process of dyeing fabric. Pure aluminium was first made in 1825 by Danish scientist Hans Øersted.

🔩 **Aluminium production** was the first industrial process to use hydroelectricity when a plant was set up on the river Rhine, in Europe, in 1887.

🔩 **Aluminium is silver** in colour when freshly made, but it quickly tarnishes to white in the air. It is very slow to corrode and is one of the lightest of all metals.

🔩 **Aluminium oxide** can crystallize into one of the hardest minerals, corundum, used to sharpen knives.

- **Aluminium melts** at 650°C and boils at 2450°C.

- **Each year** 21 million tonnes of aluminium are made, mostly from bauxite dug up in Brazil and New Guinea.

▼ Duraluminium (aluminium with a little copper and manganese) is widely used for building aircraft because it is so light and tough.

Iron and steel

⚙ **Iron is the most** common element. It makes up 35 percent of the Earth, most of it in the core.

⚙ **Iron is found** in iron ores, rather than in its pure form. The ores are heated in blast furnaces to extract the iron.

⚙ **The chemical symbol** for iron is Fe from the word *ferrum*, which is Latin for 'iron'. Iron compounds are described as ferrous or ferric.

⚙ **Iron has an atomic number** of 26 and an atomic weight of 55.85.

▼ *Molten iron is poured into a steelmaking furnace in a steel mill. The temperature of the liquid metal is about 1500°C.*

▲ *These steel cookers are made made 'stainless' by adding chromium to keep the steel permanently shiny and smooth.*

⚙ **Iron conducts heat** and electricity quite well and dissolves in water very slowly. Iron is easily magnetized, but also loses its magnetism easily.

⚙ **Iron oxide** (rust) forms when iron combines with oxygen, especially in the presence of moisture.

⚙ **Cast iron** is iron with 2–4 percent carbon and 1–3 percent silicon and is suitable for pouring into moulds. Wrought iron is almost pure. Carbon is removed to make it easy to bend and shape for railings and gates.

⚙ **Iron is made into steel** by adding traces of carbon. Steel is used in a variety of products including cars and railway lines.

⚙ **Sixty percent of all steel** is made by the basic oxygen process in which oxygen is blasted over molten iron to burn out impurities.

⚙ **Special alloy steels** such as chromium steels can be made from scrap iron (which is low in impurities) in an electric arc furnace.

Copper

- **Copper has been used** for more than 10,000 years. It was one of the first metals used by humans.

- **It is one of the few metals** that occurs naturally in a pure form, but most of the copper we use today comes from ores such as cuprite and chalcopyrite.

- **The biggest deposits** of pure copper are found in volcanic lavas in the Andes Mountains, Chile.

- **Copper is by far** the best low-cost conductor of electricity, so it is widely used for electrical cables.

▼ *Many modern buildings are coated in copper because of its attractive colour, both when new and when it corrodes to verdigris.*

▼ The familiar pale green colour of the Statue of Liberty comes from a thin coating of copper carbonate that has formed on the surface.

- ☼ **It is also** a good conductor of heat, so it is used to make saucepan bases.

- ☼ **Copper is so ductile** (easily stretched) that a copper rod as thick as a finger can be stretched out thinner than a human hair.

- ☼ **After being exposed to the air** for some time, copper gets a thin, green coating of copper carbonate. This is called verdigris, which means 'green' in Greek.

Calcium

🔩 **Calcium is a soft**, silvery-white metal. It does not occur naturally in its pure form and is the fifth most abundant element on Earth.

🔩 **Calcium is one of six** alkaline earth metals that make up group 2 of the Periodic Table.

🔩 **Most calcium compounds** are white solids called limes. These include substances such as chalk, porcelain, enamel (found on teeth), cement, seashells and limescale.

🔩 **The word** 'lime' comes from the Latin for 'slime'.

🔩 **Quicklime is calcium oxide**, so-called because when water drips on it, it twists and swells as if it is alive ('quick' is the Old English word for 'living').

◄ *You can get the calcium your body needs for healthy teeth and bones by drinking milk.*

◄ The eggshell that protects a chick until it is ready to hatch is usually made from calcium carbonate.

⚙ **Slaked lime** is calcium hydroxide. It may be called 'slaked' because it slakes (quenches) a plant's thirst for lime in acid soils.

⚙ **Limelight was the bright light** used by theatres in the days before electricity, made by applying a mix of oxygen and hydrogen to pellets of calcium. It was replaced by electric lighting, but this is why people in the public eye are often referred to as being 'in the limelight'.

⚙ **Calcium adds rigidity** to bones and teeth and helps to control muscles. Your body gets it from dairy, such as milk and cheese.

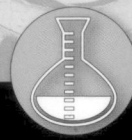

Oxygen

🔹 **Oxygen is the second** most plentiful element on Earth. It is a colourless, odourless, tasteless gas, and makes up 20.94 percent of the air.

🔹 **Oxygen is one of the most** reactive elements, so in the Earth's crust it is usually found joined with other chemicals in compounds.

🔹 **Molecules of oxygen** in the air are made from two oxygen atoms. Molecules of the gas ozone have three oxygen atoms.

🔹 **Oxygen becomes liquid** at −182.962°C. Liquid oxygen is pale blue in colour. It freezes at −218.4°C.

🔹 **Living organisms** are dependent upon oxygen because it joins with other chemicals in living cells such as glucose to create energy. This process is known as cellular respiration.

🔹 **Liquid oxygen** (LOX) is combined with fuels such as kerosene to produce rocket fuel.

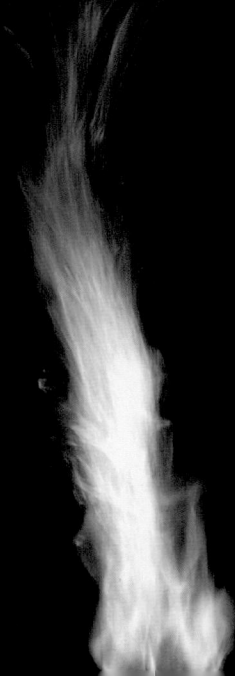

◄ Oxygen is needed for combustion to take place.

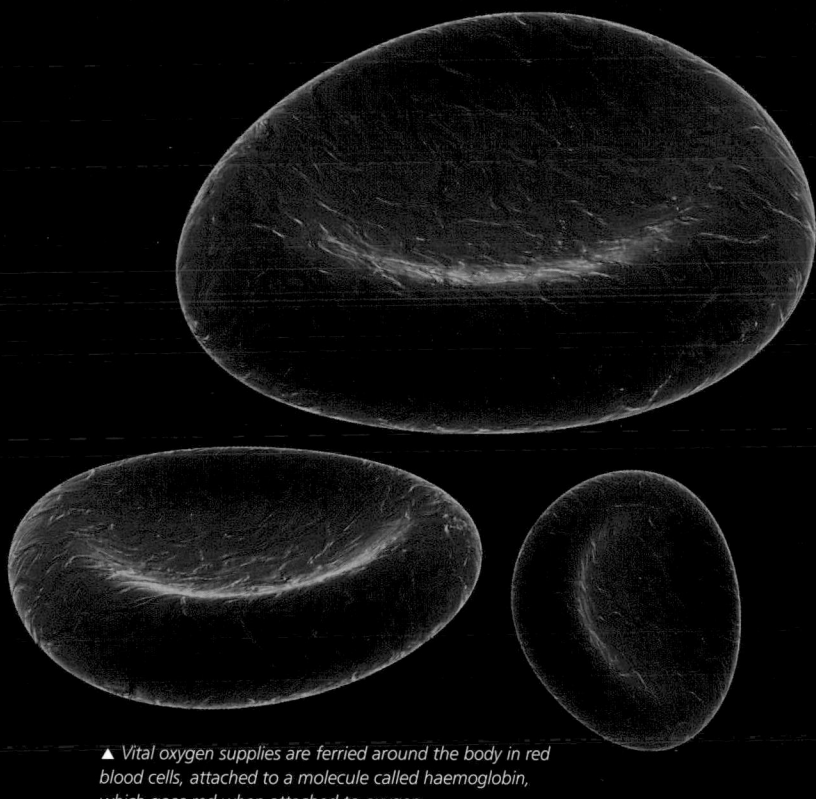

▲ Vital oxygen supplies are ferried around the body in red
blood cells, attached to a molecule called haemoglobin,
which goes red when attached to oxygen.

✱ **Oxygen was discovered** by both the Swedish chemist Carl
Scheele and the English clergyman and scientist Joseph Priestley
independently during the 1770s.

✱ **The word** 'oxygen' means acid-forming. Oxygen was named in
1779 by Antoine Lavoisier.

Nitrogen

⚙ **Nitrogen makes up** 78.08 percent of the air. Like oxygen, it is a colourless, tasteless, odourless gas.

⚙ **Unlike oxygen**, nitrogen is inert (unreactive), but it is still vital to life.

⚙ **Nitrogen becomes liquid** at −196°C and freezes at −210°C.

⚙ **Liquid nitrogen can be used** to freeze substances so quickly that they are practically undamaged by the freezing process. Foods such as fruit can be preserved (made to stay fresh for longer) by being sprayed with liquid nitrogen.

⚙ **Lightning supplies** the energy for reactions between nitrogen and oxygen. The result is nitrogen oxide, which combines with moisture to form around 250,000 tonnes of nitric acid per day, which is washed into soil by rain.

⚙ **Compounds of nitrogen** are called nitrates and nitrites. Both are important soil nutrients that help plants grow.

⚙ **During a deep-sea dive**, water pressure can affect a diver's lungs, causing extra nitrogen to dissolve in the blood. If the diver surfaces too quickly the nitrogen forms bubbles, causing a painful condition known as 'the bends', which can be fatal.

> **DID YOU KNOW?**
>
> When you 'crack' your knuckles, the noise you hear is actually popping bubbles of nitrogen gas, which is formed from the fluid in the joints.

▼ *Liquid nitrogen is so cold, it can be used to make ice cream in less than ten minutes.*

Hydrogen

⚙ **Hydrogen is the lightest** of all gases and elements – a swimming pool full of it would weigh just 1 kg.

⚙ **With just one proton** and one electron, hydrogen is the first element in the Periodic Table.

⚙ **Of every 6000** hydrogen atoms, one has a neutron as well as a proton in its nucleus, making it twice as heavy. This atom is called 'deuterium'.

⚙ **Some rare hydrogen atoms** have two neutrons as well as the proton, making them three times as heavy. These are called 'tritium'.

⚙ **The most common substance** in the Universe, hydrogen makes up more than 90 percent of the Universe's weight. It was the first element to form after the Universe began, and billions of years passed before another element formed.

⚙ **Most hydrogen** on Earth occurs in combination with other elements, such as oxygen in water. Pure hydrogen occurs naturally in a few places, such as small underground pockets and as tiny traces in the air.

⚙ **As one of the most** reactive gases, hydrogen is highly flammable, so it often bursts into flames.

⚙ **Under extreme pressure** hydrogen becomes a metal – the most electrically conductive metal of all.

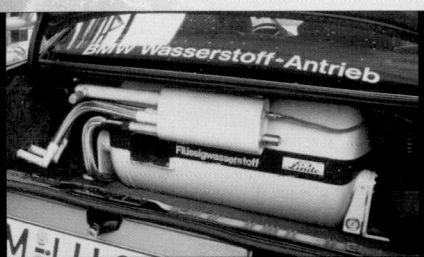

▶ BMW's 735i is one of a new generation of experimental clean cars running on hydrogen fuel.

🌣 **A hydrogen fuel cell** creates electrical power from a chemical reaction between hydrogen (the fuel) and oxygen (the oxidant).

🌣 **In the future**, many cars could be powered by hydrogen fuel cells, which – unlike regular fuels – produce water, not polluting fumes. However, until filling stations start to sell hydrogen, anyone wanting to use it has to make it from other fuels such as methanol.

🌣 **Fuel for hydrogen-powered cars** could be made by using solar cells (electric cells that convert solar energy into electricity) to split water molecules into their component parts of hydrogen and oxygen. Cars powered by this method would essentially run on a clean mixture of water and sunlight!

🌣 **A hydrogen bomb** is a thermonuclear weapon that uses a small nuclear explosion to fuse deuterium and tritium atoms together. It is called a thermonuclear weapon because of the high temperatures needed to fuse the deuterium atoms (50 million°C) and the tritium atoms (400 million°C).

◀ Hydrogen bombs are among the most destructive of all nuclear bombs, a thousand times more powerful than basic atom bombs.

Halogens

⚙️ **Halogens are the non-metal** chemical elements fluorine, chlorine, bromine, iodine and astatine, which make salts when they form compounds with metals. The word 'halogen' means salt-forming.

⚙️ **Many salts in the sea** are compounds of a halogen and a metal, such as sodium chloride and magnesium chloride.

⚙️ **Together the halogens** form group 17 of the Periodic Table – elements that have seven electrons in their outer shells.

⚙️ **Fluorine and chlorine** are both gases. Fluorine is pale yellow, while chlorine is greenish in colour. Bromine is a red liquid, and iodine is a black solid.

⚙️ **Astatine** is an unstable element that only survives by itself briefly. It is usually made artificially.

⚙️ **All halogen atoms** have one electron missing, so they take on another to become negative ions.

⚙️ **Halogens are used** in lamps. As a halogen lamp heats, its tungsten filament starts to evaporate. Halogen gas combines with the atoms of tungsten redepositing them on the filament so the lamp burns for longer.

DID YOU KNOW?

Fluorides (fluorine compounds) are often added to drinking water to prevent tooth decay.

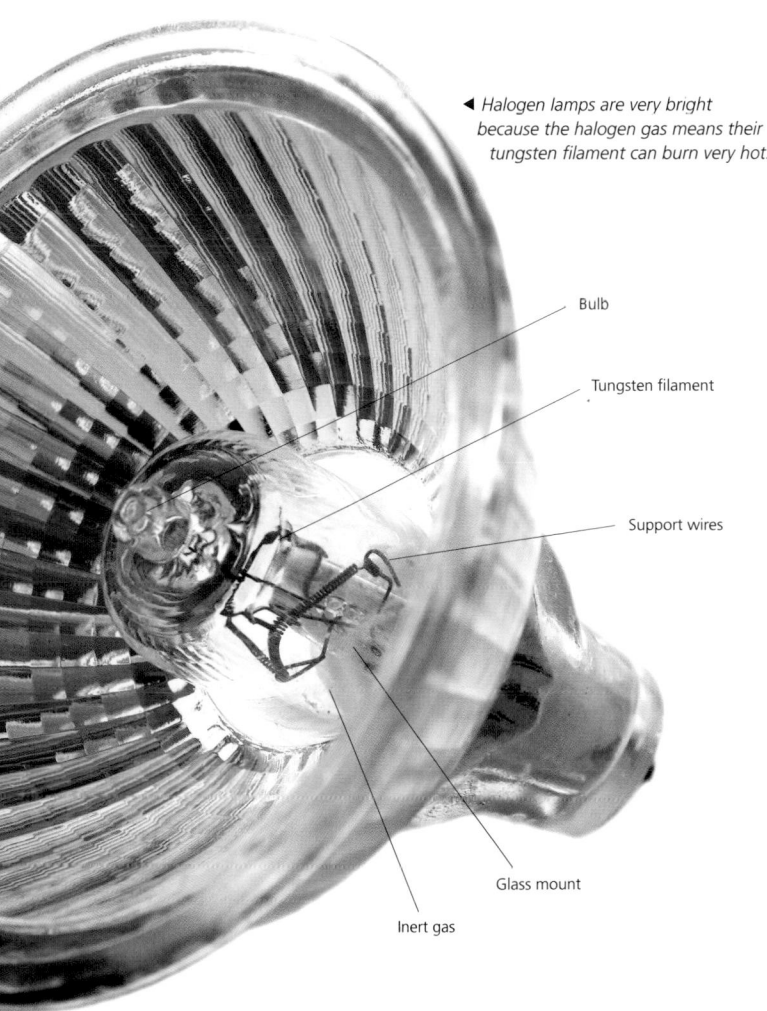

◄ Halogen lamps are very bright because the halogen gas means their tungsten filament can burn very hot.

Bulb

Tungsten filament

Support wires

Glass mount

Inert gas

Noble gases

⚙ **The noble gases** are a group of gases that are unreactive. They are named because they stay 'nobly' aloof from reactions with other elements.

⚙ **Six noble gases** – helium, neon, argon, krypton, xenon and radon – occur naturally. A seventh, called ununoctium, has recently been created.

⚙ **All noble gases** are unreactive, as their atoms have a full complement of electrons in their outer shells.

⚙ **Only a few hundred compounds** involving noble gases have ever been made.

▼ *These glowing illuminated signs are made from glass tubes filled with noble gases.*

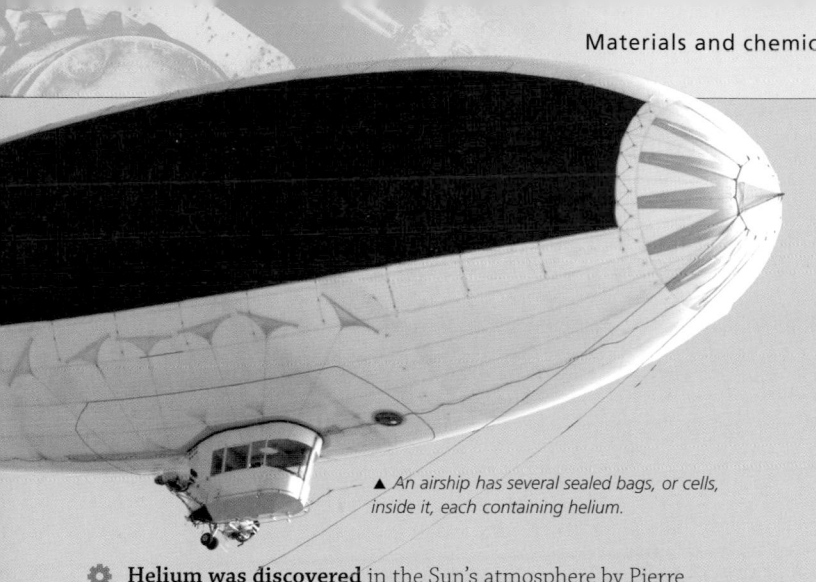

▲ An airship has several sealed bags, or cells, inside it, each containing helium.

⚙ **Helium was discovered** in the Sun's atmosphere by Pierre Janssen and Joseph Lockyer in 1868 by analyzing its colour.

⚙ **Helium is often** used to fill aeronautical balloons and airship bags because it is much lighter than air but not dangerously explosive like hydrogen.

⚙ **British chemist William Ramsay** discovered the gases argon, krypton, neon and xenon in the 1890s by distilling liquefied air.

⚙ **The highly toxic noble gas** radon was discovered in 1898 by German chemist Friedrich Dorn.

⚙ **In a gas discharge tube**, an electric current is sent through a plasma of noble gas, causing the gas to glow brightly. Each noble gas creates its own colour. Neon lights are bright red-orange. Argon lights are lavender.

DID YOU KNOW?
If you inhale the gas helium, your voice will go very high-pitched, because sound travels much faster in helium than air.

Carbon

⚙ **Carbon is the fourth** most abundant element in the Universe after hydrogen, helium and oxygen. Most of it was originally made inside stars.

⚙ **The word** 'carbon' comes from the Latin word *carbo*, meaning 'charcoal'.

⚙ **Carbon atoms have space** for four electrons in their outer shells, so carbon forms over ten million compounds.

⚙ **Pure carbon** occurs in five major allotropes (forms). These are: diamond, graphite, amorphous carbon, fullerenes and carbon nanotubes.

▼ *The hardness of diamonds comes from the very strong tetrahedron (three-sided pyramid) patterns that the carbon atoms are arranged in.*

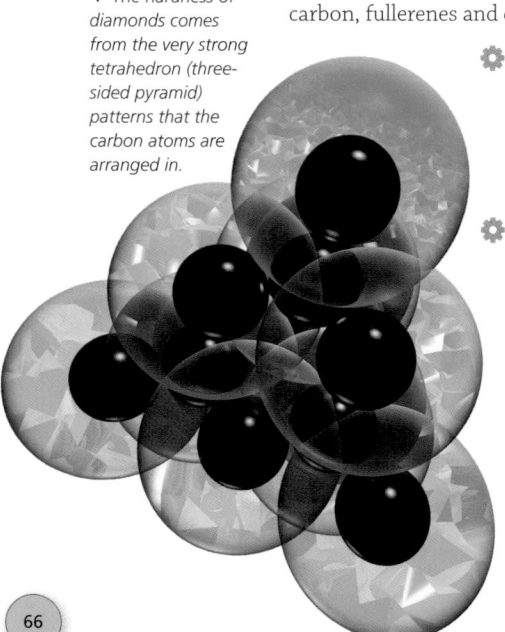

⚙ **Diamond, graphite and amorphous carbon** form naturally, while fullerenes and carbon nanotubes are mostly created artificially.

⚙ **Diamond is the hardest natural substance** on Earth. Natural diamonds were made deep in the Earth billions of years ago. They were formed by huge pressures as the Earth's crust moved, and then brought nearer to the surface by volcanic activity.

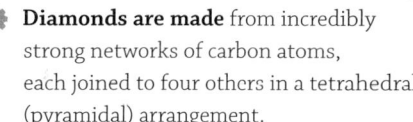

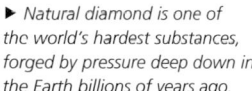
▶ *Natural diamond is one of the world's hardest substances, forged by pressure deep down in the Earth billions of years ago.*

- **Diamonds are made** from incredibly strong networks of carbon atoms, each joined to four others in a tetrahedral (pyramidal) arrangement.

- **Carbon has the highest melting** point of all elements. The melting point of diamond is about 3550°C, but it usually sublimes (goes straight from solid to gas), at around 3800°C.

- **Graphite is the black carbon** used in pencils. Its atoms are arranged in sheets that slide over each other, so it is quite soft.

- **Amorphous carbon** is the black soot residue that is left behind when candles and other objects burn.

- **Fullerenes are big molecules** made of 60 or more carbon atoms linked together in a tight cylinder or ball. The first was made in 1985. They were named after the American architect R Buckminster Fuller, who designed a geodesic (Earth-shaped) dome that is constructed on the same structural principles.

- **Carbon nanotubes** are tubes of carbon atoms measuring a few nanometres across (a nanometre is a billionth of a metre). They are 20 times as strong as steel, and can bend and conduct electricity 1000 times better than copper.

Chemicals of life

▶ *Molecules of the hydrocarbon gas ethane are made from two carbon atoms (purple) and six hydrogen atoms (orange).*

⚙ **The study** of compounds that contain carbon atoms is called organic chemistry.

⚙ **Organic chemistry** is so-called because originally scientists thought that carbon compounds occurred only in living things (the word 'organic' describes things that are related to living organisms). Organic chemicals are the basis of most life processes.

⚙ **Scientists once thought** that carbon compounds were only made by living things. However, in 1828 German chemist Friedrich Wöhler made the carbon compound urea in his laboratory.

⚙ **It is now known** that over 90 percent of all chemical compounds are organic. Organic compounds are used in a wide variety of products, including paints, plastics, food, explosives, drugs and oil.

⚙ **Most organic compounds** consist of carbon and hydrogen, often combined with other elements such as nitrogen, oxygen, phosphorus and silicon. Compounds that consist of hydrogen and carbon are called 'hydrocarbons'. These are the largest groups of carbon compounds.

⚙ **Aromatic compounds** are made from rings of six atoms (most of which are carbon), with hydrogen atoms attached. They get their name from the strong aroma (smell) of the most important of the aromatics, benzene.

⚙ **If one of two or more compounds** have the same atoms but different structures they are known as 'isomers'. The gas butane is an isomer.

⚙ **There are many** natural hydrocarbons in the human body including steroid hormones such as testosterone and cholesterol, which helps build blood vessel walls.

⚙ **Hydrocarbons and carbohydrates** are not the same. Hydrocarbons are made from carbon and hydrogen atoms, but carbohydrates contain oxygen atoms as well. The oxygen component of carbohydrates enables them to take a huge variety of forms essential for life.

⚙ **Carbohydrates such as** starches and sugars are the basic energy foods of plants and animals.

⚙ **Organic compounds** that are formed from rings of carbon atoms are called cyclic compounds. The carbon atoms of some organic compounds are arranged in chains. These are called aliphatic compounds, and include the gases ethane and propane.

▶ *Hummingbirds sip the nectar from flowers to get their essential energy source of carbohydrates.*

Oil

⚙ **Oils are liquids** that do not dissolve in water and burn easily. They are usually made from groups of carbon and hydrogen atoms. There are three main kinds of oil – essential oils, fixed oils and mineral oils.

⚙ **Essential oils** are thin, perfumed oils from plants. They are used in flavouring and aromatherapy. Fixed oils are derived from plants and animals, such as fish oils and nut oils. Mineral oils come from petroleum, which is formed underground over millions of years from the remains of tiny marine organisms such as plankton.

⚙ **Petroleum is a mixture** of organic compounds, most of which are hydrocarbons, combined with oxygen, sulphur, nitrogen and other elements.

⚙ **Petroleum is separated** into different substances such as aviation fuel, petrol and paraffin by distillation. In this process, oil is heated in a distillation column, causing a mixture of gases to evaporate. Each gas cools and condenses at a different height, becoming a liquid or fraction (a mixture of liquids of similar boiling point), which is then drawn off separately.

⚙ **There are different forms** of petroleum, such as crude oil and natural gas. Crude oil is usually thick and sticky, but it can vary in composition and colour, from jet-black Sudan oil to straw-coloured Texas oil.

1 Tiny animals die and sink to the seabed

⚙ **The simplest hydrocarbon** is methane, the main gas in natural gas. Methane molecules are comprised of one carbon atom and four hydrogen atoms.

⚙ **There are three** main kinds of hydrocarbon in oil – alkanes, aromatics and naphthenes. The proportion of each varies from oil to oil.

⚙ **Alkanes have long**, chain-shaped molecules, aromatics have small, ring molecules and naphthenes have large ring molecules.

⚙ **Lighter alkanes** are gases such as methane, propane and butane (used in camping stoves). Candles contain a mixture of alkanes and they all make good fuels.

⚙ **Ethene is the simplest alkene.** It is also called ethylene (C_2H_4) and is used to make plastics. It is the basis of many paint strippers and can be used to make ethanol – the alcohol in drinks such as wine.

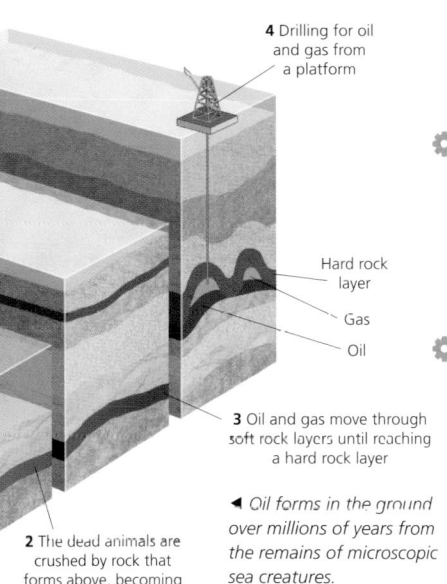

4 Drilling for oil and gas from a platform

Hard rock layer

Gas

Oil

3 Oil and gas move through soft rock layers until reaching a hard rock layer

◄ *Oil forms in the ground over millions of years from the remains of microscopic sea creatures.*

2 The dead animals are crushed by rock that forms above, becoming oil and gas

71

New materials

- **Materials that are man-made** rather than occurring naturally are known as 'synthetic'.

- **Many synthetic materials**, such as plastics, are polymers – substances with long chains of organic molecules that are made up from lots of identical smaller molecules, called monomers.

- **Some polymers** are natural, such as the plant fibre cellulose.

- **The first synthetic polymer** was Parkesine. It was invented by Alexander Parkes in 1862.

- **The first successful** synthetic polymer was celluloid. It was invented by John Hyatt in 1869, and was soon used as photographic film.

- **Polymers can be** strung together to make light, strong fibres such as lycra.

- **The polymer nylon** was the first completely synthetic fibre. It was created by Wallace Carothers of Du Pont in the 1930s.

- **Kevlar is a fibre** developed by Stephanie Kwolek of Du Pont in the 1960s, which is based on aromatic polymers. It is so light and tough it can be woven to make a bullet-proof vest.

DID YOU KNOW?
New 'smart' materials might change their properties in response to changing conditions.

⚙ **Composites are new**, strong, light materials, made by combining a polymer with another material.

⚙ **Carbon reinforced plastic** (CRP) is an incredibly strong, light material made by embedding tough fibres of carbon in a plastic.

◄ German paralympian Wojtek Czyz set a world long jump record at the 2008 Paralympics using materials in his prosthetic lower leg developed for use in space by MST Aerospace.

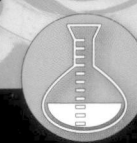

Glass

▲ *Some of the "stained" glass in this window was tinted with metallic oxides during manufacture, while the rest was coloured and painted by hand.*

- **Glass is made** from heating together sand, soda ash (sodium carbonate) and limestone (calcium carbonate).

- **Silica is a hard**, glassy solid found in sand. Glass can be made from silica alone, but it has a very high melting point (1700°C), so soda ash is added to lower its melting point. Adding a lot of soda ash makes glass too soluble in water, so limestone is added to reduce its solubility.

- **To make sheets of glass**, 6 percent lime and 4 percent magnesia (magnesium oxide) are added to the mix.

- **To make glass for bottles**, 2 percent alumina (aluminium oxide) is added to the basic mix.

⚙ **The cheapest glass** is green because it contains small impurities of iron.

⚙ **Metallic oxides** are added to the mix to make different colours.

⚙ **Unlike most solids**, glass is amorphous (not made of crystals) so it does not have the same rigid structure as other solids.

⚙ **When glass is extremely hot** it flows slowly like a thick liquid.

> **DID YOU KNOW?**
> Glass is five times as strong as steel in tension (the force under which a material is stretched).

◀ Molten glass is shaped by a process called 'glass-blowing' in which air is blown into it through a tube.

Plastics

⚙ **Plastics are synthetic** materials that can be easily shaped and moulded. Most plastics are polymers. A plastic gets its properties from the way its polymer molecules are arranged.

⚙ **Plastics are usually made** by joining carbon and hydrogen atoms to create ethene molecules, which are then joined to form plastic. Long chains of molecules that slide over each other easily make flexible plastics, whereas angled chains make rigid plastics. Many plastics are made from liquids and gases that are extracted from crude oil.

⚙ **Thermoplastics** are soft and easily moulded when warm but set solid when cool. They are used to make products such as bottles and drainpipes. Thermoset plastics, which cannot be remelted once set, are used to make telephones and pan handles.

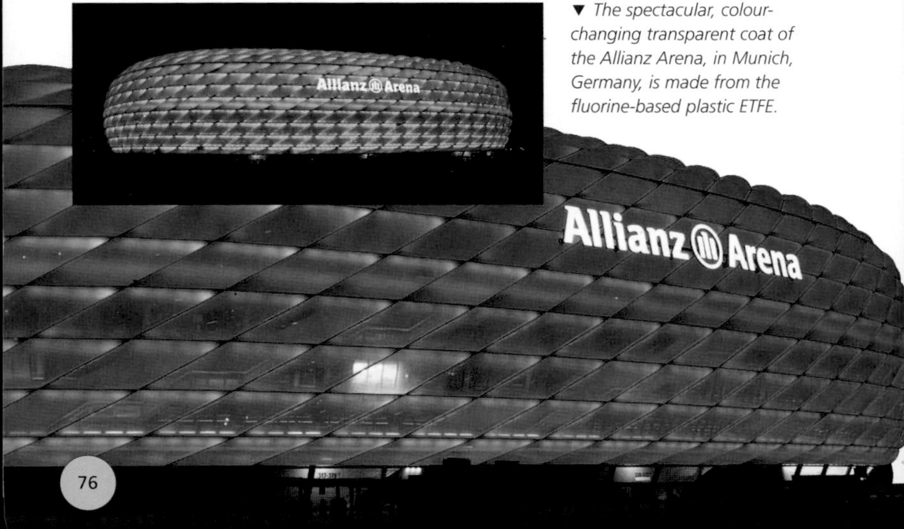

▼ The spectacular, colour-changing transparent coat of the Allianz Arena, in Munich, Germany, is made from the fluorine-based plastic ETFE.

▶ *A pole vaulter's pole benefits from the lightness, strength and flexibility of fibreglass, made from plastic reinforced with tough fibres of glass.*

⚙ **Plastic can be moulded.** Blow moulding uses compressed air to push plastic into a mould. Vacuum moulding uses a vacuum to suck plastic into a mould. In extrusion moulding, plastic pellets are heated, then shaped by being forced through a nozzle.

⚙ **Polycarbonate is easily moulded** but very durable (tough). It is used to make products such as mp3 players.

⚙ **Polystyrene is very light.** It is used to make products such as disposable coffee cups because it is a good insulator.

⚙ **Polyvinyl chloride** (PVC) is a hard plastic, so it is used to make window frames. It can be softened with plasticizers to make anything from shoes to shampoo bottles.

⚙ **Low-density polyethene** (LDPE) is a light, flexible plastic. It is used to wrap food. High-density polyethene (HDPE) is a tough but flexible plastic that is used for making products such as toys.

⚙ **Polycarbonate** is resistant to chemicals, so is used to make containers for medicine and industrial chemicals.

⚙ **Some plastics,** such as Teflon® and tetrafluorethylene (ETFE), are made from carbon and fluorine rather than hydrocarbons.

77

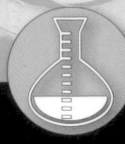

Air

- **Air is a mixture of gases**, dust and moisture.

- **The gas nitrogen** makes up 78.08 percent of the air. Nitrogen is usually unreactive, but sometimes reacts with oxygen to form oxides of nitrogen.

- **Oxygen makes up** 20.94 percent of the air. Animals breathe in oxygen, while plants give it out as they take their energy from sunlight in photosynthesis.

- **Earth's atmosphere** gained its oxygen from the billions of plantlike micro organisms that floated in the oceans of the primeval world.

- **The air contains** very small quantities of the inert gases argon, neon, helium, krypton and xenon.

- **It also contains** a number of more reactive gases, including carbon dioxide, water vapour, ozone, sulphur dioxide and nitrogen dioxide.

- **Water vapour** makes up 1–7 percent of air, while carbon dioxide makes up 0.03 percent. Carbon dioxide is being continually recycled as it is breathed out by animals and taken in by plants in photosynthesis.

▼ *The Earth's atmosphere is just 100 km deep, proportionally less thick than the skin of an apple.*

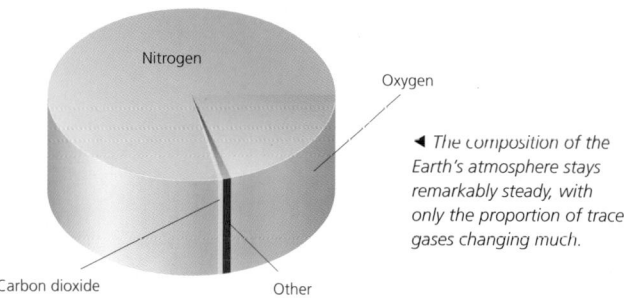

◀ *The composition of the Earth's atmosphere stays remarkably steady, with only the proportion of trace gases changing much.*

⚙ **Ozone makes up 0.00006** percent of the air. It is created when sunlight breaks up oxygen. Hydrogen makes up 0.00005 percent of the air, and is continually drifting off into space.

⚙ **Air is typically polluted** with gases, tiny solid particles (such as soot) and aerosols (tiny droplets).

⚙ **Some pollution is natural**, such as dust from storms, soot and smoke from forest fires and ash from volcanic eruptions. However, a lot of pollution is now made by humans, including motor vehicle exhaust fumes and emissions from factories and power stations.

⚙ **Man-made pollution** also adds gases such as carbon dioxide, methane, nitrous oxides and ozone to the air. Particles from motor vehicle exhausts can mix with fog to form smog, while soot particles can cause breathing problems.

⚙ **Carbon dioxide** created by burning oil and coal, and methane from cows are adding to the natural insulating effect of the atmosphere, so that the Earth is gradually getting warmer. This is called 'global warming'.

⚙ **Rain is turned to acid** by pollution with sulphur and nitrogen compounds emitted by coal and oil-burning power stations, factories and motor vehicles.

Water

Hydrogen

Oxygen

▲ *Water's V-shaped molecule has a hydrogen atom (red) at the base and an oxygen atom (green) at each tip.*

⚙ **Water is the only substance** that exists in all three states of matter – solid, liquid and gas – at normal temperatures. It melts at around 0°C and boils at around 100°C.

⚙ **The boiling point of water** varies according to atmospheric pressure. It is 100°C at sea level, but just 68°C on the top of Mount Everest (the highest point on Earth), where atmospheric pressure is low.

⚙ **Ice is much less dense** than water, which is why ice forms on the surface of ponds and why icebergs float.

⚙ **Water is one of the few substances** that expands as it freezes, which is why pipes burst during cold weather. It has a unique capacity for making mild solutions with other substances.

⚙ **Water is a compound** made of two hydrogen atoms and one oxygen atom. It has the chemical formula H_2O. A water molecule is shaped like a flattened letter 'v', with the two hydrogen atoms on each tip.

⚙ **A water molecule** is said to be polar because the oxygen end is more negatively charged.

⚙ **Substances that are similar to water**, such as ammonia (NH_3), exist as gases below 0°C.

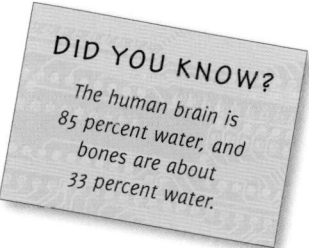

⚙ **Water stays in a liquid form** until 100°C because pairs of its polar molecules make strong bonds, as the positively charged end of one molecule is drawn to the negatively charged end of another.

⚙ **The way in which water molecules** are drawn together creates a lot of surface tension. This is what pulls water drops into globules.

⚙ **Water covers** 71 percent of Earth's surface. Most of this is in the oceans and rivers, while 1.6 percent is in the ground and 0.001 percent is in the air as vapour, clouds and rain.

⚙ **Some of the world's water** (2.4 percent) is frozen as glaciers and ice caps, but global warming may reduce this proportion.

⚙ **Liquid water** may also occur elsewhere in space – in small amounts on the Moon; under the surface of Saturn's moon, Enceladus; and on Jupiter's moon Europa. Ice is present on Mars, and on Saturn's moon, Titan.

▼ *It has been known for some time that there is water on Mars, frozen in its polar ice caps, but it is still unknown whether there is liquid water on the planet.*

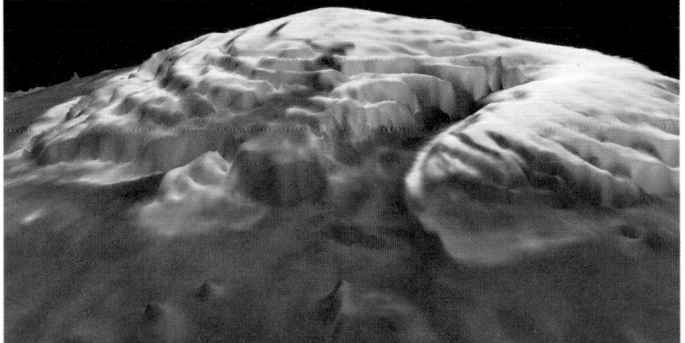

Energy, force and motion

Weight and mass

⚙ **Mass is the amount of matter** in an object. Mass is not the same as weight. In physics, 'weight' refers to the force of gravity acting on an object. An object's weight varies according to its mass and the strength of gravity.

⚙ **Objects weigh more** at sea level, which is nearer the centre of the Earth, than up a mountain.

⚙ **If you were standing on the Moon**, you would weigh only one-sixth of your weight on Earth because the Moon's gravity is one-sixth of the Earth's gravity.

⚙ **The weight of an object can vary**, but its mass is always the same, so scientists use units of mass to describe how heavy something is.

⚙ **The object** with the smallest known mass is a photon (a particle of energy), which has a mass of 5.3×10^{-63} kg.

⚙ **The mass of the Earth** is 6×10^{24} (six trillion trillion) kg. The mass of the Universe is thought to be approximately 10^{51} (10 followed by 50 zeros) kg.

◄ *Astronauts experience 'weightlessness' because they no longer feel the effect of Earth's gravity.*

- **Density is the ratio** of the mass of a substance to its volume. It is measured in grams per cubic centimetre (g/cm^3).

- **The lightest solids** are silica aerogels made for space science, with a density of 0.005 g/cm^3.

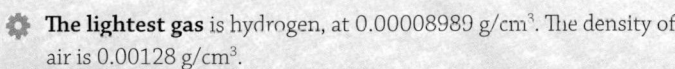

▼ Experimental aircraft allow astronauts to feel the illusion of weightlessness for testing and training purposes.

- **The lightest gas** is hydrogen, at 0.00008989 g/cm^3. The density of air is 0.00128 g/cm^3.

- **The densest solid** is osmium, at 22.59 g/cm^3. Lead is 11.37 g/cm^3. A neutron star has a density of about one billion trillion g/cm^3.

Inertia and momentum

⚙ **Inertia is the property** that causes a body to resist any change in speed caused by a force. For example, a ball on a level surface doesn't move because inertia keeps it where it is. A kick provides the force to make it move.

⚙ **Momentum is an object's mass** times its velocity (the rate at which it moves in a particular direction).

⚙ **Inertia and momentum** depend on mass, so a large force is needed to slow down or speed up a heavy object.

◀ A spinning top remains upright while it is moving because its angular momentum is greater than the pull of gravity.

▲ *This crash test shows the potential for damage caused by the force of momentum when objects collide.*

● **When a moving object** strikes another object (when you kick a ball, for example), the momentum of the moving object (your foot) is transferred to the object it strikes (the ball), making it move. This is known as the law of conservation of momentum.

● **The momentum of a spinning object** is called angular momentum. When a spinning skater draws their arms close in to their body, their spin diameter (the circle they are making) is smaller than it would be if their arms were outstretched. To conserve angular momentum, the skater's body automatically spins faster.

● **For the same reason**, a satellite orbiting close to the Earth travels faster than one orbiting farther out.

Velocity and acceleration

⚙ **When an object** is moving in one direction at a constant speed, it is described as having uniform velocity. The speed of the object can be worked out using the following formula:

$$\frac{\text{distance travelled (d)}}{\text{time (t)}} = \text{velocity (v)}$$

⚙ **Acceleration is the rate** of change of velocity. When something speeds up (accelerates), it has positive acceleration. When something slows down (decelerates), it has negative acceleration.

⚙ **Acceleration is typically measured** in metres per second per second (m/sec^2), meaning that in each second speed increases or decreases by so many metres per second per second. A rifle bullet accelerates down the barrel at 3000 m/sec^2. A fast car accelerates at 6 m/sec^2.

▼ *Electric motors accelerate this Japanese bullet-train to speeds of more than 250 kph.*

⚙ **Earth's gravitational pull** causes freely falling objects to accelerate. The rate at which this happens is called g (acceleration of gravity). On Earth this rate is 9.8 m/sec^2.

⚙ **In a rocket** travelling at 1 g the acceleration has little effect on passengers. At 3 g it becomes difficult to move, and at 4.5 g passengers black out within five seconds.

⚙ **A plane takes off** at 0.5 g, while a car brakes at up to 0.7 g. In a car crash you may survive a deceleration of up to 100 g.

▶ *A sprinter develops his muscles to accelerate his body to the maximum velocity he can achieve in the shortest possible time.*

Motion

⚙️ **Every movement** in the Universe is governed by laws. Three of the most important of these laws were described by English scientist Isaac Newton.

⚙️ **Newton's first law of motion** states that an object accelerates, slows down or changes direction only when a force is applied to it.

⚙️ **Newton's second law of motion** states that the acceleration of an object depends on how heavy the object is, and on the size of the force that is acting on it.

⚙️ **The greater the force** acting on an object, the more it will accelerate. The heavier an object is (the greater its mass), the less it will be accelerated by a particular force.

⚙️ **Newton's third law of motion** states that when a force acts one way, an equal force acts the opposite way. 'To every action, there is an equal and opposite reaction'.

⚙️ **Rocket engines** depend on Newton's law. As the hot gases shoot out of the rocket motors (the action), the rocket reacts against them and is propelled forwards (the reaction).

⚙️ **Reactions are not always visible.** When you bounce a ball on the ground, only the ball appears to move. Actually, the ground recoils (moves in the opposite direction to the ball) too, but because Earth's mass is huge compared to the ball's, the recoil is so tiny it is invisible.

▶ *Space scientists can calculate the projected flight of a spacecraft with pinpoint precision using Newton's laws of motion.*

Forces

⚙ **A force** is a push or a pull. It can make something start to move, slow down, speed up, change direction or change shape or size. The greater a force, the more effect it has.

⚙ **Force is measured** in newtons (N). One newton is the force needed to speed up a mass of one kilogram by one metre per second every second.

⚙ **When an object moves** there are usually several forces involved. When you throw a ball, the force of your throw hurls it forwards, the force of gravity pulls it down and the force of air resistance slows it down.

◄ A rollercoaster gets its speed from gravity. As it hurtles downhill, the constant pull of gravity makes it go faster and faster. When it reaches the bottom of a slope its momentum carries it on uphill.

- **The direction and speed** of any movement depends on the combined effect of all the forces involved – this is known as the resultant.

- **A force** has magnitude (size) and works in a particular direction.

- **A force can** be drawn on a diagram as an arrow, called a vector. The arrow's direction shows the force's direction and its length shows the force's strength.

- **Four fundamental forces** operate throughout the Universe. These are gravity, electric and magnetic forces (electromagnetic force) and nuclear forces.

- **A force field** is the area affected by a force. The field is strongest closest to the source.

▶ When a boxer hits a punchball, the ball is moved by the force of his punch.

Vectors

- **Vector quantities** are quantities that have magnitude (size) and direction. Velocity, force and acceleration are all vector quantities. Gravity, jet propulsion and the wind, for instance, can be seen as vectors.

- **Scalar quantities** are quantities that have a size but no direction. Temperature, density and mass are all scalar quantities.

- **When a value is given to a vector** quantity, the direction must also be shown, normally by an arrow. The length of the arrow indicates the magnitude, and the direction of the arrow indicates the direction of the force.

- **Objects can be affected** by a combination of vector quantities at the same time. For example, you sit on a chair, gravity pulls you down and the chair pushes you up with equal force, keeping you still. If someone pushes the chair, the force they are exerting combined with gravity may cause the chair to tip over.

- **When several vectors** affect a single object, they may act at different angles. The effect of vectors on an object (the resultant) can be predicted by drawing a geometric diagram.

- **The parallelogram of forces** is a diagram used to work out the resultant from two forces. An arrow is drawn for each force from the same point. A parallel arrow is then drawn from the end of each arrow, forming a parallelogram. The resultant is the diagonal of the parallelogram.

DID YOU KNOW?

Vector charts are used to predict the weather because they describe both speed and direction – invaluable for showing the course of winds or storms.

◄ Using vectors, you can draw a simple geometrical diagram of all the forces acting on this gymnast, such as her weight and momentum.

Machines

⚙ **In science**, a machine is a device that cuts down the effort needed to move a load. It works by modifying the force applied or changing its direction.

⚙ **Simple machines** include levers, gears, pulleys, screws and wedges. Complex machines, such as cranes, are built up from combinations of simple machines.

⚙ **Machines reduce the effort** by spreading the load over a greater distance or a longer time.

⚙ **The mechanical advantage** (MA) is a measure of how effective a machine is. It is the ratio of the load to the effort needed to move it.

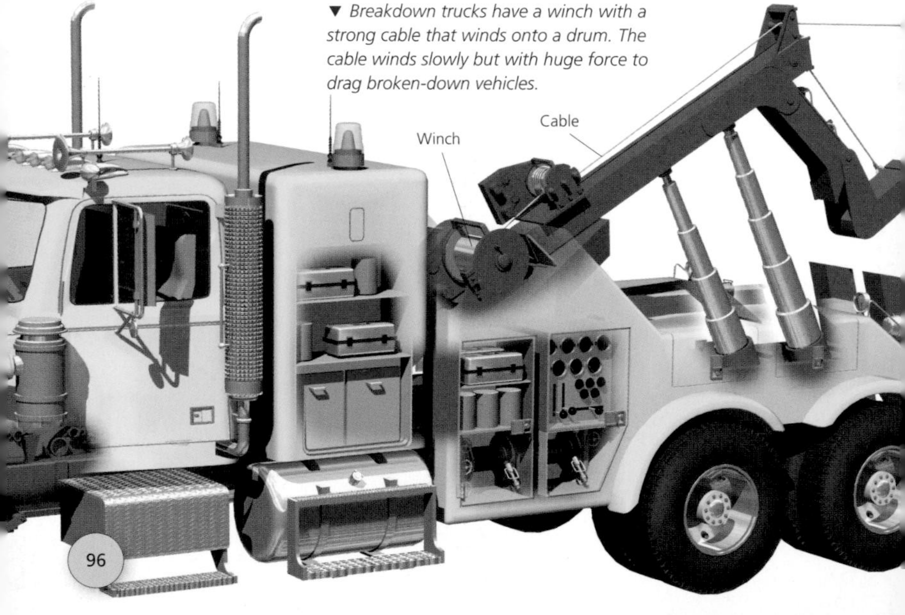

▼ Breakdown trucks have a winch with a strong cable that winds onto a drum. The cable winds slowly but with huge force to drag broken-down vehicles.

Cable

Winch

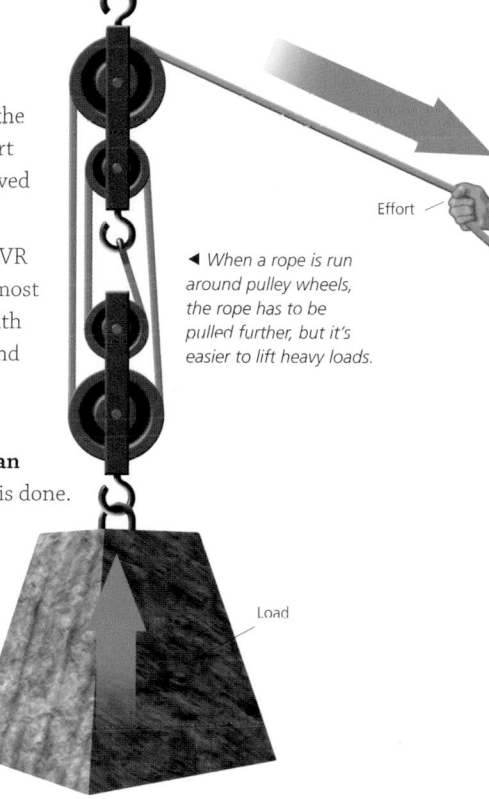

- **The velocity ratio** (VR) is the distance moved by the effort divided by the distance moved by the load.

- **In a perfect machine**, the VR would match the MA, but most machines are inefficient, with losses between the effort and the load due to forces such as friction.

Effort

◄ *When a rope is run around pulley wheels, the rope has to be pulled further, but it's easier to lift heavy loads.*

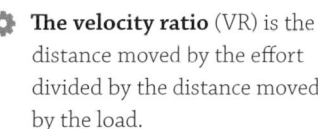

- **Whenever a force moves an object**, scientists say work is done. Work is the force applied multiplied by the distance moved.

- **The efficiency** of a machine is the ratio of the work done in moving the load to the work involved in applying the effort.

Load

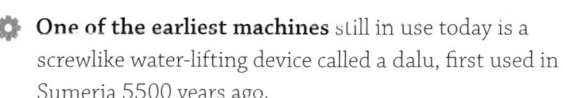

- **One of the earliest machines** still in use today is a screwlike water-lifting device called a dalu, first used in Sumeria 5500 years ago.

- **One of the biggest machines** is the SMEC Earthmover, which is used in opencast mines in Australia. It weighs 180 tonnes and has wheels 3.5 m high.

Turning forces

⚙ **Forces always act in straight lines**, but when a force acts on an object that pivots around a fixed point (a fulcrum), it creates a turning effect.

⚙ **The size of the turning effect** is called the moment by physicists and torque by engineers. The further from the fulcrum the force is applied, the greater the moment.

⚙ **A lever** is a simple machine consisting of a rigid bar that pivots about a fulcrum somewhere along its length.

⚙ **In a first-class lever** the fulcrum is between the effort and the load. Pliers and scissors are first-class levers.

⚙ **In a second-class lever**, the load is between the effort and the fulcrum. Screwdrivers and wheelbarrows are second-class levers.

⚙ **In a third-class lever**, the effort is between the load and the fulcrum. Tweezers are a third-class lever.

⚙ **A gear** is a simple machine that transmits motion through multiple rotating shafts (toothed wheels).

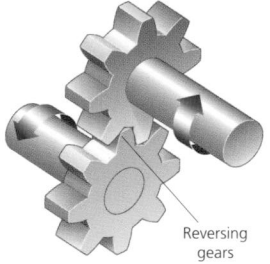

Reversing gears

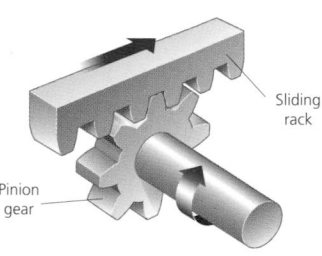

Sliding rack

Pinion gear

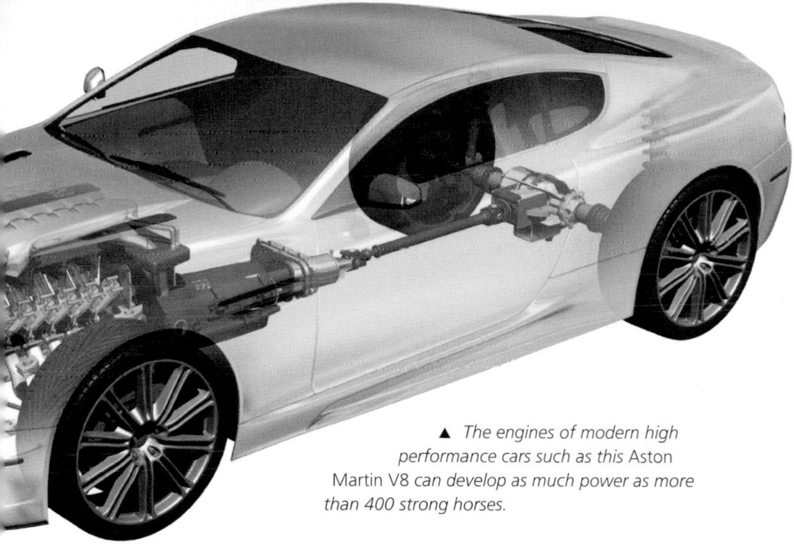

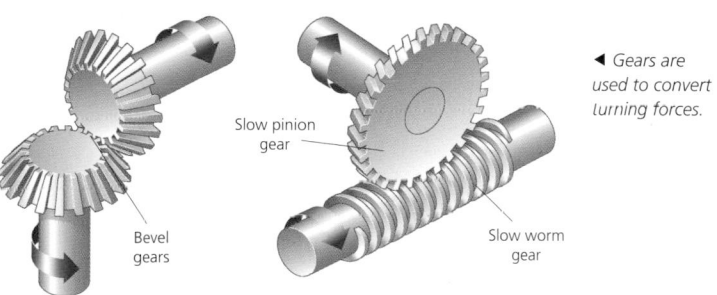

▲ *The engines of modern high performance cars such as this Aston Martin V8 can develop as much power as more than 400 strong horses.*

⚙ **The gear ratio** is the ratio of the number of teeth on two engaged gearwheels. A gear with 14 teeth turns twice in order to turn a gear with 28 teeth once, giving a gear ratio of 2:1.

⚙ **The larger the gear ratio**, the more the turning force is increased, but the slower the driven wheel turns.

◄ *Gears are used to convert turning forces.*

Slow pinion gear

Bevel gears

Slow worm gear

Stretching and pulling

⚙ **Elasticity is the degree** to which a solid can return to its original size and shape after being stretched, squeezed or deformed.

⚙ **A force** that misshapes a material is called a stress.

⚙ **All solids** have some elasticity but some, such as rubber, nylon and coiled springs, are very elastic. A solid will return to its original shape when stress stops, as long as the stress does not exceed its elastic limit (the point at which a material loses elasticity).

▶ Bungee jumpers rely on precisely judging the elastic limits of the cord to bring them gently to a halt before they hit the ground.

DID YOU KNOW?

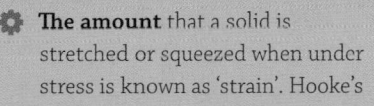

DID YOU KNOW?

Some types of rubber can be stretched 1000 times beyond their original length before reaching their elastic limit.

⚙ **The amount** that a solid is stretched or squeezed when under stress is known as 'strain'. Hooke's law, named after English scientist Robert Hooke, states that the amount of strain is directly proportional to the amount of stress.

⚙ **The amount** by which a solid stretches under a particular force – the ratio of stress to strain – is known as its elastic modulus.

⚙ **Solids that have a low** elastic modulus, such as rubber, are more elastic than those with a high modulus, such as steel.

⚙ **Steel can only be stretched** by one percent before it reaches its elastic limit. However, if steel is coiled into a spring shape, this one percent can allow a huge amount of stretching and squeezing.

◀ *The leverage of the bow string helps an archer to bend the elastic material of the bow so far that it has tremendous power as it snaps back into shape.*

101

Pressure

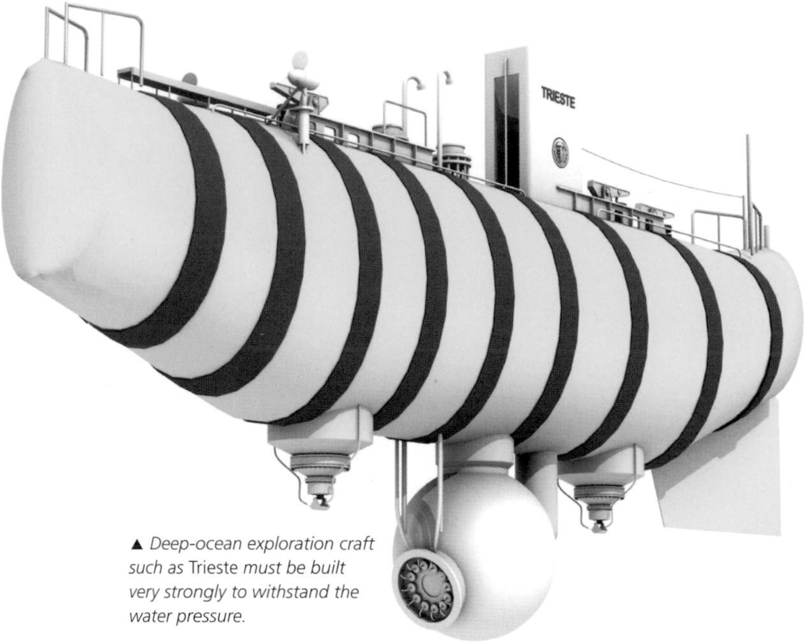

▲ *Deep-ocean exploration craft such as Trieste must be built very strongly to withstand the water pressure.*

⚙ **Pressure is force** applied to a surface. It is measured as the force acting per unit area of surface. The standard unit of pressure is a pascal (Pa) or 1 newton per sq m (N/m^2).

⚙ **The pressure at the centre of the Earth** may be 400 billion Pa. Steel can withstand 40 million Pa, while a shark bite can be 30 million Pa. The quietest sound is 200 millionths Pa. The pressure of sunlight may be 3 millionths Pa.

- **Pressure in a gas or liquid** is actually the assault of fast-moving molecules on surfaces around or within it.

- **An inflated bicycle tyre** feels firm because of the constant assault by air molecules on the inside of the tyre. Pumping pushes more air molecules into the available space and so increases pressure.

- **Pressures are greater** in liquids than in gas because liquids are denser. Pressure rises as you descend into the ocean because the density of water increases.

- **The water pressure** 10,000 m below the surface is equivalent to seven elephants standing on a dinner plate.

- **Air pressure** outside your body is balanced by the pressure of fluids inside your body. Without this internal pressure, air pressure would crush your body instantly.

▶ Balloons remain inflated because the pressure of the gas inside them is greater than the pressure of the surrounding air.

Floating and sinking

⚙ **When an object** is placed in liquid, its weight displaces (pushes away) a volume of the liquid. The displaced liquid pushes back on the solid with a force called 'upthrust'.

⚙ **If the upthrust** is equal to or greater than the object's weight it will float. This is called Archimedes' principle.

⚙ **An object sinks** until its weight is equal to the upthrust of the water, at which point it floats. The ability of an object to float is called 'buoyancy'.

⚙ **The density** of a substance is the ratio of its mass to its volume.

⚙ **An object will only float** if it has the same density or is less dense than the liquid surrounding it.

⚙ **A steel ship can float**, even though steel is denser than water, because its hull is full of air. The ship will sink to a point where enough water is displaced to match the combined weight of the steel and the air inside the hull, and then float.

⚙ **Ships float** at different heights according to how heavily they are laden and how dense the water is.

⚙ **Ships float higher** in sea water than in fresh water because salt makes sea water more dense.

⚙ **Ships float higher** in dense cold seas than in warm tropical ones.

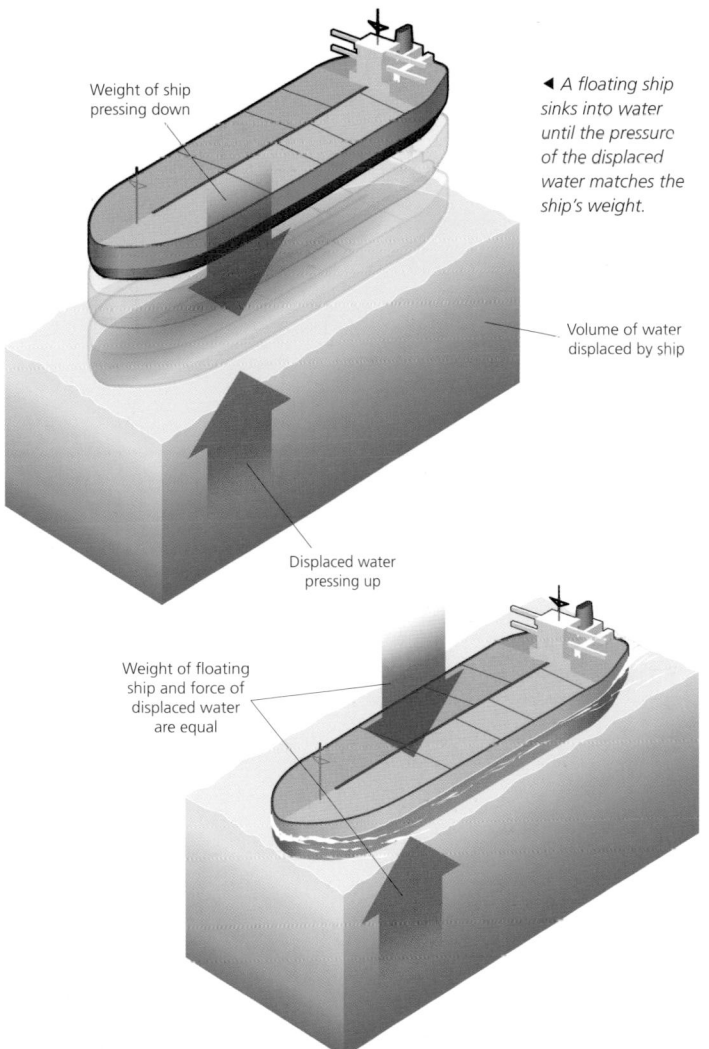

Weight of ship
pressing down

◄ A floating ship
sinks into water
until the pressure
of the displaced
water matches the
ship's weight.

Volume of water
displaced by ship

Displaced water
pressing up

Weight of floating
ship and force of
displaced water
are equal

Energy

⚙ **Energy is the capacity** of a system to do work. It has many forms, from chemical energy locked in sugar to mechanical energy in a speeding train.

⚙ **Energy conversion** is when energy changes from one form to another. When energy moves from one place to another it is known as energy transfer.

▼ *Inside the Sun, nuclear energy in atoms is converted into heat energy, making the surface ferociously hot.*

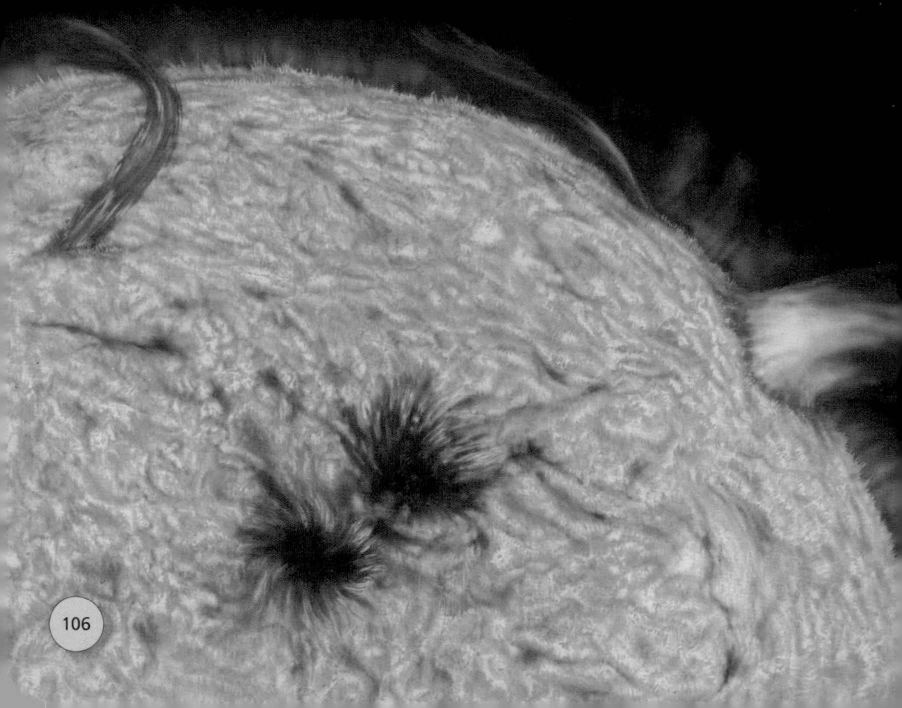

▲ *When fuels such as gas are burned, chemical energy is changed into heat energy.*

🔅 **Energy is never lost or gained**, it simply changes or moves. The total amount of energy in the Universe has always been the same. Using energy usually means converting it from one form to another.

🔅 **Potential energy** is energy that is stored up within a body or system ready for action. The energy in a coiled spring is an example of potential energy.

🔅 **Kinetic energy** is energy that is possessed by an object because it is moving. A rolling ball has kinetic energy.

🔅 **The greater an object's mass or velocity**, the greater its kinetic energy. A car has four times more kinetic energy at 40 km/h than at 20 km/h.

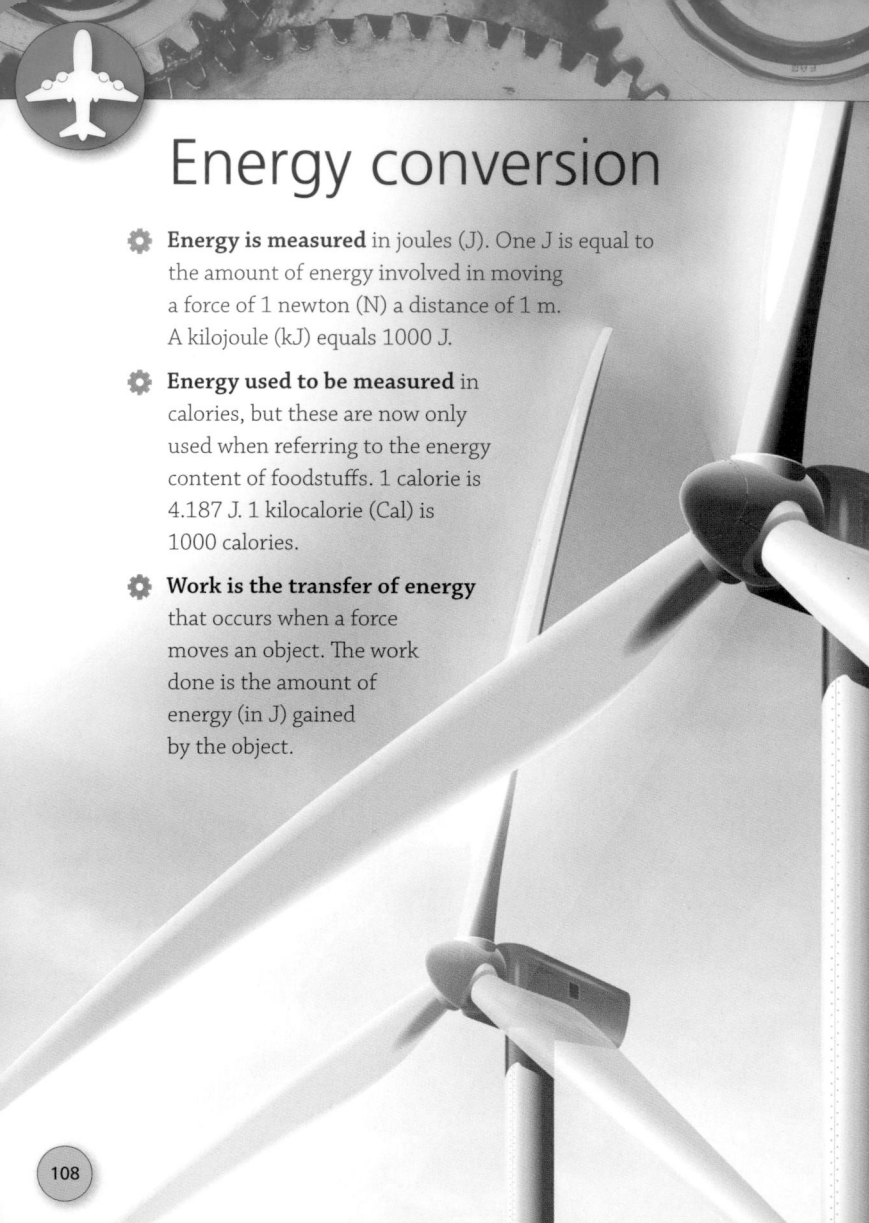

Energy conversion

⚙ **Energy is measured** in joules (J). One J is equal to the amount of energy involved in moving a force of 1 newton (N) a distance of 1 m. A kilojoule (kJ) equals 1000 J.

⚙ **Energy used to be measured** in calories, but these are now only used when referring to the energy content of foodstuffs. 1 calorie is 4.187 J. 1 kilocalorie (Cal) is 1000 calories.

⚙ **Work is the transfer of energy** that occurs when a force moves an object. The work done is the amount of energy (in J) gained by the object.

⚙ **The work rate** (the rate at which energy is changed from one form to another) is known as the power.

⚙ **The power of a machine** is the amount of work it does divided by the length of time it takes to do it:

$$\text{power} = \frac{\text{distance travelled (d)}}{\text{time (t)}}$$

⚙ **A transducer** is a device that converts electricity into different forms – such as sound, light or motion – or vice versa. A loudspeaker is an example of a transducer.

⚙ **Earth's coal reserves** contain a total of 2×10^{23} J of energy. A thunderstorm has 10^{11} J.

⚙ **While you are asleep** your body uses 60 Cals per hour. Three hours of reading or watching television uses 240 Cals, while an hour of running uses 600 Cals. Seven hours of hard physical work uses around 1000 Cals.

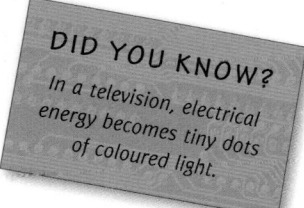

DID YOU KNOW?

In a television, electrical energy becomes tiny dots of coloured light.

▲ *A wind turbine converts the kinetic (movement) energy of the wind into electric energy.*

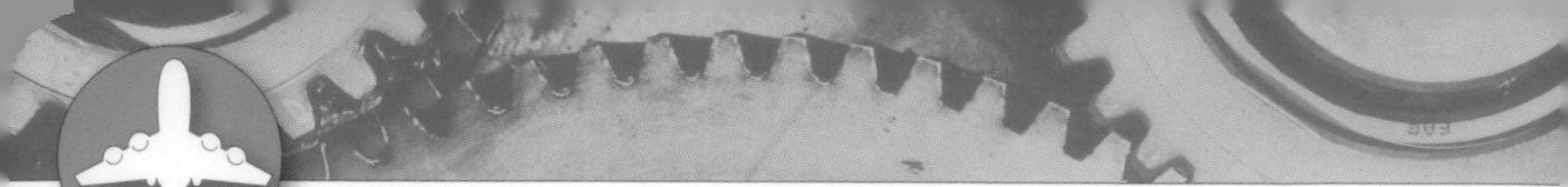

Heat

⚙ **Heat is a form of energy.** It is a result of the movement of thermal energy. Thermal energy is the combined energy of moving molecules.

⚙ **When you hold your hand** over a heater, the warmth you feel is actually the assault of billions of fast-moving molecules of air.

⚙ **Heat is the combined energy** of all the moving molecules, whereas temperature is a measure of the average energy of the molecules.

▼ The heat of the Earth's interior can melt solid rock into fiery liquid lava.

▲ *Water boils – turns from a liquid into a gas –*
when heated to 100°C.

🌼 **The coldest temperature possible** is absolute zero, or −273.15°C. At this temperature molecules stop moving.

🌼 **When you heat a substance**, its temperature rises because heat makes its molecules move faster. The same amount of heat will raise the temperatures of different substances by different amounts.

🌼 **Specific heat** is the amount of energy required (in J) to heat a substance by 1°C.

🌼 **Latent heat** is the quantity of heat energy released or absorbed whenever a substance changes state without changing its temperature.

🌼 **Sensible heat** is all the heat that is not converted to latent heat and so is free to move.

🌼 **Heat spreads out** from its source. It heats up its surroundings while the source of the heat cools down.

Heat movement

⚙ **Heat moves** in three different ways: conduction, convection and radiation.

⚙ **Conduction involves** heat spreading from hot areas to cold areas by direct contact. It works a bit like a relay race – energetic, rapidly moving or vibrating molecules bump into their neighbours, setting them moving.

⚙ **Good conducting** materials such as metals feel cool to the touch because they carry heat away from your fingers quickly.

▲ Hot liquid heats a metal spoon by conduction.

⚙ **The best conductors of heat** are the metals silver, copper and gold, in that order.

⚙ **Materials that conduct heat slowly** are called insulators. They help keep things warm by reducing heat loss. Wood is one of the best insulators. Water is also effective as an insulator.

⚙ **Radiation is the spread of heat** as heat rays, that is, invisible waves of infrared radiation.

⚙ **Radiation spreads heat** without direct contact.

⚙ **Convection is when warm** air rises through cool air, as in a hot-air balloon.

⚙ **Convection currents** are circulation patterns set up as warm air (or liquid) rises. Around the column of rising warmth, cool air (or liquid) continually sinks to replace it at the bottom.

▶ A hot-air balloon contains air that is heated by a burner. The heat makes air molecules inside the balloon spread out. This makes the air inside the balloon lighter than the air around it, so the balloon rises.

Temperature

⚙️ **Temperature is the measurement** of how hot or cold something is. The best-known temperature scales are Celsius and Fahrenheit.

⚙️ **The Celsius (C) scale** is part of the metric system of measurements. It is named after Swedish astronomer Anders Celsius, who developed it in 1742.

⚙️ **Celsius is also known as centigrade** because water boils at 100°C, and *cent* is the Latin prefix for 100. Water freezes at 0°C. On the Fahrenheit (F) scale water boils at 212°F and freezes at 32°F.

⚙️ **To convert** Celsius to Fahrenheit, divide by 5, multiply by 9 and add 32. To convert Fahrenheit to Celsius, subtract 32, divide by 9 and multiply by 5.

⚙️ **The Kelvin (K) scale** is used by scientists. It is like the Celsius scale, but it begins at –273.15°C. This means that 0°C is equivalent to 273.15K.

▶ *In this globe, sea surface temperature is indicated by colour, from the coldest waters (black) through blue, purple and red to the hottest, yellow.*

🔅 **Helium changes** from gas to liquid at −269°C. Petrol freezes at −150°C. The lowest air temperature ever recorded on Earth is −89.2°C.

🔅 **A log fire burns** at a temperature of around 800°C. Molten magma is around 1200°C. The surface of the Sun is around 6000°C, while Earth's core is over 7000°C. A lightning flash reaches 30,000°C. The centre of a hydrogen bomb reaches over 4,000,000°C.

🔅 **The blood temperature** of the human body is normally around 37°C. Body temperature above 40°C is very hot, and below 31°C is very cold. Anything hotter than 45°C hurts if it touches your skin, although some people can walk barefoot on burning coals as hot as 800°C.

▶ Temperature is measured by a thermometer. The liquid inside expands as it heats up and rises along the tube.

Friction

▲ Static friction keeps the tyres of a racing car firmly on the track, they only slide when the car skids.

🌼 **Friction is a force** that acts to oppose the motion of two surfaces that are in contact with each other.

🌼 **The type of friction** that prevents things sliding is known as static friction. The type of friction that slows sliding is called dynamic friction.

🌼 **The harder** two surfaces press together, the greater the force needed to overcome the friction.

🌼 **The coefficient of friction** (CF) is the ratio of the friction to the weight of the sliding object. Metal sliding on metal has a CF of 0.74, while ice on ice has a CF of 0.1. This means it is over seven times harder to make metal slide on metal than ice on ice.

🌼 **Friction often makes** things hot. As the sliding surfaces are forced to slow, some of the energy of momentum is turned into heat.

- ⚙ **Fluid friction** occurs between two fluids, or between a fluid and a solid. Fluid friction makes thick fluids 'viscous' (flow less easily).

- ⚙ **Oil reduces friction** by creating a film that keeps the solid surfaces apart.

- ⚙ **Brakes use dynamic friction** to slow things down.

- ⚙ **Drag is friction** between air and an object. It slows a fast car, or any aircraft moving through the air.

▼ *Ice-bikes need sharp metal spikes on their tyres to compensate for the lack of friction on the slippery ice.*

Thermodynamics

⚙ **Energy cannot be destroyed**, but it can be burned up. Every time energy is used, some of it turns into heat.

⚙ **Energy that turns into heat** dissipates (spreads out thinly in all directions) and is hard to use again.

⚙ **Scientists use the word** 'entropy' to describe how much energy has become unusable. The less energy available for doing work, the greater the entropy.

⚙ **German physicist** Rudolf Clausius invented the word 'entropy' in 1868 to describe how everything happens because energy naturally moves from hot, high energy areas to cold, low energy areas.

⚙ **Energy flows** from hot areas to cold until both are equal. Once this 'equilibrium' is reached, there is no longer any energy difference to make things happen. Entropy is said to be at a maximum.

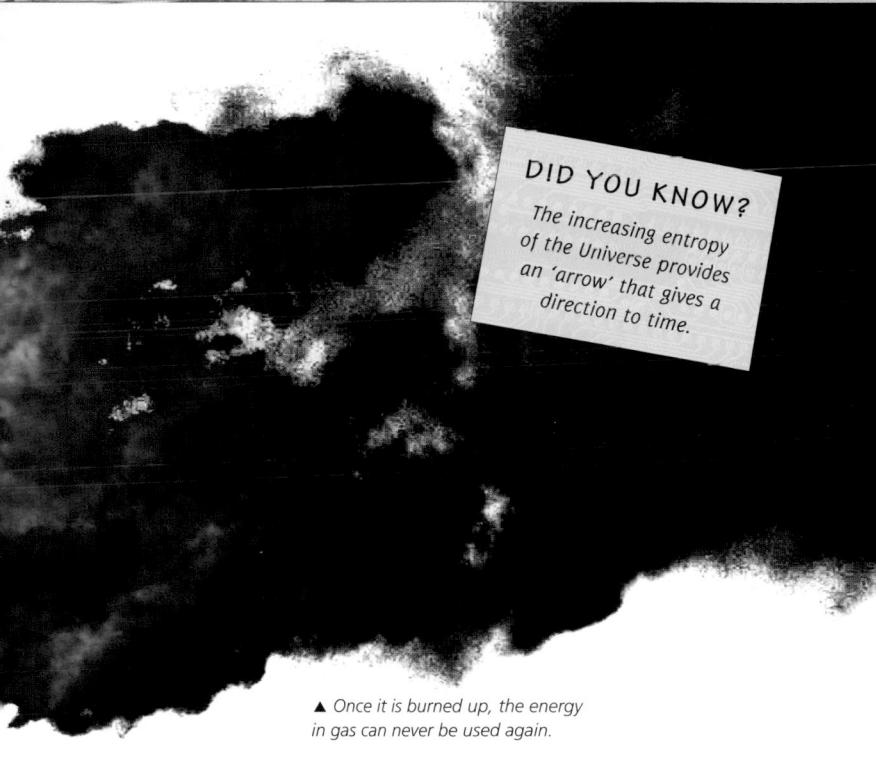

▲ Once it is burned up, the energy in gas can never be used again.

🔧 **Clausius summed this idea up** in the 1860s with two laws of thermodynamics.

🔧 **The first law of thermodynamics** says the total energy in the Universe was fixed forever at the beginning of time.

🔧 **The second law of thermodynamics** is that all energy differences tend to even out over time, so the entropy of the Universe must always increase.

Engines

⚙ **Engines are machines** that convert fuel into movement. Most work by burning fuel to make gases that expand rapidly as they get hot.

⚙ **Engines that burn fuel** to generate power are called 'heat engines'. The burning process is called 'combustion'.

⚙ **Internal combustion engines**, such as those in cars and jets, burn fuel on the inside.

⚙ **In car and diesel train engines**, hot gases swell inside a 'combustion chamber' and push against a piston or turbine.

⚙ **External combustion engines**, such as those in steam engines, burn fuel on the outside in a separate boiler that makes hot steam to drive a piston or turbine.

⚙ **The most common** fuels for motor vehicles are petrol and diesel, but reserves of these are limited. Some engines now burn biofuels such as ethanol and methanol, which are made from plants such as maize.

▼ *In a turbofan engine, cold air mixes with hot gases to produce thrust.*

Fan sucks in air

Burning fuel creates hot gases

The hot gases push the plane forwards

⚙ **Petrol, diesel and biofuels** create gases that pollute the air, so some engines now use hydrogen.

⚙ **Engines with pistons** that go back and forth inside cylinders are called reciprocating engines.

⚙ **In four-stroke engines** (used in most cars) the pistons go up and down four times for each time they are thrust down by the hot gases. In two-stroke engines, such as those on small motorcycles and lawnmowers, the piston is pushed by burning gases every time it goes down.

⚙ **In jets and rockets**, the hot gases swell, pushing against the engine as they shoot out of the back.

⚙ **In a jet engine**, air is taken in at the front, compressed by fans, then sprayed with fuel and ignited. The burning gases swell, blast past more fans (the turbine) and through the back of the engine to thrust the plane forwards.

▼ *Hot gases from a jet engine turn the propeller in a turboprop engine.*

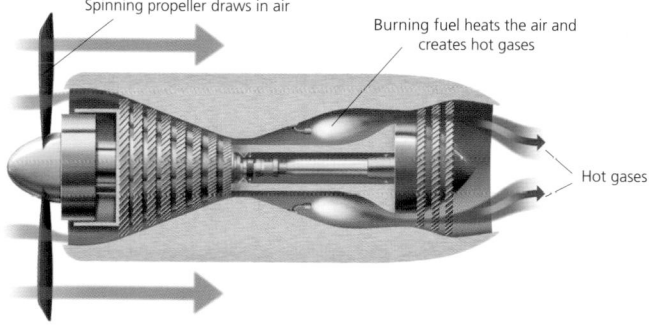

Spinning propeller draws in air

Burning fuel heats the air and creates hot gases

Hot gases

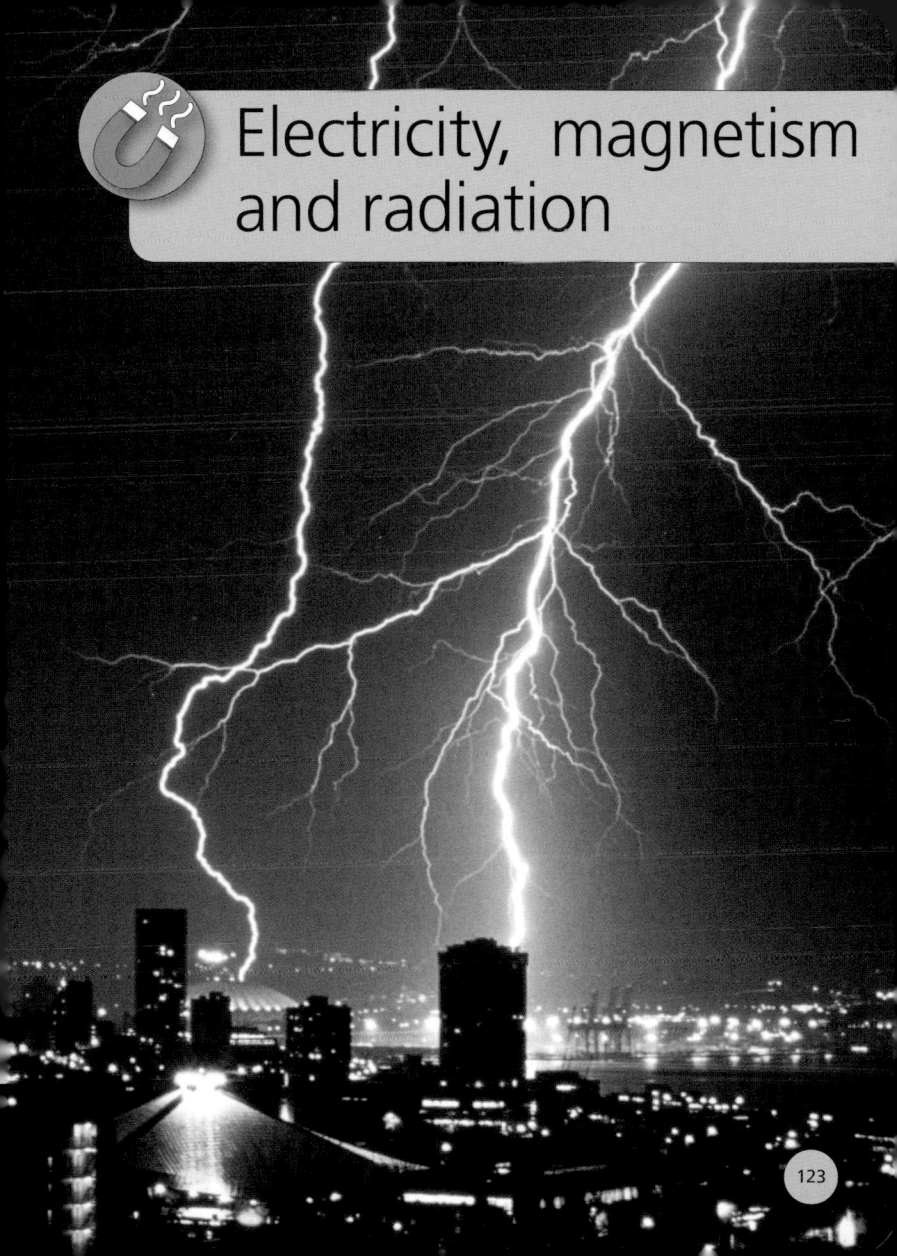

Electricity, magnetism and radiation

123

Electricity

⚙ **Electricity is energy**, and it is the major source of power for much of the world.

⚙ **All the electrons** that make up every atom carry a tiny electrical charge. This is a force, which either pulls bits of atoms together (attracts them) or pushes them apart (repels them).

⚙ **Some particles** (such as electrons) have a negative electrical charge. Others have a positive charge. Two particles with the same charge repel each other, while two particles with opposing charges attract each other.

⚙ **Most atoms** have equal numbers of positive and negative particles, so they are usually balanced.

⚙ **The movement of electrons** can produce an electric current – a flow of electricity.

⚙ **A material** through which electrons (and electrical charge) flow, such as copper, is called a 'conductor'. Materials that stop electrons passing through, such as rubber, are called insulators.

⚙ **Static electricity** is the accumulation of electric charge on an insulator. It is the result of electrons being shifted to the insulator by friction.

⚙ **Electric charge** can be detected and measured with an instrument called an electroscope.

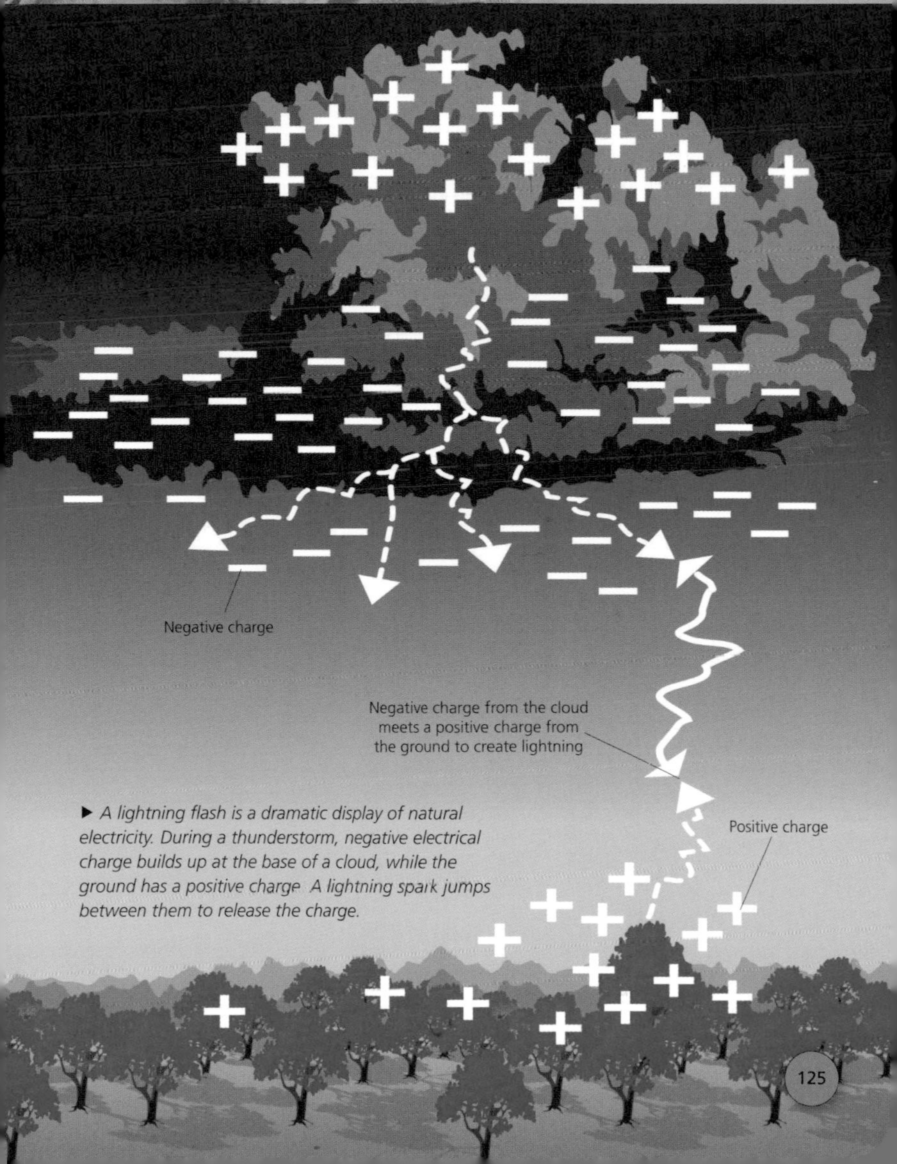

Negative charge

Negative charge from the cloud meets a positive charge from the ground to create lightning

Positive charge

▶ A lightning flash is a dramatic display of natural electricity. During a thunderstorm, negative electrical charge builds up at the base of a cloud, while the ground has a positive charge A lightning spark jumps between them to release the charge.

Electric circuits

⚙️ **An electric circuit** is an unbroken loop of conducting material along which an electric charge may flow. A current will only flow through a good conductor.

⚙️ **There are three basic components** in an electric circuit: a conductor, an energy source and an object for the circuit to power.

⚙️ **A current will only flow** if there is an energy force to push the electric charge. This force is called an electromotive force (emf).

⚙️ **An emf is created** by a battery or generator. Without an emf, charged electrons will just move randomly inside the conductor in different directions. Random movement does not produce an electric current.

▼ *Electricity is generated in a power station by spinning tightly wrapped coils of wire (the windings) in between magnets to induce a current in the wire.*

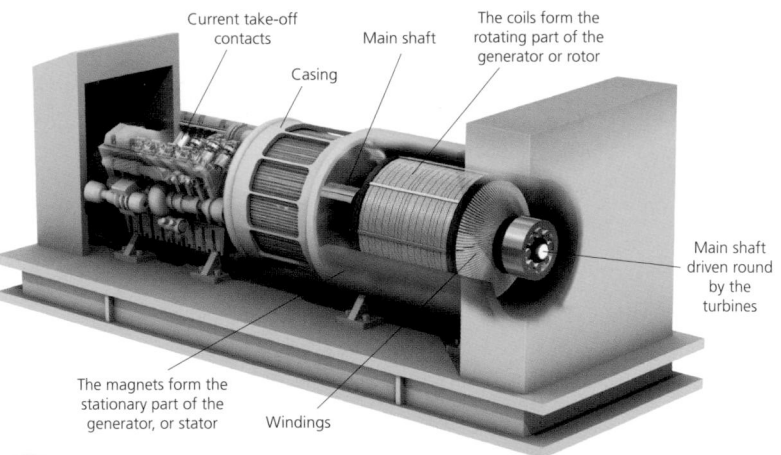

Current take-off contacts

Main shaft

The coils form the rotating part of the generator or rotor

Casing

Main shaft driven round by the turbines

The magnets form the stationary part of the generator, or stator

Windings

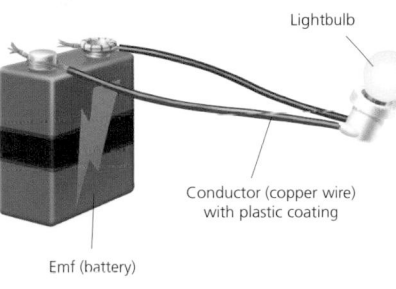

Lightbulb

Conductor (copper wire) with plastic coating

Emf (battery)

◀ A battery provides the emf for an electric current to flow through the circuit and light the bulb.

DID YOU KNOW?

The electrical resistance of dry skin is 500,000 ohms, whereas wet skin is just 1000 ohms.

⚙ **When a conductor** is connected to a battery, the negatively charged electrons are attracted to the battery's positive terminal, so they flow towards it, in one direction. The flow produces an electric current.

⚙ **Batteries give potential energy** to the electrons that come from it. The amount of electrical energy varies at different points in a circuit. This difference, called the potential difference, is measured in volts.

⚙ **The rate** at which current flows is measured in amps. It depends on the voltage and the resistance (how much the circuit obstructs the flow of current). Resistance is measured in ohms.

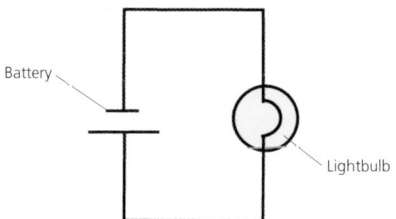

Battery

Lightbulb

◀ An electric circuit can be represented by a simple line on a diagram, with symbols for features such as the battery and bulb.

Magnetism

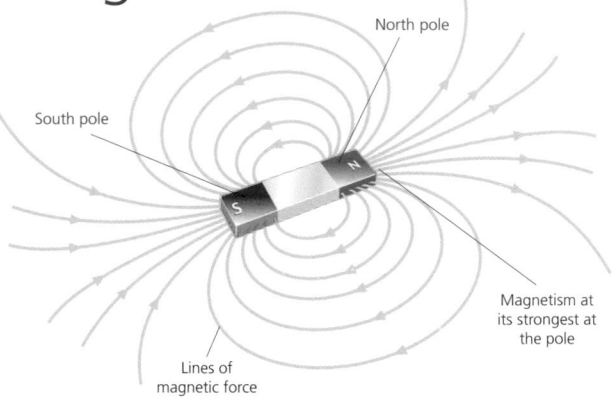

North pole

South pole

Magnetism at its strongest at the pole

Lines of magnetic force

▲ *A typical bar magnet is made of steel. Its lines of magnetic force curve from one pole to the other at each end.*

⚙ **Magnetism is the property** of some materials to attract or repel 'like' materials. A magnet is a material that has this property, such as the metal iron.

⚙ **A magnetic field** is the area around a magnet inside which its magnetic force can be detected. An electric current creates a magnetic field.

⚙ **A magnet** has north and south 'poles' near each end. The magnetic field is strongest at the poles. 'Like' poles (for example, north poles of two magnets) repel each other, and 'unlike' poles attract each other.

- **Earth has a magnetic field** created by electric currents inside its iron core. The magnetic north pole is close to the geographic North Pole.

- **If suspended freely**, a magnet will turn so that its north pole points to Earth's magnetic north pole.

- **The strength of a magnet** is measured in teslas. The Earth's magnetic field is 0.00005 teslas.

- **Magnetic materials** are made up of groups of atoms (domains). Each domain is a tiny molecular magnet with north and south poles.

▼ Charged particles from the Sun are funnelled into the atmosphere by Earth's magnetic field to create aurorae above the poles.

Electromagnetism

⚙ **Electromagnetism** is the combination of electricity and magnetism. Every electric current creates its own magnetic field.

⚙ **Scottish physicist** James Maxwell developed the electromagnetic theory. Maxwell's screw rule states that a magnetic field runs in the same way a screw turns, if it is screwed in the direction of the electric current.

⚙ **An electromagnet** is a strong magnet that is only magnetic when an electric current passes through it. It is made by wrapping a coil of wire (a solenoid) around a core of iron.

⚙ **Electromagnets are used** in most of the electric machines in use today, from ticket machines to telephones.

⚙ **Magnetic levitation** (Maglev) trains use electromagnets to support the train above the rails by magnetic repulsion.

⚙ **When an electric wire** is moved across a magnetic field, a current is created (induced) in the wire. This is the basis of every kind of electricity generation.

▶ *In a brain scan, the patient's head goes inside a ring-shaped electromagnet and radio waves reveal slight changes in the field created by the brain.*

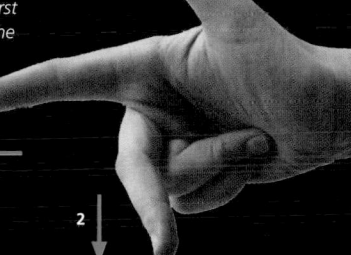

▶ *Fleming's right-hand rule, with thumb, first and second fingers at right angles, shows the direction of the current induced **2** when a wire **T** moves through a magnetic field **1**.*

⚙ **Fleming's right-hand rule** shows the direction of the flow of an electric current when a wire moves through a magnetic field (see diagram above).

⚙ **Electromagnets can be switched on and off**, unlike permanent magnets.

⚙ **'Electromagnetic field'** describes the area around an electric or magnetic object in which the electromagnetic force is effective.

Electromagnetic spectrum

⚙ **Electromagnetic radiation** is energy emitted by atoms. It travels in minute packets of energy called 'photons' that can behave either as particles or as waves.

⚙ **Waves of electromagnetic radiation** can vary in length and frequency. The electromagnetic spectrum is the entire possible range.

⚙ **The longest waves** are over 100 km in length, while the shortest are less than a billionth of a millimetre long.

⚙ **The human eye** can see just a small range of wavelengths, known as visible light. Every colour we see has its own wavelength.

⚙ **Infrared (IR)** is light given off by warm objects in waves just too long for the human eye to see. Ultraviolet (UV) is light given off by very hot objects in waves just too short for the eye to see.

⚙ **Waves longer than light include:** terahertz (used for security body scans), microwaves (used in microwave ovens), and radio waves (used by radios, televisions, mobile phones and wireless networks). Longer waves are less energetic than short waves.

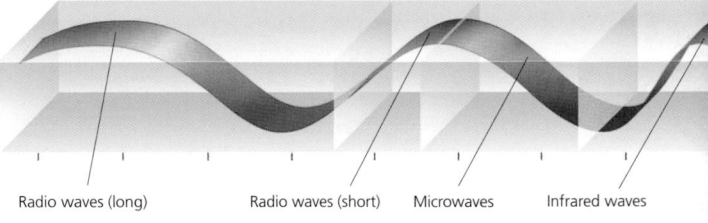

Radio waves (long)   Radio waves (short)   Microwaves   Infrared waves

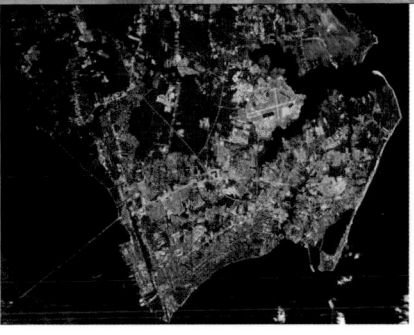

◀ *This satellite photo clearly shows all the 'near' IR (IR with waves shorter than heat) reflected by healthy vegetation, shown in red.*

✿ **Waves shorter than light**, such as UV, X-rays and gamma rays, are very energetic, and can penetrate some solid materials that block light. That makes exposure to them dangerous.

✿ **UV in sunlight** in small doses tans the skin, but in large doses can cause skin cancer.

✿ **X-rays are harmless in brief doses** and are short enough to pass through most body tissues except bone. This is why they can be used to make medical X-ray photos.

✿ **Gamma rays** are dangerous even in small doses but they can be used in some body scans and to 'irradiate' seeds to stop them growing until needed.

▼ *The electromagnetic spectrum ranges from long wavelength, low-energy radio waves to short wavelength, high-energy gamma rays.*

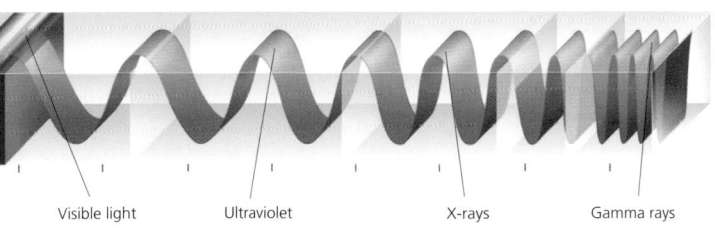

Visible light   Ultraviolet   X-rays   Gamma rays

Electronics

⚙ **Electronics is the technology** of electrical control systems, at the heart of everything from mobile phones to personal computers.

⚙ **Electronic components** control operations by switching tiny electrical circuits on and off.

⚙ **Transistors are the key components** of every electronic system. They control the flow of electricity.

⚙ **A transistor controls** currents automatically because it is made from a material called a semiconductor that can change its ability to conduct electricity.

⚙ **Diodes are transistors** with two connection points: an 'in' and an 'out'. They are simple switches, turning the current on or off.

⚙ **Triodes are transistors** with three connection points: an 'in', an 'out' and a 'control'. They can amplify the current or reduce it.

◀ *Mobile phones were made possible by the invention of the silicon chip, which miniaturized electronic circuits. Inside the phone, a chip translates speech into digital form for wireless transmission to the nearest phone mast.*

⚙ **A silicon chip** consists of thousands of transistors linked by thin metal strips, integrated (contained) within a single crystal (chip) of the semiconductor silicon.

⚙ **The electronic areas** of a chip are those treated with traces of chemicals, such as boron and phosphorus, which alter the conductivity of silicon.

▼ *Tiny electronic circuits are made by printing the circuit pattern on a copper-coated board, then dissolving away unwanted bits.*

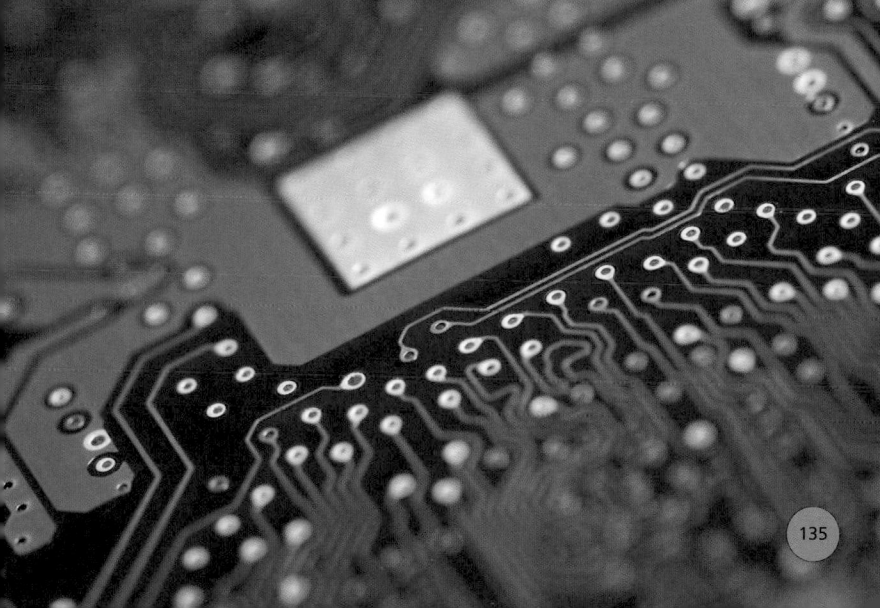

Radiation

⚙ **Radiation is an atom's way** of getting rid of excess energy. Electromagnetic radiation is energy that travels as photons at the speed of light. Particulate radiation is bigger particles shot out by atoms at slower speeds.

⚙ **Particulate radiation** includes cosmic rays (streams of particles from the stars) and 'radioactivity' that occurs when certain large atoms degrade (break down).

⚙ **Radiation can be harmful.** It can damage and kill human, animal and plant cells.

⚙ **Bacteria can survive** a dose of radiation 10,000 times stronger than that which a person would survive.

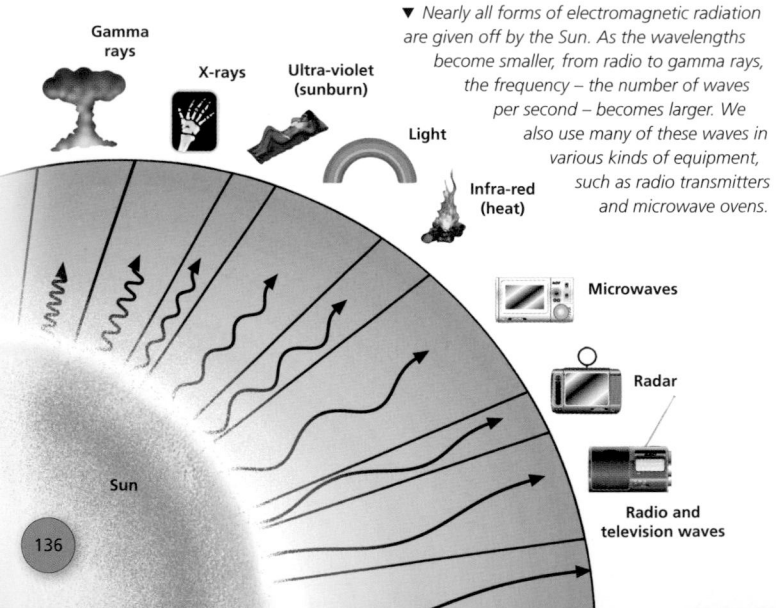

▼ Nearly all forms of electromagnetic radiation are given off by the Sun. As the wavelengths become smaller, from radio to gamma rays, the frequency – the number of waves per second – becomes larger. We also use many of these waves in various kinds of equipment, such as radio transmitters and microwave ovens.

Gamma rays

X-rays

Ultra-violet (sunburn)

Light

Infra-red (heat)

Microwaves

Radar

Sun

Radio and television waves

▲ *Some of the fuel burned in nuclear power stations becomes highly radioactive when spent (after being used) and must be disposed of safely.*

⚙ **The radiation released** by radioactivity is commonly measured in becquerels. The radiation dose a victim receives is measured in roentgens. The dose the victim absorbs is measured in grays.

⚙ **An accident** at the Chernobyl nuclear power station in the Soviet Union in 1986, released large amounts of radiation into the atmosphere, killing 32 people outright and contaminating millions of acres of land

⚙ **The natural radioactivity** of a Brazil nut is about six becquerels. This means that six atoms in the nut break up every second.

Visible light

⚙ **When we refer to 'light'** we usually mean visible light, which is the only form of electromagnetic radiation that we can see.

⚙ **During the day** light appears to be all around us, but only a few things are actually sources of light. Light sources include stars, such as our Sun, and electric lights.

⚙ **Most objects** are visible to us because they reflect the light that is produced by light sources. If something is not a light source and does not reflect light, we cannot see it.

⚙ **Light travels** in straight lines, called rays. Light rays change direction if they are reflected off or pass through an object or substance, but still remain straight.

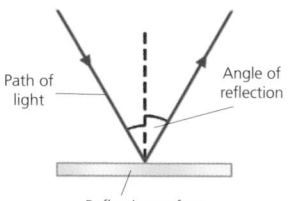

Path of light

Angle of reflection

Reflective surface

◀▼ *We see light rays reflected together from a mirror at the same angle that they arrived, so they show a clear image (left). A mirror that isn't flat reflects them at different angles, distorting the image (below).*

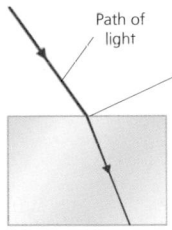

Path of light — Light bends as it leaves the air and enters the glass block

▲▶ *Light travels more slowly through glass than air, and if a ray enters glass at an angle it is bent or refracted, which is why the drinking straw shown here appears to be broken.*

⚙ **When light strikes a surface**, some or all of it is reflected. Most surfaces scatter light in all directions, which simply makes the surface visible to the human eye.

⚙ **Mirrors and other shiny surfaces** reflect light in exactly the same pattern in which it arrived, producing a visible 'mirror image'.

⚙ **When light passes** into transparent substances, such as glass or water, it changes direction slightly. This is known as 'refraction'.

⚙ **If the path of a light ray** is blocked, a shadow forms. Most shadows have two regions – the umbra and penumbra. The umbra is the dark part where light rays are blocked altogether. The penumbra is the lighter rim where some rays reach.

Light sources

⚙ **The main source** of natural light on Earth is the Sun. The hot gases on its surface glow fiercely.

⚙ **The brightness** (or 'luminous intensity') of a light source is measured in candelas (Cd), with 1 Cd having about the same luminous intensity as a small candle.

⚙ **The Sun's surface** pumps out 23 billion Cd per m². Laser lights are even brighter, but very small.

⚙ **The amount of light** falling on a surface is measured in lux, with 1 lux equalling the amount of light from a source of 1 Cd, from 1 m away. You need around 500 lux to read by.

▼ *At a concert, laser beams send out brilliant coloured shafts of light, each of a single wavelength.*

- **Electric lightbulbs** are incandescent, which means that their light comes from a thin tungsten wire (filament) that glows when heated by an electric current.

- **Electric lights** were invented independently in 1878 by English physicist and chemist Sir Joseph Swan and American inventors Thomas Edison and Hiram Maxim.

- **A fluorescent light** has a glass tube coated on the inside with powders called phosphors. Electricity causes the gases inside the tube to send out UV rays, which hit the phosphors, making them glow (fluoresce).

- **In a neon light**, a huge electric current makes the gas inside the tube electrically charged, causing it to glow.

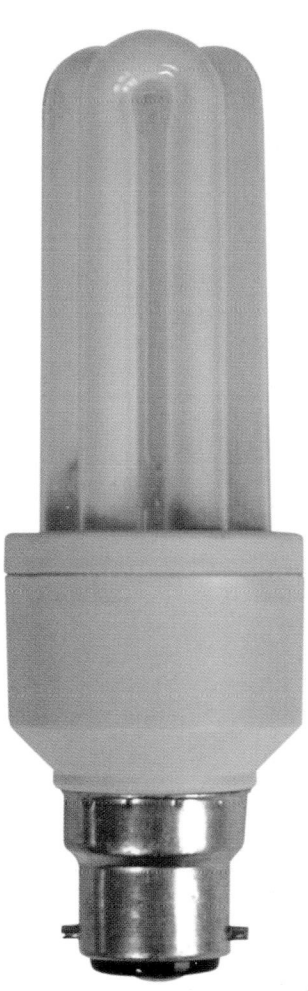

▶ *This low-energy lightbulb uses a glowing gas to emit light, instead of the old-fashioned glowing filament of wire.*

141

Moving light

⚙️ **Light is the fastest thing** in the Universe, travelling at a speed of 299,792,458 m/sec. One method used to remember this figure is from the number of letters in each word of the following sentence: 'We guarantee certainty, clearly referring to this light mnemonic'.

⚙️ **For centuries** scientists debated whether light travels as waves or as particles (photons). It is now thought to do both.

⚙️ **Light waves** have peaks and troughs, like waves in the sea.

⚙️ **If two beams of light meet**, they interfere with each other.

⚙️ **Constructive interference** occurs when the peaks of two light waves align, creating a single, brighter beam.

⚙️ **Destructive interference** occurs when the peaks of a light wave align with the troughs of another. This causes the beams to cancel each other out, leading to a pattern of light and shade known as an 'interference pattern'.

⚙️ **Light rays from the Sun** can be converted into other forms of energy. Solar photovoltaic (PV) converter panels are made of two or more layers of semi-conducting material, such as silicon. When incoming solar rays strike the silicon, it produces electrons that are conducted away by a metallic grid as an electric current.

> **DID YOU KNOW?**
> An area the size of a pin head in direct sun receives one thousand billion photons in a single second.

▼ *In solar panels, the impact of photons of light on atoms generates electricity.*

Solar panels

Light and atoms

⚙ **Atoms give out light** when they gain energy by absorbing light or other electromagnetic waves, or when hit by other particles.

⚙ **Normally, atoms** are in a 'ground' state in which their electrons circle close to the nucleus, where their energy is at its lowest ebb.

⚙ **An atom emits light** when it is excited (raised from the ground state) by taking in energy. When they gain energy, electrons move further away from the nucleus.

⚙ **An atom** only stays excited for a fraction of a second before the electron drops back towards the nucleus.

⚙ **When electrons** drop back, they release the energy they gained as a packet of electromagnetic radiation (a photon). Electrons drop towards the nucleus in steps.

◄ *Astronomers can tell what distant stars are made of from the colour of light emitted by their atoms.*

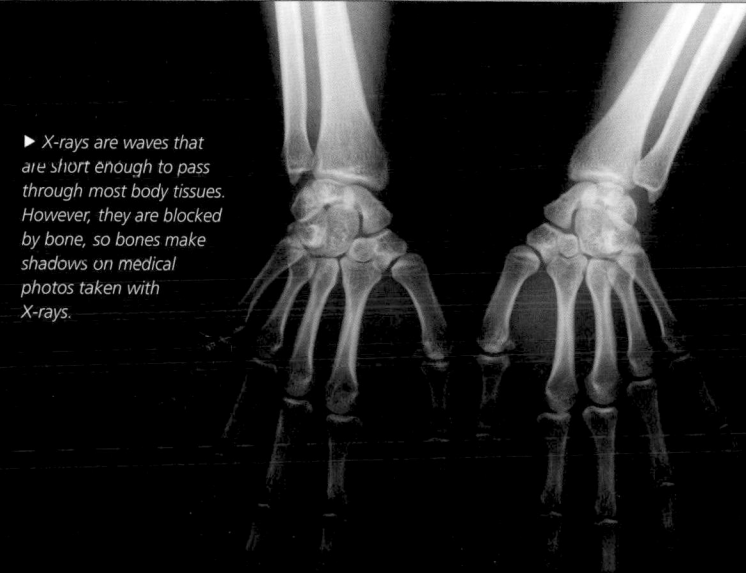

▶ *X-rays are waves that are short enough to pass through most body tissues. However, they are blocked by bone, so bones make shadows on medical photos taken with X-rays.*

⚙ **Each 'step'** has a its own energy level, so the energy of a photon depends precisely on how big the steps are. Big steps send out higher-energy short-wave photons such as X-rays.

⚙ **The colour of the light** that an atom sends out also depends on the size of the steps its electrons jump down.

⚙ **Each kind of atom** has its own range of electron energy steps, so each sends out particular colours of light. The range of colours each kind of atom sends out is called its emission spectrum.

⚙ **Atoms absorb light** as well as emitting it. A particular atom can only absorb particular colours. This is known as an atom's absorption spectrum.

Colour

- **Colour is** the way our eyes see different wavelengths of light.

- **We see the longest light waves** as the colour red. Waves that appear red are about 700 nanometres (nm) in length (1 nm = 1 billionth of a metre).

- **The shortest light waves** – about 400 nm in length – are seen by human eyes as the colour violet.

- **Some light**, such as sunlight and the light from torches and ordinary lightbulbs, is actually a mixture of every colour, and is called white light.

- **The world around us** appears to us to be different colours because molecules in different surfaces reflect and absorb particular wavelengths of light.

- **Red blood** and deep blue printers' inks are vividly coloured because both have molecules shaped like four-petalled flowers, with a metal atom at each centre.

- **The shimmering rainbow colours** that flash on surfaces such as peacock feathers, butterfly wings and CDs are known as iridescence.

- **Iridescence can be caused** by the way a surface breaks the light hitting it into colours. It can also be caused by interference, which occurs when an object has a thin, transparent surface layer. Light waves reflected from the top surface are slightly out of step with waves reflected from the inner surface, creating a pattern of light.

▶ The shimmering blue of this butterfly is iridescence set up by tiny air pockets in the scales on its wings.

Spectrum

⚙ **A spectrum** is a range of different wavelengths of electromagnetic radiation.

⚙ **The white light of sunlight** can be broken up into its spectrum of colours using a prism.

⚙ **When a prism** is lit by a beam of white light it refracts short wavelengths of the light more than longer ones. This causes the light to split into bands ranging from violet (shortest wavelength) to red (longest).

⚙ **The order of colours** in a spectrum is always red, orange, yellow, green, blue, indigo, violet. You can remember this from the first letter of each word in the phrase: 'Richard Of York Gained Battles In Vain'.

▶ *In a darkened room, a narrow beam of white light is split into a spectrum by refraction as it passes through a prism.*

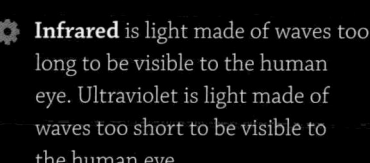

- **Infrared** is light made of waves too long to be visible to the human eye. Ultraviolet is light made of waves too short to be visible to the human eye.

- **Spectral analysis** is the study of the spectrum created when a solid, liquid or gas glows.

- **Every substance** produces its own unique spectrum, so spectral analysis helps to identify substances.

Mixing colours

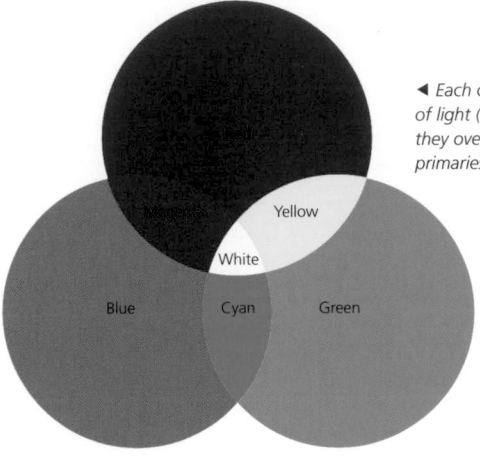

◄ Each circle is a primary colour of light (red, green, blue). Where they overlap you see the subtractive primaries (magenta, cyan, yellow).

🔧 **There are three** primary (basic) colours of light – red, green and blue. These three colours can be mixed to make any other colour by varying their proportions.

🔧 **The primary colours** of light are called additive primaries because they are added together to make other colours.

🔧 **Each additive primary** is one third of the spectrum of white light, so combining all three makes white.

🔧 **When two additive primaries** are added together they make a third colour, called a subtractive primary.

🔧 **The three subtractive primaries** are magenta (red plus blue), cyan (blue plus green) and yellow (green plus red). They too can be mixed in various proportions to make other colours.

⚙ **Surfaces appear as certain colours** to human eyes because they soak up some colours of white light and reflect the others. The colour the eye perceives is a combination of the colours reflected.

⚙ **Each subtractive primary** soaks up one-third of the spectrum of white light and reflects two-thirds of it. Mixing two subtractive primaries soaks up two-thirds of the spectrum. Mixing all three subtractive primaries soaks up all colours of the spectrum, making black.

⚙ **Two subtractive primaries** mixed make an additive primary. Cyan and magenta make blue, yellow and cyan make green, yellow and magenta make red.

▼ *The substances used to create the different colours of oil paint are known as pigments.*

Sound

⚙ **Most sounds** you hear, from the whisper of the wind to the roar of a jet, are actually moving air.

⚙ **Every sound** originates with something vibrating, like the strings of a guitar twanging to and fro. This makes the air vibrate too and the vibrations in the air carry the sound to your ears.

⚙ **The vibrations** that carry sound through the air are called sound waves, which move by alternately squeezing air molecules together and then stretching them apart.

⚙ **The parts of the air** that are squeezed are called condensations, and the parts of the air that are stretched are called rarefactions.

⚙ **Sound waves** travel faster through liquids and solids than through air because molecules in liquids and solids are more closely packed together than air molecules.

▼ *When an aircraft travels faster than sound, it squashes the air in front until it causes a 'sonic boom' as the air pops like a balloon.*

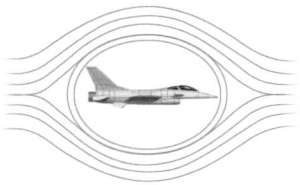

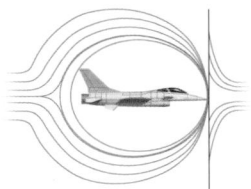

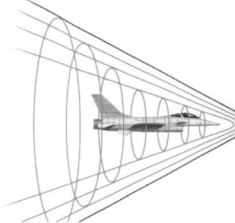

1 Sound waves spread outwards as the plane moves

2 Sound waves are squashed as the plane increases speed

3 The plane flies through the sound barrier, and a sonic boom is heard

▲ *A loudspeaker turns electrical signals into corresponding patterns of sound waves.*

- ⚙️ **There is complete silence** in a vacuum (a space empty even of air) because there are no molecules to carry sound.

- ⚙️ **Sound travels** at 344 m/sec in air at 20°C, but 386 m/sec in air at 100°C. It travels at 1500 m/sec in water and about 6000 m/sec in steel.

- ⚙️ **The speed of sound** is around a million times slower than light. This is why you hear thunder after you see a flash of lightning.

Sound measurement

⚙ **The loudness (volume) of a sound** is usually measured in decibels (dB). One decibel is one-tenth of a bel, the unit of sound named after Scottish-born American inventor Alexander Graham Bell.

⚙ **Decibels** were originally only used to measure sound intensity, but are now used to compare electronic power output and voltages too.

⚙ **An increase** of 10 points on the decibel scale means that a sound has increased by ten times.

⚙ **The quietest sound** audible to human ears is 0 dB, and we can only hear a change in a sound's volume if it is of 1 dB or more.

⚙ **A rustle of leaves** or a quiet whisper is 10 dB. Quiet talking is 30–40 dB, and loud talking is about 60 dB.

◄ *Workers protect themselves from damaging sound waves by wearing ear protectors.*

Atom bomb: 210 dB

Jet take-off: 140 dB

Thunder: 100 dB

City street: 70 dB

Talking: 40 dB

Rustling leaves: 10 dB

DID YOU KNOW?

Listening to sound levels of over 100 dB for long periods of time causes deafness in humans.

⚙ **The noise level** on a city street is about 70 dB. Thunder is around 100 dB, while the loudest scream ever recorded was 128.4 dB. A jet taking off is 110–140 dB. The loudest sound ever made by human technology was an atom bomb, at 210 dB.

⚙ **The amount of energy** in a sound is measured in watts per m² (W/m²). A sound of 0 dB is one thousand billionths of 1 W/m².

◄ A range of different sounds on the decibel scale.

Echoes and acoustics

⚙️ **An echo** is a reflection of sound off an object or surface that is heard slightly after the direct sound.

⚙️ **Our ears** can only hear an echo if it comes back more than 0.1 seconds after the original sound. In 0.1 seconds, sound travels 34 m, so our ears can only hear echoes that are reflected back from surfaces at least 17 m away.

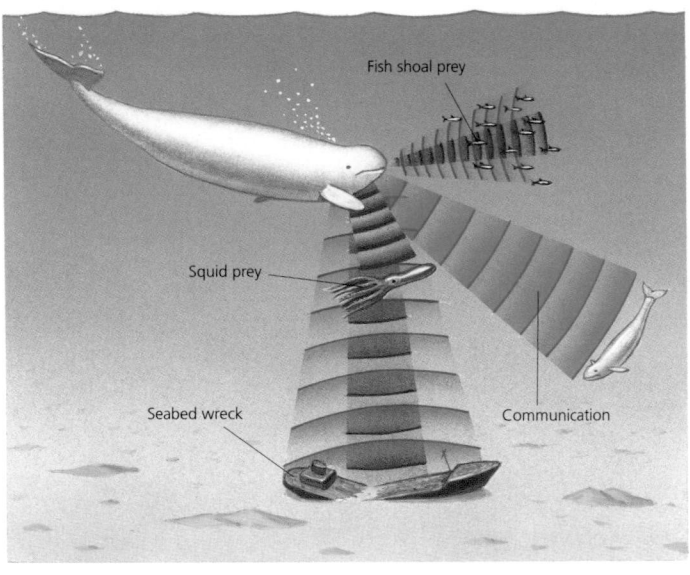

Fish shoal prey

Squid prey

Seabed wreck

Communication

▲ *Hunting whales such as the beluga send out sonic clicks. These pulses bounce back as echoes to give the whale information about the position of any objects that might be nearby.*

▶ *Acoustic engineers have installed sound cushions to reduce echoes from the vast dome of London's Royal Albert Hall and improve sound quality.*

- **Smooth, hard surfaces** give the best echoes because they cause a minimum amount of disruption to the sound waves reflecting off them.

- **Acoustics** is the study of how sounds are created, transmitted and received. It also refers to the sound properties of a building.

- **Concert halls** are designed to use echoes effectively to project sound. If a hall has too much echo, echoing sounds will interfere with new sounds, but a complete absence of echoes results in a muffled, lifeless sound.

- **The sound of live music** can be heard fading after musicians have stopped playing. This delay is called the reverberation time. Concert halls typically have a reverberation time of 2 sec. A cathedral may reverberate for up to 8 sec, giving a less defined sound.

Musical sounds

⚙ **Like all sound**, a musical note is created by a vibration of air. Musicians control the frequency and volume of these vibrations to play tunes.

⚙ **The pitch** (level) of a musical note depends upon the frequency of the vibrations.

⚙ **Sound frequency** is measured in hertz (Hz), which refers to the number of cycles or waves per second.

⚙ **Human ears** can hear sounds within a frequency range of 20–20,000 Hz.

⚙ **Middle C** on a piano measures 262 Hz. A piano has a frequency range from 27.5–4186 Hz.

⚙ **The highest singing** voice can reach the E above a piano top note (4350 Hz), while the lowest is 20.6 Hz.

⚙ **Few sounds** have only one pitch. Most have a fundamental (low) pitch and higher overtones.

Mouthpiece

⚙ **The frequency** at which an object naturally vibrates is called its resonant frequency. A musical note can shatter glass if its frequency coincides with the resonant frequency of the glass.

▶ *The shape of the saxophone controls the vibrations of air blown into it to create a musical sound.*

▶ The sound of a violin is created by the regular vibrations of the strings as the bow is drawn across them.

Bow

Time

- **Time is measured** in seconds, minutes, hours, days, months and years.

- **A clock** is a device used to measure time.

- **Clocks are controlled by mechanisms** with repeating motions. No clock keeps perfect time, usually gaining or losing at least a fraction of a second every day.

▼ ▶ *The idea of time zones began in the 1880s, to standardize timekeeping for railway timetables. Airplane travel made them even more important. The time is the same everywhere within one time zone, but different to all the other time zones.*

NEW YORK LONDON ISTANBUL NEW DELHI

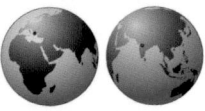

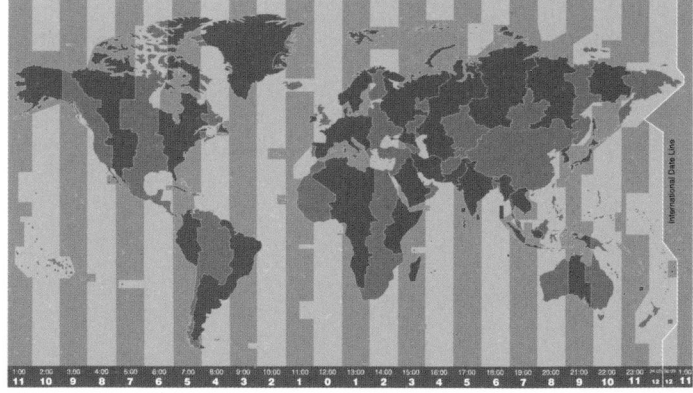

◄ The strontium atomic clock is thought to be more accurate than anything previously achieved.

⚙ **The standard worldwide time** has been set by atomic clocks since 1967. These are accurate to 0.001 sec in 1000 years.

⚙ **Atomic clocks** are kept regular by the movement of certain atoms. Caesium atoms vibrate at a rate of 9,192,631,770 times a second, while strontium atoms are even faster (and therefore even more accurate), at 429,228,004,229,952 times a second.

⚙ **The strontium atomic clock** at JILA, a scientific institute in Colorado, USA, is the most accurate clock on Earth. It could run for 200 million years without gaining or losing a single second!

⚙ **Some scientists** think time is the fourth dimension (the other three being length, width and height). This suggests the theory that time could run in any direction.

⚙ **Distant stars** are so far away that their light can take many years to reach us. This means we see them as they were years ago, not as they are now. So time actually varies according to where you are.

⚙ **Einstein's theory** of general relativity shows that time is affected by gravity, and runs slower nearer strong gravitational fields such as stars.

Space

* **A flat surface is two-dimensional**. The two dimensions – length and width – are at right angles to each other.

* **Any point** on a flat surface can be pinpointed exactly with two figures, one showing how far along the point is and the other how far across.

* **There are three dimensions** of space at right angles to each other: length, width and depth.

* **Any point** in space can be pinpointed with three figures, one showing how far along it is, one how high it is and a third how far across it is.

* **If an object is moving**, three dimensions are not enough to locate it. You need a fourth dimension – time – to pinpoint its location.

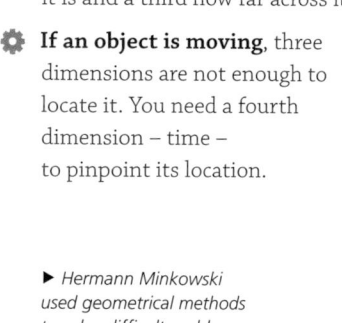

▶ *Hermann Minkowski used geometrical methods to solve difficult problems in number theory, in mathematical physics and the theory of relativity.*

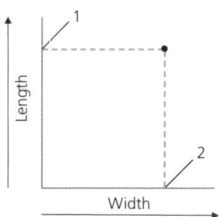

◀ You can pinpoint a position on a surface with just two figures: length and width.

Calculating the position of a point on a 2D plane

▶ You can pinpoint a position in space with three figures: length, width and depth.

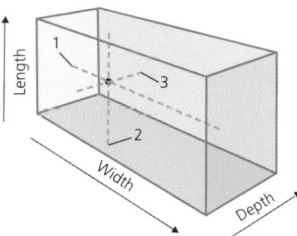

Calculating the position of a point in a 3D shape

⚙ **German mathematician** Hermann Minkowski laid the foundations for Albert Einstein's special theory of relativity in the early 1900s, when he realized that the three dimensions of physical space need to be combined with time. Four-dimensional space is called space-time.

⚙ **After Minkowski's breakthroughs**, mathematicians began to develop special geometry to describe four dimensions.

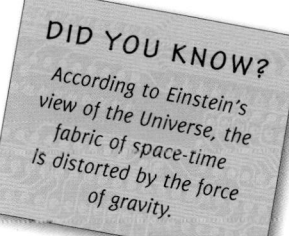

DID YOU KNOW?

According to Einstein's view of the Universe, the fabric of space-time is distorted by the force of gravity.

Relativity

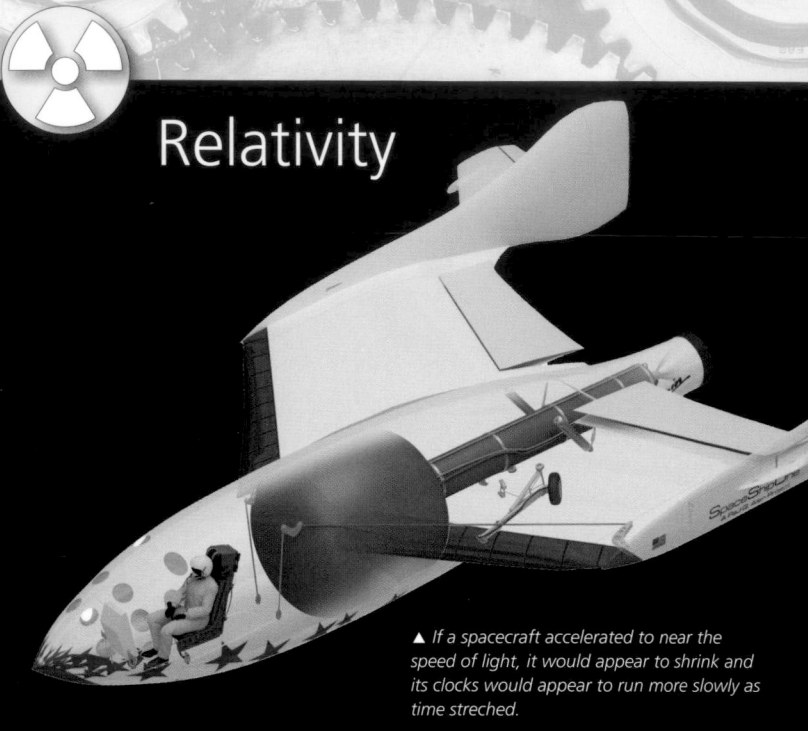

▲ If a spacecraft accelerated to near the speed of light, it would appear to shrink and its clocks would appear to run more slowly as time streched.

⚙ **Einstein was the creator of two theories** of relativity that have revolutionized scientists' way of thinking about the Universe. These are called the special theory of relativity (1905) and the general theory of relativity (1915).

⚙ **Time is relative.** It depends entirely on where you are and how you are moving when you measure it. Someone elsewhere will get a different measurement.

⚙ **Distance and speed** are also relative. For example, if you are in a car and another car whizzes past you, the slower you are travelling, the faster the other car seems to be moving.

⚙ **In his special theory of relativity**, Einstein showed that you cannot even measure speed relative to light, the fastest thing in the Universe. This is because the speed of light is constant – it doesn't depend on how fast the source of the light is moving, or the speed of someone looking at the light.

⚙ **Einstein realized** that the constant speed of light would result in some strange effects on other objects moving at very high speeds.

⚙ **Einstein's general theory of relativity** showed that gravity bends space-time, leading scientists to predict the existence of black holes (points in space where gravity is so strong even light is pulled into them).

⚙ **An eclipse of the Sun** in 1919 gave English scientist Arthur Eddington the opportunity to observe the Sun's gravity bending light, proving Einstein's general theory of relativity.

▶ *With his theories of relativity, Einstein overturned our common sense understanding of the nature of time and space.*

167

Time travel

⚙ **Einstein showed** that time runs at different speeds in different places, and that it is just another dimension like length, width and depth. This has led to the suggestion that at some point it may be possible for humans to travel through time to the past or future.

⚙ **Einstein stated that** it is impossible for anyone to move through time, because it would involve moving faster than light. Even if they reached light speed, time would stop and they would not be alive.

⚙ **The concept of time travel** causes theoretical problems for the relationship between cause and effect. A famous example is the idea of a man who travels back to a time before his parents were born and kills his grandfather. That would mean one of his parents could not have been born, and therefore he himself could not have been born. If so, then how could he have killed his grandfather? It's impossible to answer this paradox.

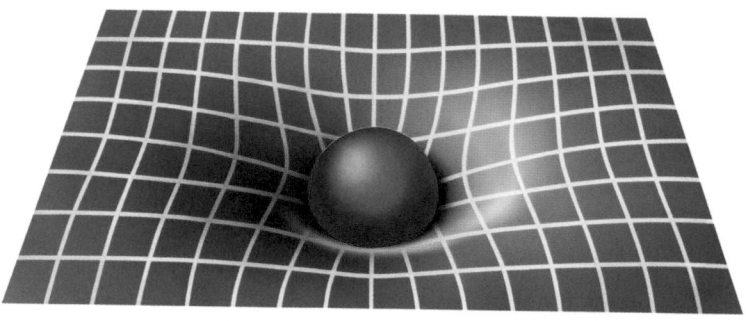

▲ *Gravity bends the fabric of space-time. Could it ever be bent so much that we could travel through time just as we travel through space?*

- **During the 1930s**, American mathematician Kurt Gödel suggested that time travel might be possible by bending space-time. Scientists have since suggested all kinds of weird ideas for technology that could bend space-time, including gravity machines. The most powerful benders of space-time are black holes.

- **English physicist** Stephen Hawking believes black holes cannot be used for time travel because everything that goes in to a black hole shrinks to a singularity (an unimaginably small point).

- **Some scientists believe** black holes may be linked by wormholes (tunnels through space-time) to reverse black holes called white holes, where matter is ejected.

▶ *Black holes in space suck in even light, but could artificially created black holes be the doors to wormholes, tunnels through space-time that could be used for time travel?*

Quantum physics

🔘 **In the 1890s**, German physicist Max Planck showed that radiation from a hot object is not in the form of waves as everyone then thought. Instead it is emitted in tiny chunks of energy called quanta, which together behave like waves.

🔘 **When light strikes certain atoms**, it creates electricity in what is called the photoelectric effect. Einstein realized this can be explained if light travels in quanta, not waves.

🔘 **To Planck**, quanta were just a mathematical idea. Einstein showed they were real. Light quanta were later called photons.

▼ *Scientists experiment with Bose-Einstein condensates, a fifth state of matter predicted in the 1920s by Einstein and Bose from quantum ideas.*

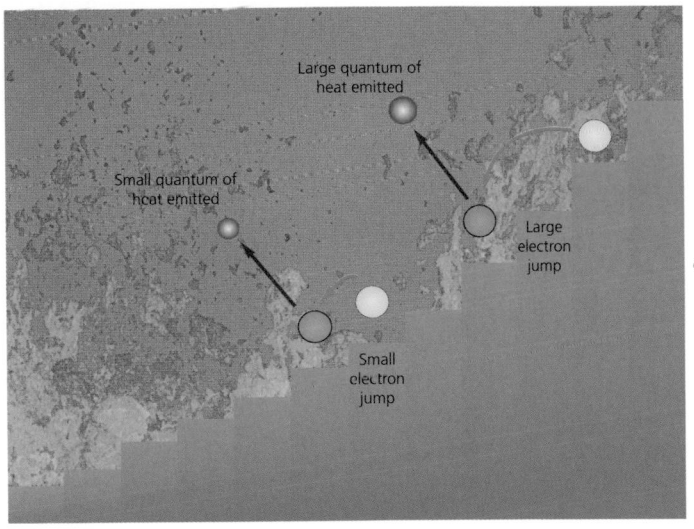

▲ *Quantum physics shows how radiation from a hot object is emitted in little chunks that are called quanta.*

Electron energy levels

⚙ **In 1913**, Danish physicist Niels Bohr showed how the different energy levels for electrons in an atom can also be explained by quanta.

⚙ **During the 1920s**, Erwin Schrödinger and Werner Heisenberg developed the idea of quantum energy levels in atoms to create a new branch of physics, called quantum physics.

⚙ **Quantum physics** explains how electrons emit radiation. It shows that an electron is both a particle and a wave, depending on how you look at it.

⚙ **The development** of the technologies that gave us lasers and transistors came from quantum physics.

Nuclear energy

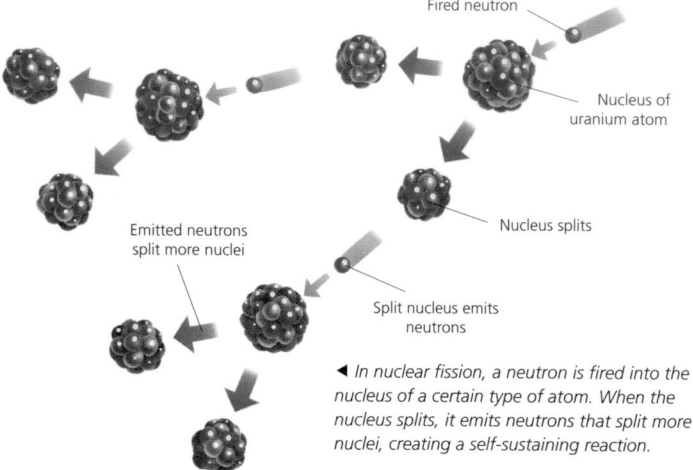

Fired neutron

Nucleus of uranium atom

Nucleus splits

Emitted neutrons split more nuclei

Split nucleus emits neutrons

◀ *In nuclear fission, a neutron is fired into the nucleus of a certain type of atom. When the nucleus splits, it emits neutrons that split more nuclei, creating a self-sustaining reaction.*

🔩 **The nucleus** at the centre of each atom is bound together with huge amounts of energy.

🔩 **Releasing the energy** from the nuclei of millions of atoms can generate a huge amount of power, known as nuclear power. Any reaction that causes a change in the nucleus of an atom is known as a nuclear reaction.

🔩 **Nuclear power** is used as an energy source for the creation of electricity and the explosion of atomic bombs.

🔩 **Nuclear fusion** is the process in which small atoms such as deuterium, a form of hydrogen, are fused together to release nuclear energy. It is a natural form of this process that causes stars to glow.

- **Nuclear fission** is a process in which neutrons are fired at the large nuclei of atoms such as uranium and plutonium so that they split, releasing energy.

- **As neutrons crash** into (bombard) atoms and split their nuclei, the nuclei emit more neutrons. These neutrons bombard other nuclei, which emit more neutrons, and so on. This is called a chain reaction.

- **An atom bomb** (A-bomb) is one of the two main kinds of nuclear weapon. It works by an explosive, unrestrained fission of uranium-235 or plutonium-239.

- **A hydrogen bomb** (H-bomb), or thermonuclear weapon, uses a conventional explosion to fuse the nuclei of deuterium atoms in a gigantic nuclear explosion.

▼ *The explosion of a nuclear weapon produces a characteristic 'mushroom cloud' that towers above the site of the explosion.*

Radioactivity

🔘 **Radioactivity** is the spontaneous disintegration of a certain kind of atom. As it breaks up, the atom emits little bursts of radiation.

🔘 **Isotopes** are atoms of the same element that contain the same number of protons and electrons as each other (as in normal atoms) but different numbers of neutrons.

🔘 **A radioactive isotope** is called a radioisotope. Some atoms, such as uranium, are so unstable that all their isotopes are radioisotopes. These emit three kinds of radiation, called alpha, beta and gamma rays.

New level of uranium-235

🔘 **When a large**, unstable atomic nucleus disintegrates, it emits alpha and beta particles and becomes the atom of another element. This is called radioactive decay.

New level of lead-207

🔘 **Alpha rays** are streams of alpha particles. These are made from two protons and two neutrons. Alpha rays can be stopped by a sheet of paper.

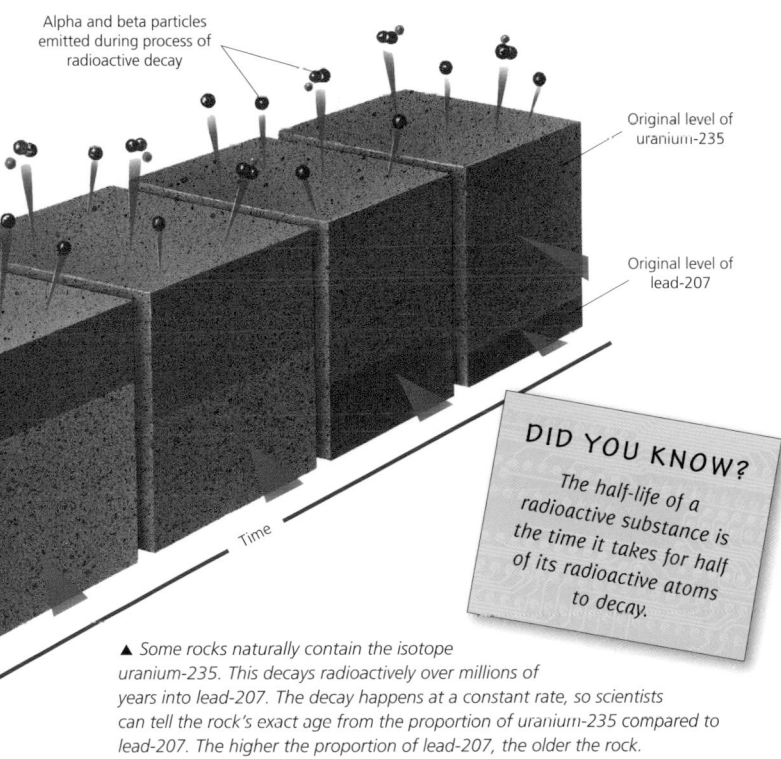

Alpha and beta particles emitted during process of radioactive decay

Original level of uranium-235

Original level of lead-207

Time

DID YOU KNOW?
The half-life of a radioactive substance is the time it takes for half of its radioactive atoms to decay.

▲ Some rocks naturally contain the isotope uranium-235. This decays radioactively over millions of years into lead-207. The decay happens at a constant rate, so scientists can tell the rock's exact age from the proportion of uranium-235 compared to lead-207. The higher the proportion of lead-207, the older the rock.

✿ **Beta rays** are streams of beta particles – electrons that are emitted as a neutron decays into a proton. Beta particles can penetrate aluminium foil.

✿ **Gamma rays** are electromagnetic waves of short wavelength and high energy. They can penetrate most materials and are the most dangerous form of radiation.

175

Splitting the atom

🔘 **Atoms were thought to be solid** and unbreakable until the 1890s. Then in 1897, British physicist J J Thomson discovered that atoms contained even smaller particles, which he called electrons.

🔘 **Scientists thought** electrons were embedded in the surfaces of atoms. Then in 1909, New Zealand physicist Ernest Rutherford fired alpha particles at gold foil. Most went straight through the foil, but a few bounced back.

🔘 **Rutherford concluded** that atoms are empty space (which the alpha particles passed through) but that each has a tiny, dense nucleus at its centre.

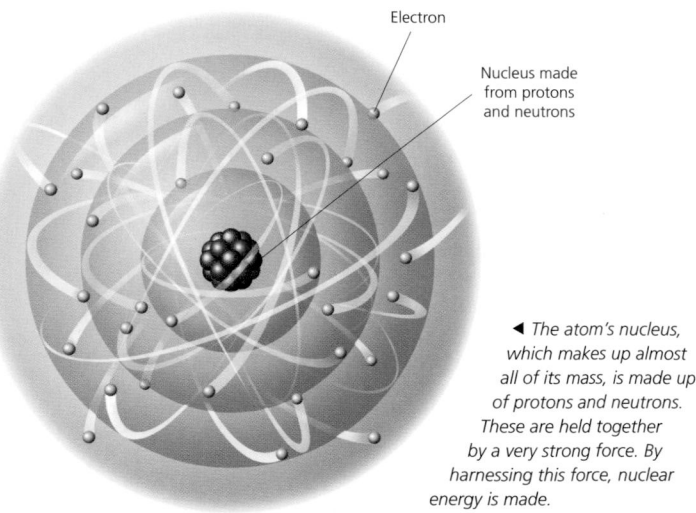

Electron

Nucleus made from protons and neutrons

◄ The atom's nucleus, which makes up almost all of its mass, is made up of protons and neutrons. These are held together by a very strong force. By harnessing this force, nuclear energy is made.

▲ *You cannot actually see subatomic particles, but after they collide, they leave tracks behind them that can be recorded photographically.*

⚙ **In 1919**, Rutherford split the nucleus of a nitrogen atom with alpha particles and in 1932, James Chadwick showed the nucleus was made of two kinds of particle: neutrons and protons.

⚙ **In 1933**, new atoms formed when Enrico Fermi bombarded the nuclei of uranium atoms with neutrons.

⚙ **German scientists** Otto Hahn and Fritz Strassman repeated Fermi's experiment in 1939 and found that the atoms created were a radioactive form of the much lighter element barium. This indicated that the uranium atom had split into two lighter atoms, a discovery that opened the way to releasing nuclear energy by fission.

Quarks

⚙ **Quarks are the tiny elementary**, or fundamental, particles from which protons and neutrons are made up.

⚙ **They are too small** for their size to be measured, but scientists have been able to measure their mass. The biggest quark is as heavy as an atom of gold. The smallest quark is 35,000 times lighter.

⚙ **There are six** kinds (flavours) of quark, known as up, down, bottom, top, strange and charm.

⚙ **Down, bottom and strange** quarks each carry one-third of the negative charge of electrons, while up, top and charm quarks each carry two-thirds of the positive charge of protons.

⚙ **Quarks only exist** in combination with one or two other quarks. Groups of quarks are known as hadrons.

⚙️ **Three-quark hadrons** are called baryons and include protons and neutrons. Rare two-quark hadrons are called mesons.

⚙️ **A proton** consists of two up quarks (two parts positive, two-thirds of a charge) and one down quark (one part negative, one-third of a charge), so has a positive charge of 1.

⚙️ **A neutron** is made from two down quarks (two parts negative, one-third of a charge) and an up quark (one part positive, two-thirds of a charge). The charges cancel each other out, so a neutron has no charge.

⚙️ **The theory of quarks** was first proposed by American physicists Murray Gell-Mann and George Zweig in 1964.

◄ *Protons and neutrons are both made from different combinations of three quarks.*

Particle physics

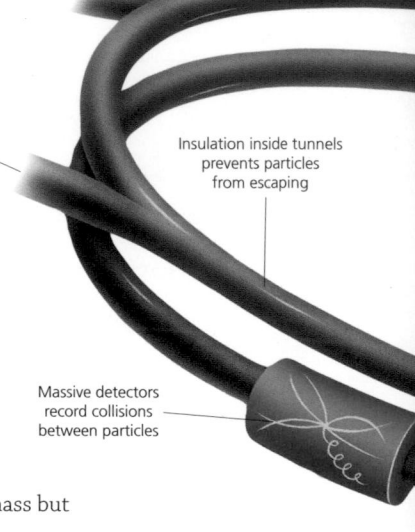

▶ *Particle accelerators at Fermilab near Chicago, USA, and CERN in Switzerland accelerate particles to near light speed.*

New particles are fed in

Insulation inside tunnels prevents particles from escaping

Massive detectors record collisions between particles

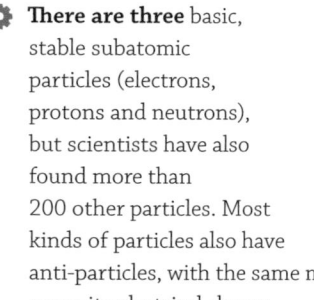

🔅 **There are three** basic, stable subatomic particles (electrons, protons and neutrons), but scientists have also found more than 200 other particles. Most kinds of particles also have anti-particles, with the same mass but opposite electrical charge.

🔅 **Cosmic rays** contain short-lived particles. These include muons, a type of particle that flashes into existence for a few microseconds just before the cosmic rays reach the ground.

🔅 **Smashing atoms** inside particle accelerators creates short-lived, high-energy particles such as taus and pions and three kinds of quark – charm, bottom and top.

🔅 **Particle accelerators** are massive machines set inside tunnels. They use powerful magnets to accelerate particles through a tube at huge speeds, and then smash them together.

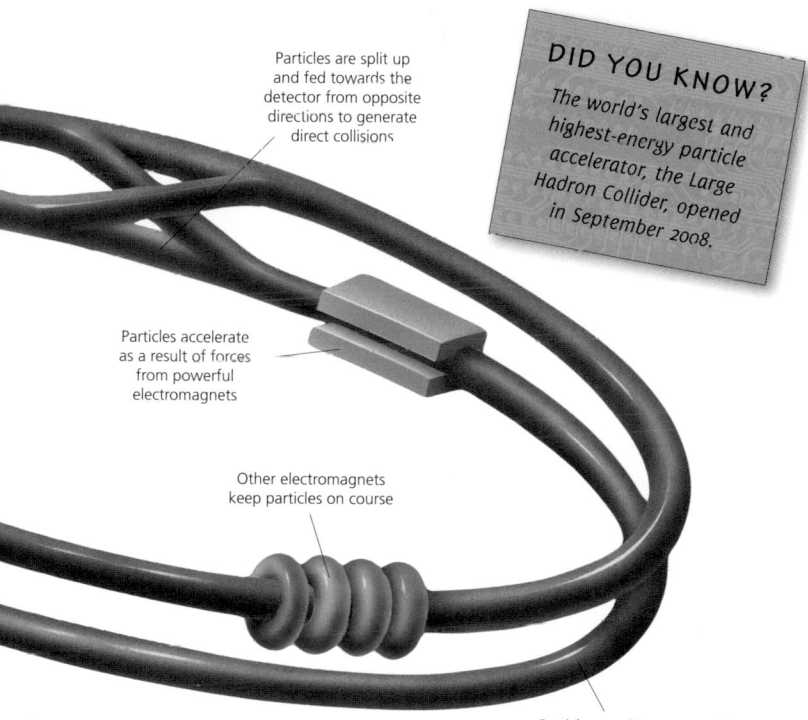

Particles are split up and fed towards the detector from opposite directions to generate direct collisions

DID YOU KNOW?
The world's largest and highest-energy particle accelerator, the Large Hadron Collider, opened in September 2008.

Particles accelerate as a result of forces from powerful electromagnets

Other electromagnets keep particles on course

Particle speed increases with each circuit of the tunnel

⚙ **Scientists classify particles** using a framework called the Standard Model, in which they are divided into elementary particles and composite particles.

⚙ **Elementary particles** are basic particles that cannot be broken down into anything smaller. There are three groups of elementary particles – quarks, leptons and bosons.

Nuclear power

🔅 **Nuclear power** harnesses the huge amount of energy that binds together the nucleus of every atom in the Universe. It is an incredibly concentrated form of energy.

🔅 **Nuclear energy is released** through nuclear fission, in which the nuclei of atoms are split.

🔅 **Nuclear reactors** do not burn fuel to produce their energy. Instead, they use pellets or rods of a fuel called uranium dioxide, an isotope of uranium.

🔅 **Just 3 kg of uranium fuel** provides enough energy for a city of one million people for one day.

🔅 **The earliest nuclear reactors** were designed to make plutonium for use in nuclear weapons. Magnox reactors make plutonium and electricity.

🔅 **Like coal- and oil-fired power stations**, nuclear power stations heat water to make steam to drive the turbines that generate electricity. But in nuclear power stations the heat comes from splitting uranium atoms in the fuel in a slow, controlled nuclear reaction.

🔅 **Every stage of the nuclear process** creates dangerous radioactive waste that may take 10,000 years to become safe. Some mildly radioactive liquid waste is pumped out to sea. Gaseous waste is vented into the air. Solid waste is mostly stockpiled underground.

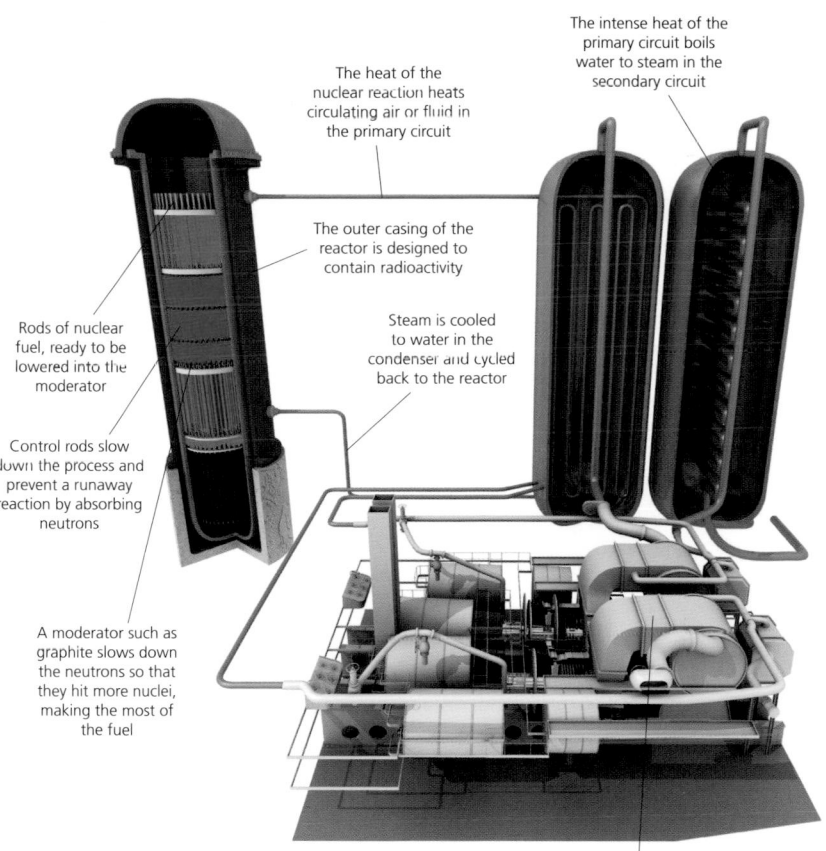

The intense heat of the primary circuit boils water to steam in the secondary circuit

The heat of the nuclear reaction heats circulating air or fluid in the primary circuit

The outer casing of the reactor is designed to contain radioactivity

Steam is cooled to water in the condenser and cycled back to the reactor

Rods of nuclear fuel, ready to be lowered into the moderator

Control rods slow down the process and prevent a runaway reaction by absorbing neutrons

A moderator such as graphite slows down the neutrons so that they hit more nuclei, making the most of the fuel

Steam is blasted over the turbines, driving them round and generating electricity

▲ *The exact layout of nuclear power plants varies, but they are all essentially giant boilers, designed to use nuclear reactions to heat water, which creates steam to drive the turbines that generate electricity.*

183

Genetic engineering

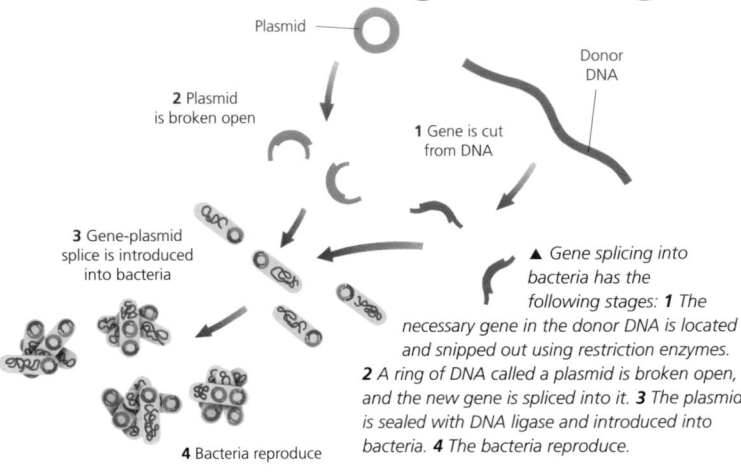

Plasmid

Donor DNA

2 Plasmid is broken open

1 Gene is cut from DNA

3 Gene-plasmid splice is introduced into bacteria

4 Bacteria reproduce

▲ *Gene splicing into bacteria has the following stages:* **1** *The necessary gene in the donor DNA is located and snipped out using restriction enzymes.* **2** *A ring of DNA called a plasmid is broken open, and the new gene is spliced into it.* **3** *The plasmid is sealed with DNA ligase and introduced into bacteria.* **4** *The bacteria reproduce.*

⚙ **Genetics is the science of heredity**, dealing with how organisms pass on traits to their offspring.

⚙ **A gene** is the basic unit of inheritance that tells an organism how to grow and live. It comes as a short section of chemical code on special molecules in every living cell called DNA.

⚙ **Genetic engineering** involves deliberately manipulating the genes of organisms to give them different characteristics.

⚙ **Scientists alter genes** by snipping them from the DNA of one organism and inserting them into the DNA of another. This is called gene splicing. The altered DNA is called recombinant DNA.

⚙ **Genes are cut** from DNA using biological 'scissors' called restriction enzymes. They are spliced into DNA using biological 'glue' called DNA ligase.

🔧 **Once a cell** has altered DNA, every new cell it produces will also have the altered DNA.

🔧 **Genetically modified (GM) food** is produced from animals or plants that have had their genes altered. For example, a food crop can be genetically modified to make it resistant to pests or frost.

🔧 **Gene therapy** is an experimental science in which human genes are altered in order to cure diseases that are inherited from parents, or caused by faulty genes.

🔧 **Cloning** means creating an organism with exactly the same genes as another. In nature, organisms contain a mixture of genes from two parents. Cloning takes DNA from a single donor and uses it to 'grow' a new life. The new life has exactly the same genes as the donor of the DNA. Cloning has been achieved in plants and animals, but not in humans.

▶ Genetic engineers have created mice that glow green by giving them a gene from jellyfish called GFP (Green Fluorescent Protein).

Cutting edge

⚙ **For a long time** it was assumed that light was the fastest thing in the Universe and that its speed could not be altered. This changed in 2001 when Danish scientist Lene Vestergaard Hau became one of the most celebrated female physicists when she halted a pulse of light by passing it through a Bose-Einstein condensate.

⚙ **In recent years**, scientists have sent laser pulses much faster than the speed of light.

⚙ **In 2000**, Lijun Wang and colleagues at the NEC Research Institute, New Jersey, USA, sent pulses of laser light through a container of caesium gas at 310 times the speed of light. Some bits of the pulses travelled so fast they emerged from the container before they entered!

▶ *Laser beams have helped scientists conduct experiments with light in which they have both made light travel faster than light speed and slow to a standstill.*

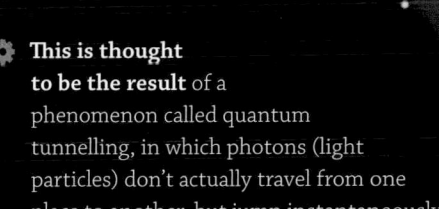

▶ *The movement of the galaxies has revealed to astronomers the presence of a colossal amount of invisible 'dark matter'.*

⚙ **This is thought to be the result** of a phenomenon called quantum tunnelling, in which photons (light particles) don't actually travel from one place to another, but jump instantaneously.

⚙ **The concept of teleporting** (making something disappear in one place and reappear instantly in another) was once thought to be science fiction, but scientists succeeded in teleporting photons across a laboratory in Rome in 1997.

⚙ **Teleporting of particles** occurs through 'quantum entanglement,' in which two particles are linked as one. When the particles are moved apart, a change in one instantly creates a change in the 'entangled' particle.

⚙ **It is thought** that barely 4 percent of all matter in the Universe is 'ordinary' visible matter, such as atoms. Scientists think 23 percent is invisible 'dark matter'. Dark matter provides the gravity needed to stop galaxies drifting apart. A force known as dark energy is thought to make up the remaining 73 percent of matter, which is thought to be pushing matter in the Universe apart.

Technology

Electric power

⚙ **In a power station**, electricity is created by a generator. In a generator, coils of wire are typically driven around between electromagnets to induce an electric current in the coils.

⚙ **The magnets in the generator** in most large power stations are turned by turbines, which have blades like fans. In some power stations, the turbine blades are turned either by steam heated by burning fossil fuels such as coal or with nuclear fuel, or by the flow of natural gas. In others, they are turned by moving water (hydro-electric power) or wind.

⚙ **Simple dynamos** generate a direct current (DC) – an electric current that always flows in the same direction.

⚙ **Power station generators** are alternators. They give an alternating current (AC) – a current that continually swaps direction.

⚙ **Electricity from power stations** is distributed around a country in a network of cables known as the grid.

DID YOU KNOW?
The world's biggest hydro-electric power station is the Three Gorges Dam, on the Yangtze River, China. It has a generating capacity of 22,500 megawatts.

⚙ **Power station generators** generate upwards of 25,000 volts. This is too much to be used safely in homes, but too little to transmit over long distances.

⚙ **To transmit** electricity over long distances, the voltage is boosted to 400,000 volts by transformers. It can then be transmitted through high-voltage cables. Near its destination, voltage is reduced to a level safe for use in homes.

▼ Some power station transformers deal with half a million volts. Step-up transformers boost voltage, while step-down transformers reduce it for daily use.

Computers

⚙️ **The information** (data) that a computer requires to work is stored in microchips – tiny structures of electronic components and their connections, produced in or on a small slice of silicon.

⚙️ **Microchips known as ROM** (read-only memory) carry a computer's basic working instructions.

Cooling fan

▶ *A typical home computer costs one-quarter of its price 20 years ago – and it is ten times more powerful.*

RAM (random access memory) chips

⚙️ **Microchips known as RAM** (random access memory) receive new data and instructions when needed.

⚙️ **At the heart** of every computer is a powerful microchip called the CPU (central processing unit). This carries out the main processing – altering data (information) according to instructions from the application (program).

⚙ **Computers use a binary system**, storing and adding information as a series of on/off (one/zero) electronic pulses known as binary code.

Optical drive tray

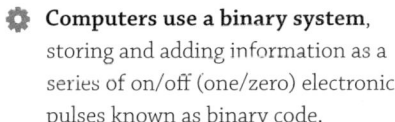

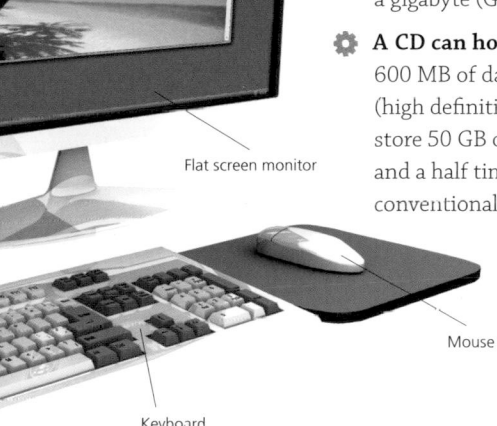

Flat screen monitor

⚙ **A single digit** of binary code is known as a bit and eight bits make a byte. One million bytes is a megabyte (MB) and one billion bytes is a gigabyte (GB).

⚙ **A CD can hold** about 600 MB of data. A Blu-ray (high definition) disc can store 50 GB of data – ten and a half times as much as a conventional DVD.

Mouse

Keyboard

Robotics

⚙ **Robots are machines** that can be programmed to perform specific tasks, and which are automatic (do not require human control once activated).

⚙ **American scientist** William Grey Walter developed some of the first electronic, autonomous robots in 1948–1949, at the Burden Neurological Institute, UK. Called Elmer and Elsie, the robots were shaped like tortoises and used light to steer.

⚙ **The first programmable robot** was an industrial robot called Unimate, made in the 1950s. It had an arm that could pick things up.

⚙ **Machine robots** perform tasks and are not designed to mimic human appearance and movement. Millions are in use in factories and homes around the world.

⚙ **Machine robots** can perform tasks too difficult, unpleasant, boring or dangerous for humans to do. For example, robot submarines and spacecraft can go to places that would be too dangerous for people to explore.

⚙ **Scientists are developing nanobots** (microscopic robots). One day this nanotechnology may be used to perform surgery from inside a person's body.

- **Farmers in Japan** can now wear robotic suits to assist their movement.

- **Scientists at MIT**, USA, have developed a robot that can respond to actions with facial expressions. Known as Kismet, it can display anger, sadness and happiness.

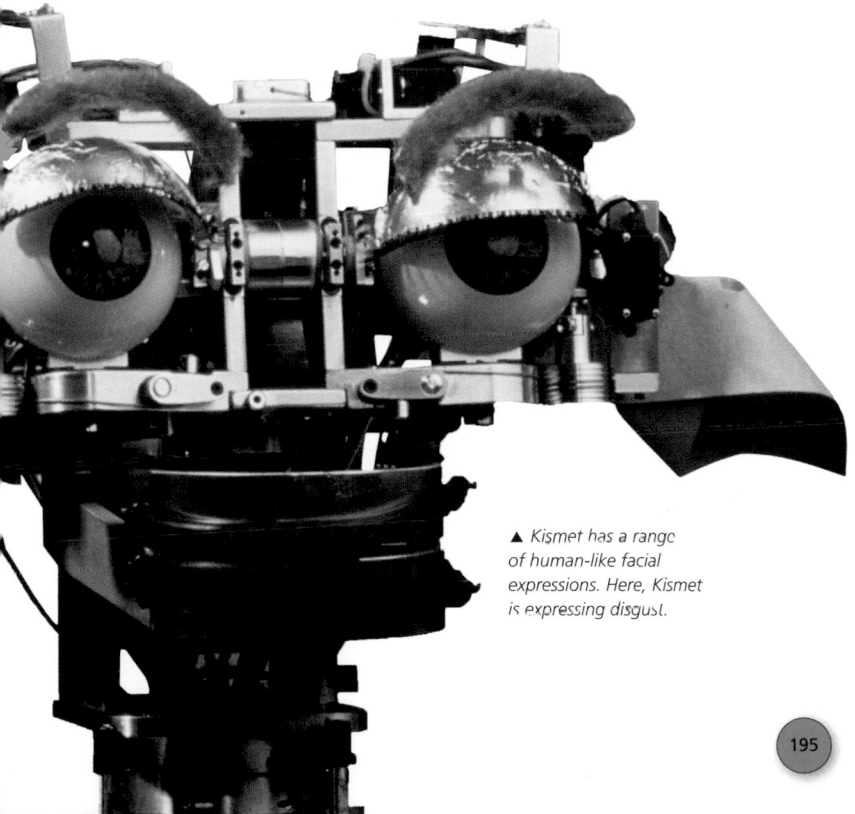

▲ Kismet has a range of human-like facial expressions. Here, Kismet is expressing disgust.

Seeing the microworld

⚙ **Microscopes are devices** used for looking at things that are normally too small for the human eye to see.

⚙ **An optical microscope** uses a lens to bend light rays apart, enlarging what you see. The latest optical microscopes can make a single molecule visible.

⚙ **Electron microscopes** fire electrons at an object, which bounce off the object onto a screen, making them visible.

⚙ **An electron microscope** can focus on an object that is 1 nanometre (one-billionth of a metre) across and magnify it five million times.

⚙ **Scanning Electron Microscopes** (SEMs) work by scanning the surface of an object to magnify it by up to 100,000 times. They are so powerful that they can make individual atoms visible.

◄ *A microscope enlarges objects and events that are too small for the human eye to see.*

⚙ **Transmission Electron Microscopes** shine electrons through thin slices of an object to magnify it millions of times.

⚙ **The world's most powerful** transmission electron microscope is called the TEAM 0.5 microscope. It can make objects smaller than a hydrogen atom (the smallest of all atoms) visible.

⚙ **Scanning Acoustic Microscopes** use sound waves to see inside tiny opaque objects.

▼ *A scanning tunnelling micrograph can reveal the exact shape of a fragment of DNA.*

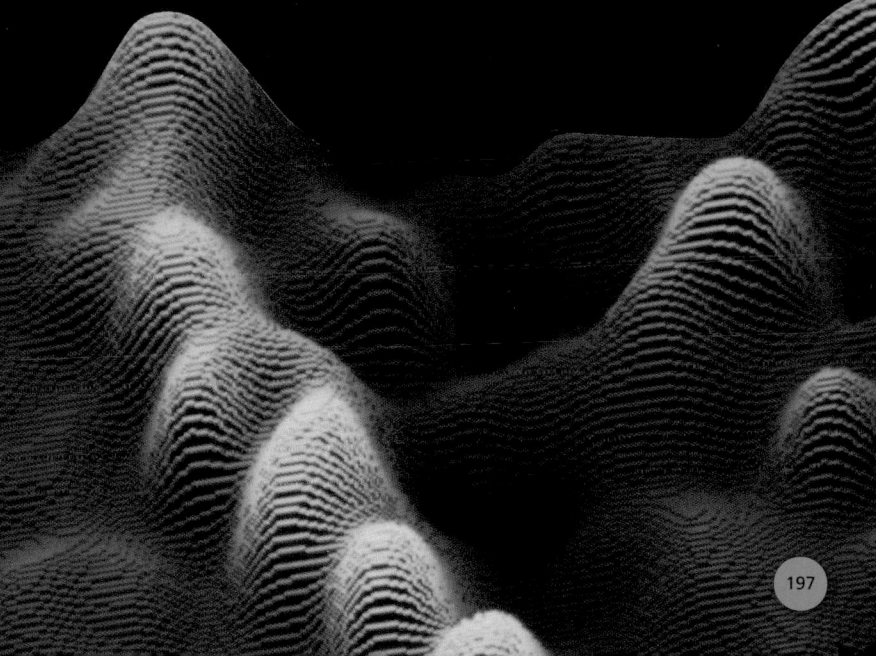

Lasers

⚙ **A laser** is a device that creates a bright artificial light.

⚙ **A beam of laser light** is so intense that it can punch a hole through steel, and is brighter than the Sun, in relation to its size.

⚙ **The word 'laser'** is an abbreviation of Light Amplification by Stimulated Emission of Radiation.

⚙ **Laser light** is the only known 'coherent' source of light. Coherent means that its light waves are all of the same frequency (wavelength) and all the same phase (the peaks and troughs of the waves all align).

▼ *Lasers provide a beam of energy so concentrated that it can cut through steel.*

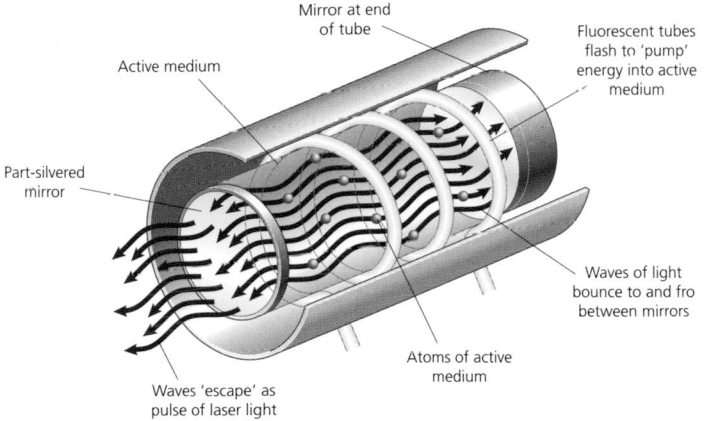

▲ In one type of laser, energy is put into the active medium of a ruby rod as flashes of ordinary light.

⚙ **Inside a laser** is a small space filled with a lasing material – either a gas, such as helium and neon, or a liquid or solid crystal, such as ruby.

⚙ **A burst of photons** (particles of electromagnetic radiation) excites atoms in the lasing material. The excited atoms emit photons. When the photons hit other atoms, they fire off photons too, which reflect up and down inside the space using mirrors.

⚙ **The powerful laser beam** finally exits the space through a small hole in one of the mirrors.

⚙ **Gas lasers** give a lower-powered beam suitable for delicate work such as eye surgery, while chemical lasers make intense beams for weapons.

⚙ **Some lasers** send out a continuous beam, while pulsed lasers send out a high-powered beam at regular intervals.

Light fibres

⚙ **Optical fibres** are threads of transparent glass. Bundles of these threads are called fibre optic cables, and are used to transmit messages.

⚙ **For data to be transmitted** using fibre optics, it must be turned into a digital form (a series of on/off signals).

⚙ **These signals** power a light source at the end of a fibre to pulse on and off. This coded light signal then travels along optical fibres until it reaches its destination, where circuits turn it back into an electrical signal.

⚙ **A thin layer of wrapping** (cladding) surrounds each fibre to stop light spilling out. The cladding reflects all light back into the fibre, no matter how much the fibre twists and turns. This is called total internal reflection.

⚙ **Single-mode fibres** are very narrow, so they require a laser light source, and are used for long-distance transmissions. Multi-mode fibres are wider than single-mode fibres, so they don't have to use lasers. They are less expensive, but unsuitable for long distances.

◀ Optical fibres allow huge amounts of information to be transmitted at the speed of light.

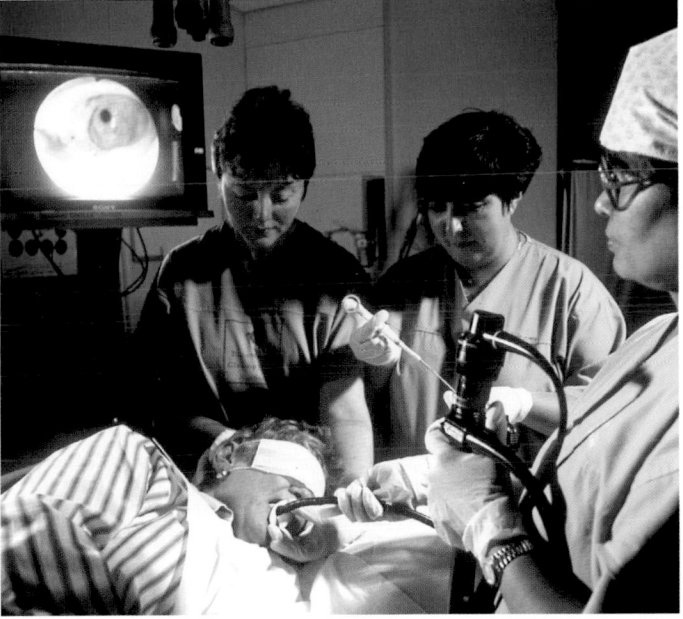

▲ *An endoscope is a tube that can be inserted into the body to view internal organs. Images from inside the body are sent along flexible optical fibres to a viewing screen.*

⚙ **The largest cables** can carry hundreds of thousands of phone calls or hundreds of television channels.

⚙ **Fibre optic cables** have been laid under the Atlantic and Pacific Oceans.

⚙ **Optical fibres** have medical uses. An endoscope is a flexible tube containing bundles of optical fibres. Lenses at each end allow surgeons to view inside a patient's body.

Holograms

⚙ **Holograms** are three-dimensional photographic images made with laser lights.

⚙ **Holography was invented** by Hungarian-born British physicist Dennis Gabor in 1947, but their use was limited until laser light became available in 1960.

⚙ **The first holograms** were made in 1963 by American scientist Emmett Leith and his University of Michigan research partner Juris Upatnieks, and Russian scientist Yuri Denisyuk.

⚙ **Holograms are made** by splitting a beam of light from a laser in two. One part is reflected off the subject onto a photographic plate. The other (called the reference beam) is shone directly onto the plate.

⚙ **The interference** between the light waves in the reflected beam and the light waves in the reference beam creates the hologram in microscopic stripes on the plate.

▶ Holograms are very hard to forge, so are used on banknotes to prevent counterfeiting.

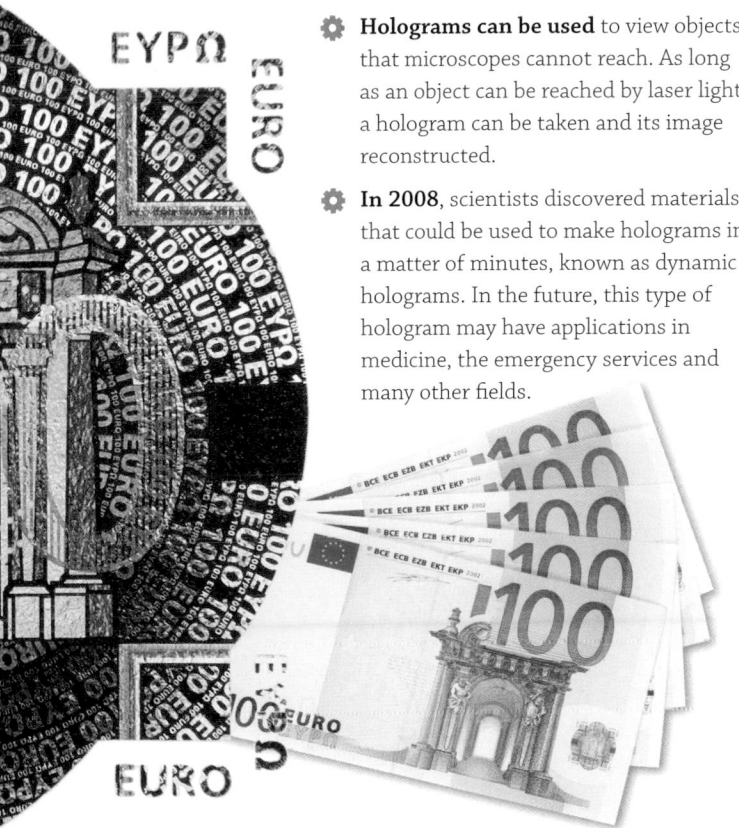

🔅 **Some holograms** only show up when laser light is shone through them, while others, such as those used in credit cards to stop counterfeiting, work in ordinary light.

🔅 **Holograms can be used** to view objects that microscopes cannot reach. As long as an object can be reached by laser light, a hologram can be taken and its image reconstructed.

🔅 **In 2008**, scientists discovered materials that could be used to make holograms in a matter of minutes, known as dynamic holograms. In the future, this type of hologram may have applications in medicine, the emergency services and many other fields.

Television

Clear cover

Outer frame

Remote sensor detects the infrared beam from the remote-control handset

Receiver tunes into channels and filters and strengthens the signals received by the aerial

▲ Plasma screens provide a brilliant flat picture built up from millions of tiny cells filled with a plasma of gas.

⚙️ **Television (TV) relies** on a phenomenon called the photoelectric effect, in which electrons are emitted by a substance when it is struck by photons.

⚙️ **TV cameras** have three sets of tubes containing photocells. Each set reacts to a colour of light – red, green or blue – to convert the picture into electrical signals. The sound signal from microphones is then added.

⚙️ **Older TV broadcasting** (analogue) used the varying strength of radio signals to carry information for pictures and sound.

⚙️ **Digital broadcasting** carries information in the form of millions of on/off signals every second.

⚙️ **Most new TV sets** have flat screens, which took over from older, heavier, box-like glass-screen displays known as CRTs (cathode-ray tubes).

⚙️ **A plasma screen** has millions of tiny compartments (cells), and two sets of wire-like electrodes at right angles to each other.

⚙️ **Each cell** can be 'addressed' by sending electrical pulses along two electrodes that cross that cell.

⚙️ **These electrical pulses** heat the cell's gas into plasma, making a coloured substance (phosphor) glow. Millions of pulses every second at different 'addresses' all over the screen build up the overall picture.

DID YOU KNOW?
The first purely electronic television systems, with no moving parts, were developed in the 1920s–30s.

Digital recording

⚙ **Digital recording** is a process in which sounds or pictures are recorded as a series of digits.

⚙ **Early sound and picture recordings** were analogue, in which the signals are recorded continuously as matching physical changes on a tape or a disc. When the sound is loud, for instance, the changes are big.

⚙ **Analogue recordings** add 'noise' (interference) during recording. If a quiet recording is amplified (increased in strength), the added noise is also amplified.

⚙ **With digital systems**, there is no noise added during reproduction or amplification. This is because the recorder simply sends just the digital code of the recording to the player, which may be a TV, a computer or a music system. The player recreates the original sound from the digital code.

◀ *Digital recording and compression allows huge amounts of recorded music to be stored on a tiny music player.*

▲ Using keyboard instructions, computers can change digital images. For example, the computer can be instructed to change all areas of a certain shade of red in an image to a blue colour.

- **Digital radio and TV broadcasts** can be very clear, because the digital code is always the same no matter how strong or faint the signal.

- **Digital imaging** allows faint sounds and pictures to be amplified without any distortion.

- **It is possible** to process digital images by computer to accentuate some qualities and play down others.

- **Astronomers have used** digital imaging techniques to identify very distant, faint stars and galaxies.

- **Mathematically compressing** the digits in a digital recording allows very detailed 'high resolution' recordings to be made and transmitted, including mp3 sound recordings and High Definition TV pictures.

Scanning

⚙ **A scanner** is an electronic device that traces out and builds up an image in lines.

⚙ **Image scanners** convert pictures or text into a digital form that computers can read.

⚙ **A photoelectric cell** inside the scanner measures the amount of light reflected from each part of the picture or document and converts this into a digital code.

⚙ **Complex scanning devices** are used in medicine to produce pictures of internal organs or body parts. These include CT scanners, PET scanners and MRI scanners.

▼ *Unlike X-rays, a MRI scanner does not produce potentially harmful radiation.*

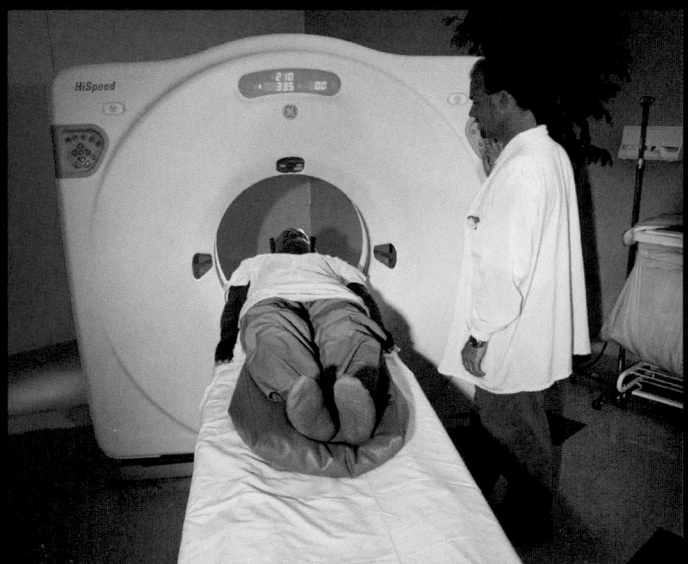

- **CT stands for** Computerized Tomography. In CT scanning, an X-ray beam rotates around the patient and is picked up by detectors on the far side to build up a 3-D image of the inside of the patient's body.

- **PET stands for** Positron Emission Tomography. In PET scanning, the scanner picks up positrons (positively charged electrons) sent out by substances injected into the blood. PET scans can show a living brain in action.

- **MRI stands for** Magnetic Resonance Imaging. MRI scans work in a similar way to CT scans, but use magnetism, not X-rays. In an MRI, the patient is surrounded by magnets, which cause all the protons in the body to line up.

- **An MRI scan starts** as a radio pulse that knocks protons briefly out of alignment. The scanner then detects radio signals sent out by the protons as they snap back into line.

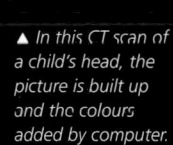

▲ In this CT scan of a child's head, the picture is built up and the colours added by computer.

209

Internet

⚙ **The Internet** is a vast network (organized system) connecting millions of computers around the world.

⚙ **Devised in the 1960s** when the US Army developed a network called ARPAnet to link computers, the Internet is now used by people for everything from buying cinema tickets to keeping in touch with friends.

⚙ **To link to the Internet** via phone lines, a home computer's output must sometimes be translated into the right form with a modem or router.

⚙ **Computers** access the Internet via a local phone to a large computer called the Internet Service Provider (ISP).

⚙ **Each ISP** is connected to a giant computer called a main hub. There are about 100 main hubs worldwide.

⚙ **Some links between** hubs are made via phone lines while others are made via satellite. Links between hubs are called fast-track connections.

⚙ **The World Wide Web** was invented in 1989 by English computer programmer Tim Berners-Lee of the CERN laboratories in Switzerland.

⚙ **The web makes special links** (hyperlinks) between web pages via key words. Words linked to other pages are shown highlighted in blue. Clicking on a 'link' allows someone to find their way to data on other sites.

▶ Mobile phones can now access the Internet by picking up radio signals sent out from service providers.

Telecommunications

🔹 **Telecommunications** is the process in which data is transmitted almost instantaneously by electronic means.

🔹 **Every communication system** requires three things to function – a transmitter, a communications link and a receiver.

🔹 **Transmitters convert data** (text, images or sounds) into an electrical signal and send it. Transmitters can be telephones or computers.

🔹 **Receivers pick up** the electrical signal and convert it back into its original form.

▼ Using a GPS (Global Positioning System) receiver, a ship can pinpoint its location and navigate from place to place. The GPS is a network of about 30 satellites, plus the equipment to control and co-ordinate them.

Communications links carry the signal from the transmitter to the receiver in two main ways. Some give a direct link through telephone lines and other cables, while others are carried on radio waves through the air, via satellite or microwave links.

DID YOU KNOW?

To avoid delays, telephone calls crossing oceans are transmitted via satellite in one direction and via underwater cable in the other direction.

In the past, telephone lines have been mainly comprised of electric cables, which carried the signal as pulses of electricity. Today, telephone lines are usually fibre optics, which carry the signals as coded pulses of light.

Communications satellites are satellites orbiting the Earth in space. Telephone calls are beamed up on radio waves to the satellite, which then beams them back down to another part of the world.

Microwave links use very short radio waves to transmit telephone and other signals directly from one dish to another in a straight line across Earth's surface.

Mobile or cellular phones transmit and receive phone calls directly via radio waves. Calls are picked up and sent on from a local aerial.

The information superhighway is the network of high-speed links that might be achieved by combining telephone systems, cable TV and computer networks. TV programmes, films, data, direct video links and the Internet could all enter homes using one big network.

Planet Earth

Formation and age

⚙ **The story of the Earth began** about 4.6 billion years ago when dust whirling around the newborn Sun started to clump into lumps of rock called planetesimals. Pulled together by their mutual gravity, the planetesimals then clumped together to form the Earth and other planets.

⚙ **When the Earth first formed**, it was little more than a red-hot ball of churning molten rock.

⚙ **About 4.5 billion years ago**, a rock the size of Mars crashed into Earth. Splashes of material from this crash clumped together to form the Moon.

⚙ **The Earth was so shaken by the impact** that all the elements in it separated. The dense metals, iron and nickel, collapsed to the centre to form the Earth's core.

⚙ **The molten rock** formed a thick mantle about 3000 km thick around the metal core. The core's heat keeps the mantle warm and churning, like boiling porridge.

◀ *The Moon was also hit by rocks in space. These made huge craters, and mountain ranges of up to 5000 m high.*

◄ *When the Earth formed from a whirling cloud of planetesimals, the pieces rushed together with such force that they formed a fiery ball. It slowly cooled down, and the continents and the oceans formed.*

✿ **After about 100 million years** the surface of the mantle cooled and hardened to form a thin crust.

✿ **A mass of erupting volcanoes** and smoke appeared on the young Earth. Streams of lava (molten rock) turned the Earth's surface into churning, red-hot oceans.

✿ **An atmosphere containing poisonous gases**, such as methane, hydrogen and ammonia, soon wrapped around the planet, rising from the volcanoes on the surface.

✿ **After about one billion years**, the air began to clear as water vapour that had gathered in the clouds fell as rain, to create the oceans.

DID YOU KNOW?

Earth's first atmosphere would have been poisonous to animals. Early microscopic plants gradually converted carbon dioxide gas into oxygen gas for animals to breathe.

Internal structure

- **The Earth is not a solid ball.** The Earth's crust rests on a layer of hot, partly molten rock called the mantle, which in turn surrounds two cores, one inside the other.

- **The Earth's crust** is a thin, hard outer shell of rock, which is a few dozen kilometres thick. Its thickness in relation to the Earth is about the same as the skin on an apple.

- **Oceanic crust** is the crust beneath the oceans. It is much thinner – just 7 km thick on average. It is also young, with none being more than 200 million years old.

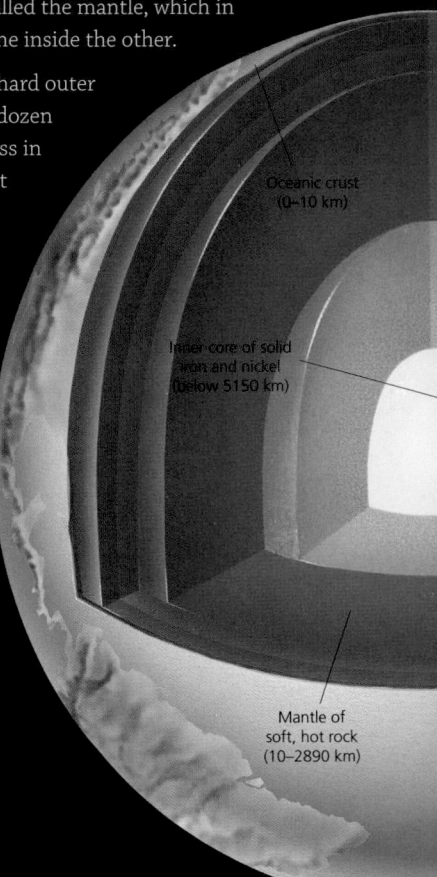

Oceanic crust
(0–10 km)

Inner core of solid
iron and nickel
(below 5150 km)

Mantle of
soft, hot rock
(10–2890 km)

- **Continental crust** is the crust beneath the continents. It is up to 50 km thick and mostly old.

- **The mantle** makes up the bulk of the Earth's interior. Temperatures in the mantle climb steadily as you move through the mantle, reaching 4500°C near the core.

- **Mantle rock** is so warm that it churns slowly round like very, very thick treacle boiling on a stove. This movement is known as mantle convection currents.

- **Beneath the mantle** is a core of hot iron and nickel. The outer core is so hot – climbing from an amazing 4500°C to 6000°C – that it is always molten.

- **The inner core** is even hotter (up to 7000°C) but it stays solid because the pressure is 6000 times greater than on the surface.

- **The only time we see** the hot molten rock of the mantle is when it bursts out through the crust in a volcanic eruption.

- **Our knowledge of the Earth's interior** comes mainly from studying how earthquake waves vibrate right through the Earth.

Continental crust
(0–50 km)

Outer core of
liquid iron and
nickel
(2890–5150 km)

◄ The main layers inside the Earth from the hot core to the rocky surface.

Moving plates

⚙ **Slowly, the Earth's surface is moving** around beneath our feet. Continental drift is the name for the slow movement of the continents around the world.

⚙ **It is not just the continents that are moving.** The ocean beds are also moving. In fact, the whole of the Earth's surface is on the move.

⚙ **The Earth's crust** is made of curved rocky plates, which float like pieces of gigantic jigsaw on the molten layer of hot rock in the mantle.

⚙ **There are seven large plates** and some 20 smaller ones, and they move very slowly on currents circulating within the mantle.

▼ *Along the boundaries where the plates push together or slide past each other earthquakes and volcanoes occur.*

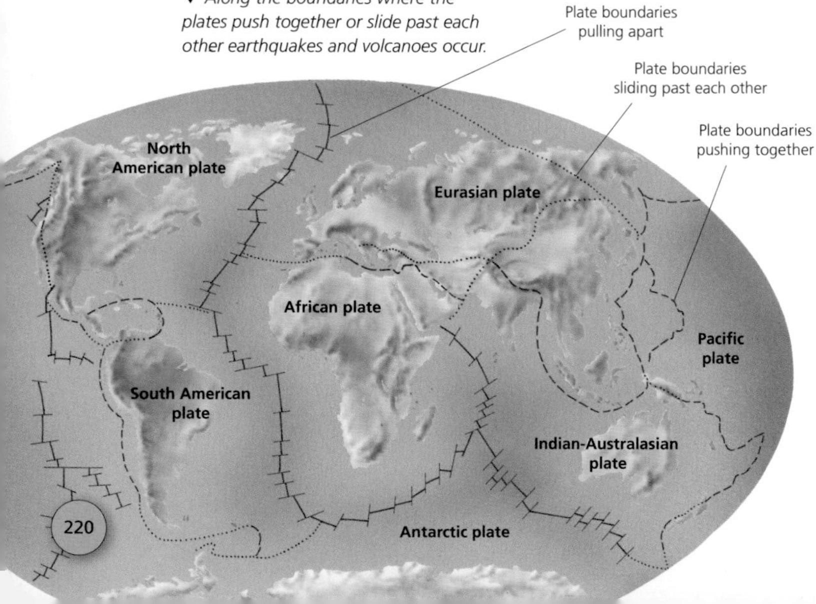

Plate boundaries pulling apart

Plate boundaries sliding past each other

Plate boundaries pushing together

North American plate

Eurasian plate

African plate

Pacific plate

South American plate

Indian-Australasian plate

Antarctic plate

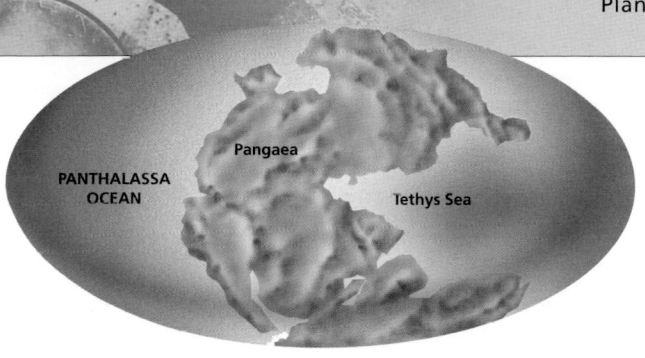

▲ *About 220 mya all the world's continents were joined together in one huge landmass that geologists call Pangaea. Pangaea gradually split up into today's continents.*

🌐 **Rates of continental drift vary.** South America is moving 20 cm farther from Africa every year. On average, continents move at about the same rate as a fingernail grows.

🌐 **Scientists know** that the continents were once all joined up because identical fossils of prehistoric plants and reptiles have been found in Africa, India, South America and Antarctica.

🌐 **Some tectonic plates have moved so far**, they have travelled half way around the globe.

🌐 **In some places, tectonic plates** are crunching together. Where this happens, one of the plates – typically the one carrying a continent – rides over the other and forces it down into the Earth's interior. This process is called subduction.

🌐 **Where one plate dives beneath the other**, there is often a deep trench in the ocean floor.

🌐 **In some places**, usually in mid ocean, tectonic plates move apart or diverge. As they move apart, molten magma from the Earth's interior wells up and solidifies: so the seabed grows wider and wider.

Mountains

⚙ **Mountains look solid and unchanging**, but they are constantly being built up, then worn away by the weather. The Himalayas, for instance, were built up in the last 40 million years, and are still growing.

⚙ **All the world's great mountain ranges**, such as the Andes and Rockies, were made by the crumpling of rock layers as tectonic plates pushed against each other. Such mountains are called fold mountains.

⚙ **The most ancient mountain ranges** have long been worn flat, or reduced to hills, such as New York's Adirondacks, which are now over one billion years old.

⚙ **The Himalayan range** in Asia has the world's 20 highest mountains, including Mount Everest, which rises to 8848 m.

The Himalayas

India moving north

Asian plate

Folded rock layers

◄ The Himalayas were thrown up by the collision between India and the rest of Asia. Layer upon layer of rock in Asia's southern edge has crumpled.

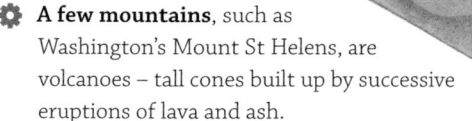

▶ *Fault block mountains are made when a section of rock tilts or is pushed up during a tremor. This happens along faults or breaks in the Earth's crust.*

- **The Andes is the longest mountain range**, stretching for 7240 km along the western side of South America. The highest peak is Mount Aconcagua in Argentina at 6960 m.

- **A few mountains,** such as Washington's Mount St Helens, are volcanoes – tall cones built up by successive eruptions of lava and ash.

- **The tallest mountain** measured from its base under the sea is Mauna Kea in Hawaii. From base to tip it measures 10,205 m, but only 4205 m is above the sea.

- **One side of a mountain range is often very wet.** Approaching winds rise over the mountains, cooling and dropping rain on the windward side. The other side gets very little rain.

- **The air is thinner on mountains**, so the air pressure is lower, and climbers may need oxygen masks to breathe.

- **Temperatures drop** 0.6°C for every 100 m you climb, so mountain peaks are very cold and often covered in snow.

Volcanoes

⚙ **Volcanoes are places where hot molten rock** (magma) wells up to the surface from deep within the Earth's interior.

⚙ **Active volcanoes erupt often.** Dormant volcanoes do so only occasionally. Extinct volcanoes are dead and will not erupt again.

> **DID YOU KNOW?**
> The most active volcano in the world is Kilanea on Hawaii in the Pacific Ocean. It has erupted continuously since 1983 and produces lava at a rate of 5 cu m every second.

⚙ **When a volcano erupts,** molten magma explodes from the main vent. Ash and lava pour out and flow down the side of the volcano. Gas, dust and rock 'bombs' are thrown into the sky.

⚙ **There are more than 800 active volcanoes** in the world. The country with the most is Indonesia, which has about 200.

⚙ **Around the Pacific** there is a ring of explosive volcanoes called the Ring of Fire. It includes Mount Pinatubo in the Philippines and Mount St Helens in Washington, USA.

⚙ **Successive eruptions** can build up such a huge cone of ash and lava around the volcano that it becomes a mountain.

⚙ **Eruptions begin with a build-up of pressure** in the magma chamber beneath the volcano. Bubbles of steam and gas form and swell rapidly inside the magma, then burst out.

⚙ **As the steam and gas jet out,** they carry with them clouds of ash and larger fragments of the broken plug of magma, called rock bombs or tephra.

⚙ **With the volcanic plug out of the way**, magma surges up and out of the volcano, and flows down as lava.

⚙ **If the level of magma** in the magma chamber drops, the top of the volcano's cone may collapse into it, forming a giant crater called a caldera.

▼ *The biggest volcanic eruptions are powered by a combination of steam and carbon dioxide gas. As the plug of magma breaks, the pressure is suddenly released, creating an explosion big enough to send chunks of rock the size of houses many thousands of metres up into the air.*

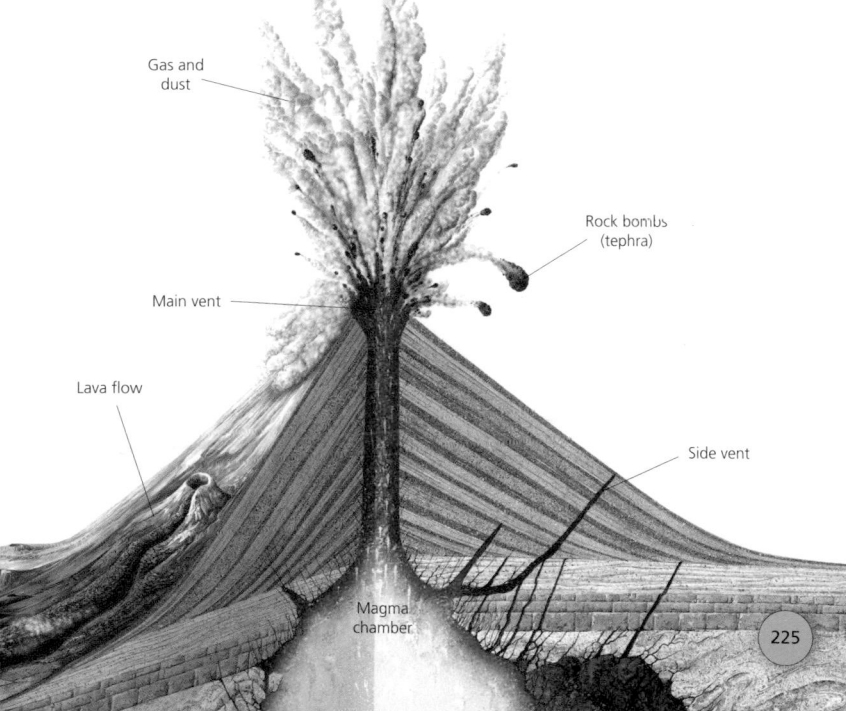

Gas and dust

Rock bombs (tephra)

Main vent

Lava flow

Side vent

Magma chamber

225

Earthquakes

⚙ **Earthquakes are a shaking of the ground.** Some are slight tremors that are hardly noticed. Others are so violent, they can tear down mountains and cities.

⚙ **Small earthquakes** may be set off by landslides, volcanoes or even just heavy traffic. Bigger earthquakes are set off by the grinding together of the vast tectonic plates that make up the Earth's surface.

⚙ **Tectonic plates** typically slide 4–5 cm past each other in a year. In a slip that triggers a major quake, they can slip more than 1 metre in a few seconds.

⚙ **In an earthquake, shock waves radiate** out in circles from its origin or hypocentre (focus).

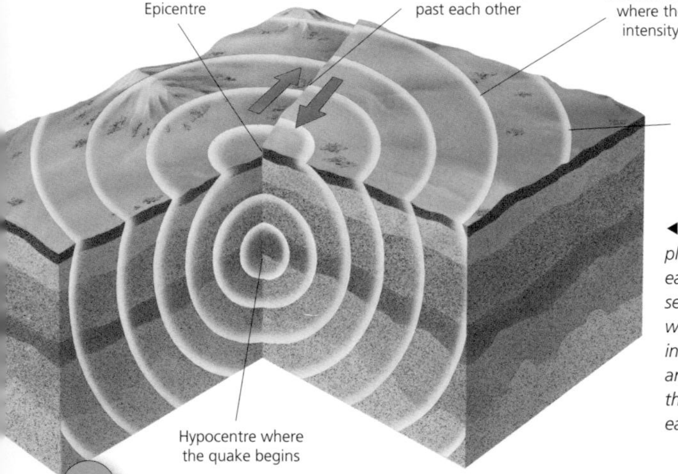

Epicentre

Tectonic plates slip past each other

Isoseismic lines show where the quake's intensity is equal

The quake's intensity is reduced away from the epicentre

◀ As two tectonic plates jolt past each other, they send out shock waves that radiate in circles outwards and upwards from the focus of the earthquake.

Hypocentre where the quake begins

◀ An earthquake has caused the second floor of this building to fall to street level in San Francisco, California, USA.

- **Damage is most severe at the epicentre** – the point on the surface directly above the focus – where the shock waves are strongest. But they can often be felt up to thousands of kilometres away.

- **In most quakes** a few minor tremors (foreshocks) are followed by an intense burst lasting just one or two minutes.

- **A second series of minor tremors** (aftershocks) occur over the next few hours. While aftershocks are less powerful than the main quake they can often add to the damage.

- **Undersea earthquakes** can produce waves, called tsunamis. These waves move at up to 800 km/h, and in shallow waters, the waves build into colossal walls of water up to 30 m high, which rush inland, drowning everything in their path.

- **Seismologists** (scientists who study earthquakes) measure the strength of the shock waves with a device called a seismometer. They then grade the severity of the quake on the Richter scale, from 1 (slight tremor) to over 9 (devastating quake).

- **Each year around 800,000 earthquakes are detected** by sensitive instruments worldwide, but less than 1000 actually cause damage.

227

Caves

- **Caves are holes in the ground**, usually hollowed out by water as rainwater trickles down through the ground and dissolves the minerals in rocks, such as limestone.

- **Some caves are very long passages**, and some are huge open spaces called caverns.

- **Much more common are 'pot-holes'**, which are deep, narrow passages, sometimes leading to caverns. Explorers crawl through pot-holes, or even swim through flooded sections of a cave, using flashlights to penetrate the gloom.

- **The world's longest caves** are the Mammoth Caves of Kentucky in the USA, first explored in 1799. This system has 560 km of caves and passages.

- **The biggest cave chamber** is called the Sarawak Chamber, in a cave system in Sarawak, Malaysia. It is 700 m long, has an average width of 300 m and is about 70 m from floor to roof.

▼ *Some cave systems contain huge caverns, large enough for people to stand in. Others are cramped and narrow, and can only be crawled through by cave explorers.*

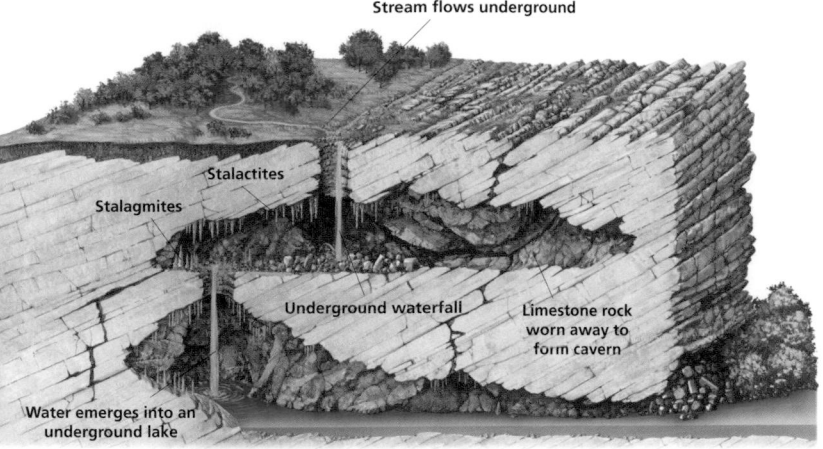

Stream flows underground

Stalactites

Stalagmites

Underground waterfall

Limestone rock worn away to form cavern

Water emerges into an underground lake

▲ *Limestone caverns and cave systems are eroded (worn away) by chemical weathering.*

⚙ **The longest underwater cave system** in the world is the Nohoch Nah Chich system in Mexico. Over 51 km of underwater passages have been mapped by cave-diving teams.

⚙ **Stalactites hang down** like huge icicles from the roofs of caves. They form as water drips down and deposits calcium carbonate.

⚙ **Stalagmites grow up** from the floors of caves as water drips down from the roof and deposits calcium carbonate.

⚙ **A stalagmite more than 30 m tall** – higher than a house – was measured inside a cave in Slovakia.

⚙ **Cave animals** include bats, birds and even fish. Many cave species are blind and so rely on smell, touch or echolocation (using echoes from sound to judge distances and obstacles) to find their way around in the darkness.

Deserts

⚙ **Desert**, where the land gets less than 250 mm of rainfall in a year, covers almost one-eighth of the Earth's surface. Many are hot, but one of the biggest deserts is Antarctica.

⚙ **The driest place on Earth** is the Atacama Desert in Chile, South America. Intervals between showers may be as long as 100 years, and in some areas it has not rained for more than 400 years!

⚙ **Dallol in Ethiopia** is called the hottest place on Earth with an average temperature of 34°C. But the hottest temperature ever measured was 58°C in the shade, in Libya in 1922.

⚙ **Temperatures in the desert** can be scorching hot by day but near-freezing at night.

⚙ **The biggest desert** is the Sahara in north Africa, at 5000 km across and up to 2250 km north to south.

▲ *Loose sand is blown by the wind and piles up in wave-shaped formations called dunes.*

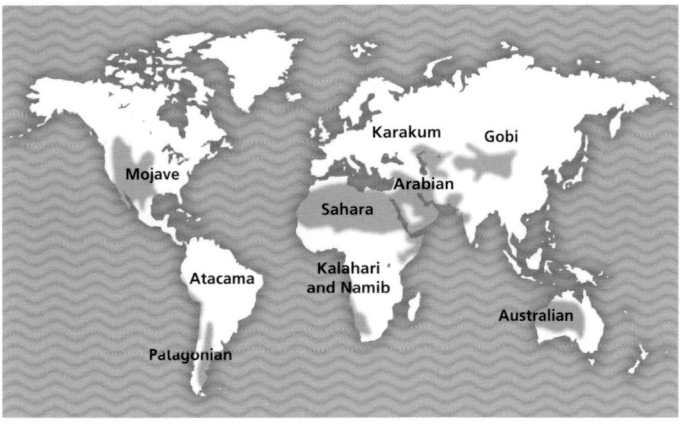

▲ Hot, dry deserts occur in warm areas where cool air sinks, warms up and absorbs moisture from the land. The world's biggest deserts are shown here.

- **The Sahara** desert has the world's biggest sand dunes, some more than 400 m high.

- **In the Arabian Desert** is the world's biggest area of sand dunes – the Rub' al-Khali, which means 'Empty Quarter' in Arabic.

- **Like waves of water**, sand is blown over the crest of the dune and down the steeper far side. Dunes move across the desert in this way.

- **Only about 20 percent of the Earth's deserts** are sandy. The rest are rocky, stony, covered by scrub and bush, or ice-covered.

- **An oasis is a green 'island'** in the desert, a haven for thirsty travellers. Plants can grow there by tapping water from a well or underground spring.

Glaciers and ice sheets

⚙ **Glaciers are rivers of slowly moving ice.** Nowadays, glaciers only form in the highest mountains and in polar regions. But in the past, in cold periods called ice ages, glaciers were far more widespread.

⚙ **Glaciers form** when new snow, or névé, falls on top of old snow. The weight of the new snow compacts the old snow into denser snow called firn.

⚙ **In firn snow,** all the air is squeezed out so it looks like white ice. As more snow falls, firn gets more compacted and turns into glacier ice that flows slowly downhill.

⚙ **Glaciers begin in small hollows** in the mountain called cirques, or corries. They flow downhill, gathering huge piles of debris called moraine on the way.

⚙ **The fastest-flowing glacier** is the Columbia Glacier in Alaska, USA. It moves at 35 m per day and has doubled its speed in the last 20 years.

⚙ **When a glacier goes over a bump** in the rock below it, or round a corner, the ice often breaks making deep cracks in the ice. These cracks are called crevasses.

⚙ **Icebergs are big lumps of floating ice** that calve, or break off, from the end of glaciers or polar ice caps.

⚙ **Icebergs float out to sea** where they can be a danger to shipping because nine-tenths of the iceberg are hidden beneath the water.

⚙ **Ice ages** are periods lasting millions of years when the Earth is so cold that the polar ice caps grow huge.

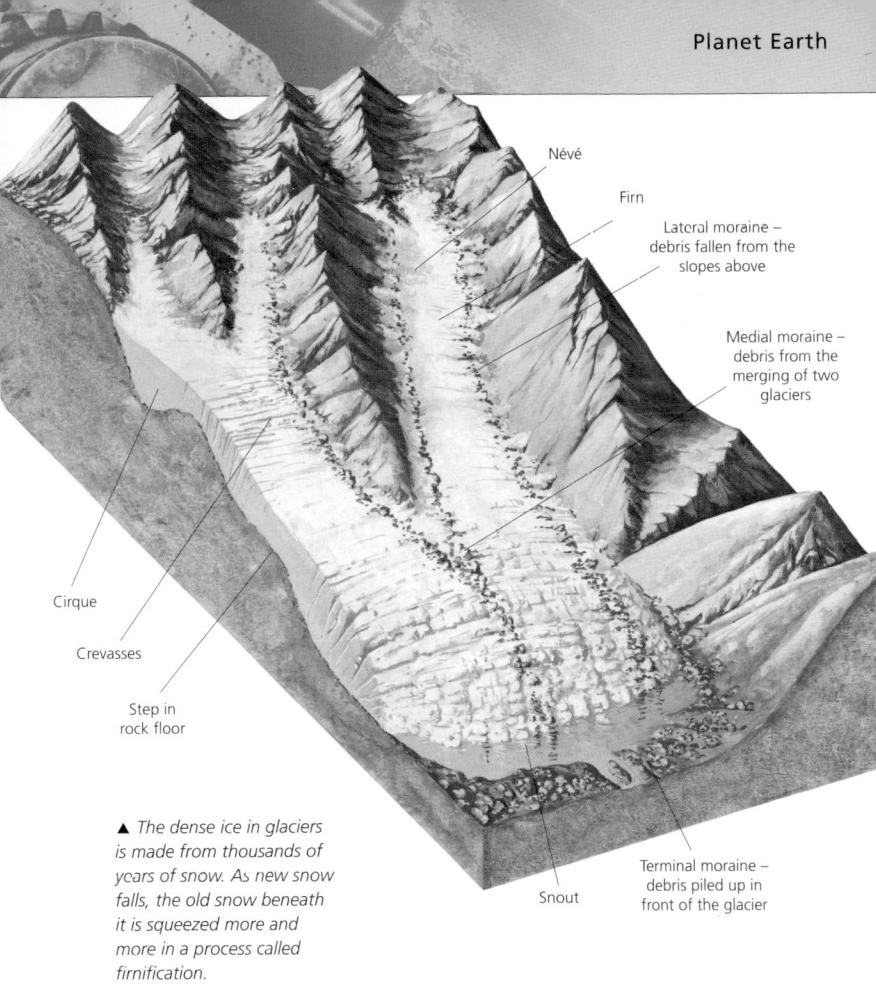

Névé

Firn

Lateral moraine – debris fallen from the slopes above

Medial moraine – debris from the merging of two glaciers

Cirque

Crevasses

Step in rock floor

Snout

Terminal moraine – debris piled up in front of the glacier

▲ The dense ice in glaciers is made from thousands of years of snow. As new snow falls, the old snow beneath it is squeezed more and more in a process called firnification.

⚙ **The most recent ice age** – called the Pleistocene Ice Age – began about 2 mya. Ice covered 40 percent of the world and glaciers spread over much of Europe and North America.

Rivers

⚙ **Rivers are filled with water** from rainfall running directly off the land, from melting snow or ice, or from a spring bubbling out water that has soaked into the ground. When there is enough rain or melting snow to keep them flowing, rivers run down to the sea.

⚙ **High up in mountains** near their source (start), rivers are usually small. They tumble over rocks through narrow valleys, which they carved out over thousands of years.

⚙ **All the rivers in a certain area** flow down to join each other, like branches on a tree. The branches are called tributaries. The bigger the river, the more tributaries it is likely to have.

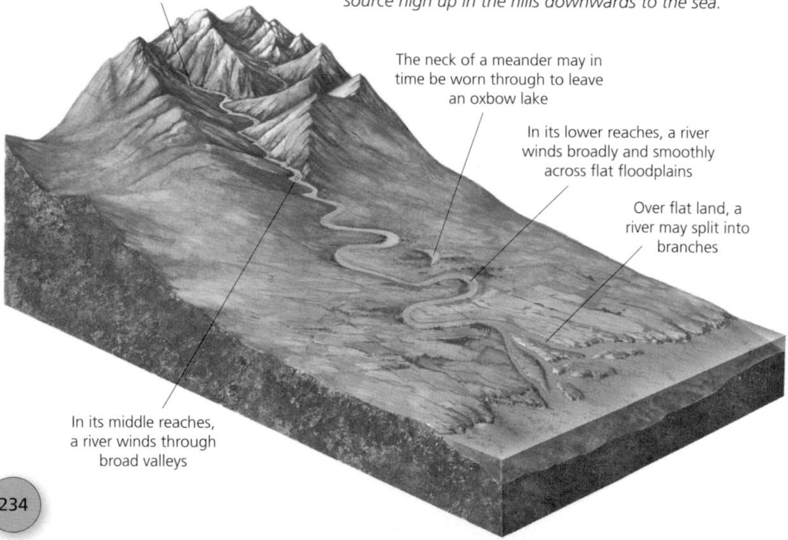

In its upper reaches, a river tumbles over rocks through steep valleys

▼ *A river changes in many ways as it flows from its source high up in the hills downwards to the sea.*

The neck of a meander may in time be worn through to leave an oxbow lake

In its lower reaches, a river winds broadly and smoothly across flat floodplains

Over flat land, a river may split into branches

In its middle reaches, a river winds through broad valleys

▲ *Near its source, the river tumbles over rocks, wearing them away to smooth pebbles.*

Rivers wear away their banks and beds, mainly by battering them with bits of gravel and sand and by the sheer force of the moving water.

Waterfalls occur when a river flows over a band of hard rock, and then over softer rock, which is more quickly worn away by the water. The hard rock forms a step over which the river pours. The highest falls are the Angel Falls in Venezuela, South America, with a drop of 979 m.

Oxbow lakes form when a river meanders (changes course), cutting off patches of water before linking back up.

A river slows down as it flows into the sea, so it can no longer carry the load of silt it has collected along the way. Often, the silt is dumped in a fan shape, or a delta.

Every year, the world's rivers carry about 8000 million tonnes of sediment, tiny particles of rock and debris, into the oceans.

The world's rivers wear the entire land surface down by an average of 8 cm every 1000 years.

235

Lakes

⚙ **A lake is a big expanse of water** surrounded by land. Some lakes are so big they are called inland seas. Most lake water is fresh rather than salty, but in some lakes so much water evaporates that the remaining water becomes salty.

⚙ **Most lakes last only a few thousand years** before they are filled in by silt or drained by changes in the landscape.

⚙ **Most of the world's great lakes** lie in regions that were once glaciated. The glaciers carved out deep hollows in the rock in which water collected. The Great Lakes of the USA and Canada are partly glacial in origin.

⚙ **The world's deepest lakes** are often formed by faults in the Earth's crust, such as Lake Baikal in Siberia and Lake Tanganyika in East Africa.

⚙ **The Aral Sea**, a large lake in central Asia, is rapidly shrinking because the rivers that feed it have been diverted to irrigate farmland. The water level has dropped by over 12 m since 1960 and its area has shrunk by over one-third.

◄ *A salt island of crystal formations in the Dead Sea.*

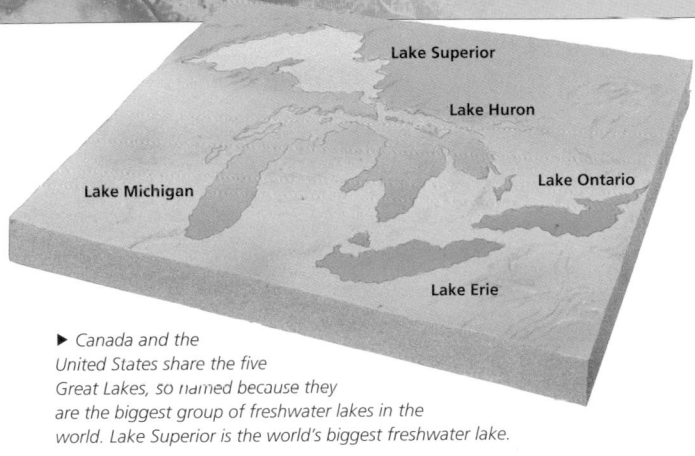

▶ Canada and the United States share the five Great Lakes, so named because they are the biggest group of freshwater lakes in the world. Lake Superior is the world's biggest freshwater lake.

🌼 **Lake Baikal in Siberia**, Russia, is about 25 million years old. It is 1637 m deep and contains about one-fifth of all the world's freshwater. The water is carried there by 336 rivers that flow into it.

🌼 **High in the Andes Mountains** of Peru, straddling the border with Bolivia, is Lake Titicaca – the highest navigable lake in the world. It is 3810 m above sea level.

🌼 **Some lakes, called crater lakes**, form as water collects in the hollow of an old volcano, like Crater Lake in Oregon, USA, which is 9 km across.

🌼 **The Dead Sea** in Israel and Jordan is well named. This saltwater lake is the lowest lake on Earth – about 400 m below sea level. In summer, scorching heat causes high evaporation, making the water so salty that a person cannot sink.

🌼 **The largest underground lake** in the world is Drauchenhauchloch, which is inside a cave in Nambia.

Oceans

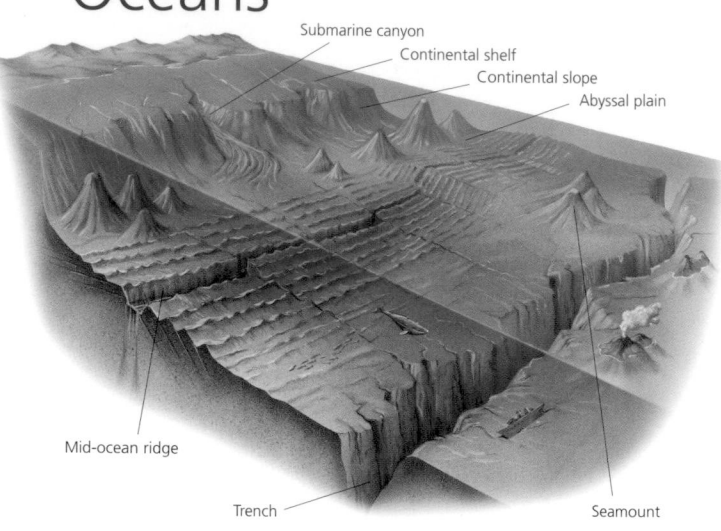

Submarine canyon
Continental shelf
Continental slope
Abyssal plain
Mid-ocean ridge
Trench
Seamount

▲ *Surveys have revealed a hugely varied landscape on the oceanbed, with high mountains, wide plains and deep valleys.*

⚙ **Viewed from space, the Earth** looks like a planet of blue ocean – more than 70 percent is water. About 97 percent of all the Earth's water is in the oceans, which cover more than 360 million sq km of the planet.

⚙ **There are five oceans**, which all connect to make one vast body of water. The three biggest oceans are the Pacific, Atlantic and Indian oceans. They meet in the Southern or Antarctic Ocean. The Pacific and the Atlantic also meet in the smaller Arctic Ocean.

⚙ **The Pacific** is the world's largest ocean. It is twice as large as the Atlantic (the next largest) and covers an area of 181 million sq km – one-third of the world.

⚙ **Seas, such as the Baltic Sea**, are smaller areas of saltwater, but most seas are joined to an ocean, such as the Mediterranean Sea, which is linked to the Atlantic Ocean at the Strait of Gibraltar.

⚙ **Around the edge of the ocean** is a shelf of shallow water called the continental shelf.

⚙ **At the edge of the shelf**, the oceanbed plunges steeply to the deep ocean floor – the 'abyssal plain'.

⚙ **This plain is vast**, but not completely flat. In the Pacific especially, it is dotted with huge mountains, called seamounts.

⚙ **Most of the Arctic Ocean** is permanently covered with a vast floating raft of sea ice. Temperatures are low all year round, averaging –30°C in winter and sometimes dropping to –70°C.

⚙ **All around the world**, the sea rises and falls slightly twice every day in 'tides'. Tides are caused by the pull of the Moon's gravity on the oceans' waters as the Earth spins around.

⚙ **Spring tides** (high tides) happen twice a month. They occur as the Moon and Sun line up with each other, combining their gravitational pull.

▶ *Where the ocean meets the land, waves batter the coast wearing it away and forming strange rock shapes. When a sea arch collapses, it leaves behind tall pillars called stacks.*

The atmosphere

Exosphere 500–800 km
Contains hardly any gas; low-level satellites orbit here

Thermosphere 80–500 km
Becomes roasted by the Sun to up to 1800°C, but is so thin in gases that it contains little real heat

Mesosphere 50–80 km
Is too thin to soak up much heat, but is thick enough to stop meteorites that burn up leaving fiery trails in the sky

Stratosphere 10–50 km
Contains the ozone layer and becomes hotter higher up; little water and no weather; airliners cruise here in the still air

Troposphere 0–10 km
Contains three-quarters of the atmosphere's gases and nearly all its water

⚙ **Surrounding the Earth** is a layer of gases called the atmosphere. It is held in place by the Earth's gravity, which keeps most of the gases in the atmosphere close to the ground.

⚙ **The atmosphere contains** oxygen, nitrogen and tiny amounts of other gases – argon, carbon dioxide, carbon monoxide, hydrogen, ozone, methane, helium, neon, krypton and xenon.

⚙ **Oxygen is the most important gas** in the atmosphere because people and animals need to breathe it. When we breathe, we take in oxygen and breathe out carbon dioxide. Green plants, such as trees, take in carbon dioxide and give off oxygen during their food-making process (photosynthesis).

⚙ **The atmosphere can be divided** into five main layers: troposphere (the lowest), stratosphere, mesosphere, thermosphere and exosphere.

◄ *The atmosphere absorbs the Sun's warmth, yet shields the Earth from its most harmful rays. It gives us fresh, clean water to drink and provides us with the air that we need to breathe.*

- **At the bottom is the troposphere** – only 10 km thick, but containing over 70 percent of the atmosphere's gases by weight. All of Earth's weather, including clouds, is produced in this lowest layer of the atmosphere.

- **In the upper levels of the atmosphere** is a layer of ozone (a form of oxygen), which forms a protective layer blocking out harmful ultraviolet rays from the Sun.

- **With each layer** the gases become thinner and thinner, until at about 800 km up they are so thin or 'rarified' that it is hard to tell where the atmosphere ends and where empty space begins.

- **The atmosphere protects** the Earth from space rocks. About 100 tonnes of rocks and dust enter the atmosphere every day, but almost all of it burns up when it hits the atmosphere at high speed.

- **The sky looks blue** because light from the Sun is scattered by tiny particles of dust and moisture in the air. This breaks up the sunlight into its rainbow colours. The blue rays scatter most, so we see blue more and the sky looks blue.

- **The Aurora Borealis**, or Northern Lights, makes the night sky glow green, gold, red or purple. The effect is caused by solar wind – radiation from the Sun – hitting Earth's atmosphere.

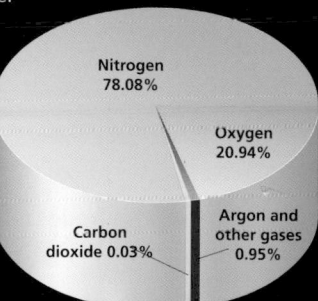

▶ *Nitrogen and oxygen together make up about 99 percent of the Earth's atmosphere.*

Nitrogen 78.08%

Oxygen 20.94%

Argon and other gases 0.95%

Carbon dioxide 0.03%

Climate

⚙ **The nearer a place is to the Equator**, the warmer the climate tends to be. The effect is to give the world three broad climate bands which fall either side of the Equator: the warm tropics, the cold polar regions, and a moderate 'temperate' zone in between.

> **DID YOU KNOW?**
> One of the most pleasant climates in the world is Quito in Ecuador. It rarely drops below 8°C at night, nor rises above 22°C during the day. 100 mm of rain falls reliably each month of the wet season.

⚙ **Climates are warm near the Equator**, where the Sun climbs high in the sky. Tropical climates are warm climates in the tropical zones on either side of the Equator. Average temperatures of 27°C are typical.

⚙ **Temperate climates** are mild climates in the temperate zones between the tropics and the polar regions. Summer temperatures may average 23°C, and winter 12°C.

⚙ **The climate is cool near the poles**, where the Sun never climbs high in the sky. Average temperatures of −30°C are typical.

⚙ **Antarctica has the coldest climate.** It is so cold that almost nothing grows and nobody lives there.

⚙ **An oceanic climate** is a wetter climate near oceans, with cooler summers and warmer winters.

⚙ **A continental climate** is a drier climate in the centre of continents, with hot summers and cold winters.

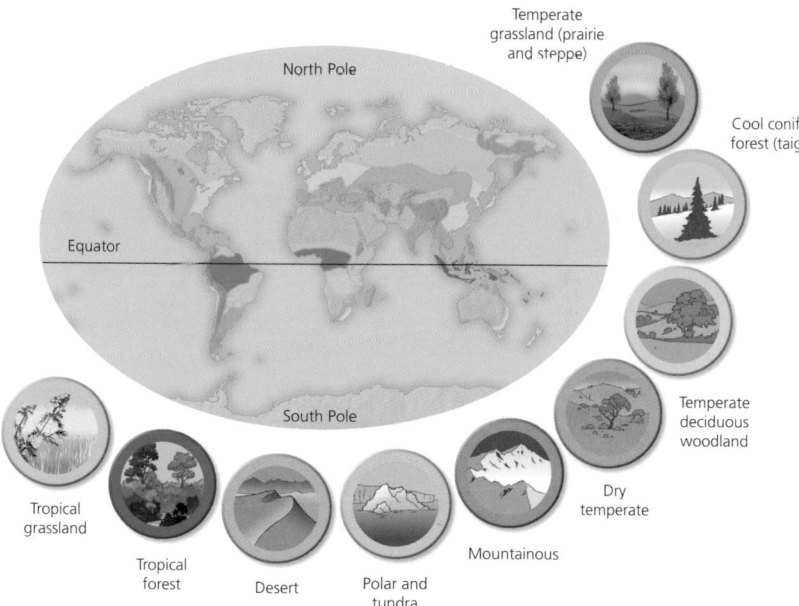

Temperate grassland (prairie and steppe)

North Pole

Cool conifer forest (taiga)

Equator

Temperate deciduous woodland

South Pole

Dry temperate

Tropical grassland

Mountainous

Tropical forest

Desert

Polar and tundra

▲ *The warmth of a region's climate depends on how close it is to the Equator. But oceans and mountain ranges have a huge influence, too, so the pattern of climate is complicated, with many local variations.*

⚙ **A monsoon climate** is a climate with one very wet and one very dry season. Hot air rising over the land pulls in warm moist winds off the sea, bringing heavy rain. Then the winds change, blowing cool dry weather from the mountains.

⚙ **Volcanic eruptions** can send enough dust into the atmosphere to change the world's climate for a short time. After Mount Pinatubo erupted in the Philippines in 1991 many parts of the world had cooler weather in 1992.

Weather

⚙ **At a warm front**, warm air rises over cold, giving rain. At a cold front, cold air pushes warm air upwards, giving heavy showers.

⚙ **The more of the Sun's energy there is in the air**, the windier it is. This is why the strongest winds may blow in the warm tropics.

⚙ **Rainbows are caused** by sunlight passing through falling raindrops. The water acts like a glass prism, splitting the light. White light is made up of seven colours – red, orange, yellow, green, blue, indigo and violet – so these are the colours, from top to bottom, that make up the rainbow.

▲ *A satellite view of a large hurricane approaching Florida, USA. The yellow eye is the centre of the storm.*

⚙ **A drought is a long period** when there is little or no rain. During a drought the soil dries out, streams stop flowing, groundwater sinks and plants die. Drought bakes the soil so hard that it shrinks and cracks.

⚙ **Winter weather is cold** because the days are too short to give much heat. The Sun always rakes across the ground at a low angle, spreading out its warmth.

⚙ **Fresh snow can contain up to 90 percent air**, which is why snow can actually insulate the ground and keep it warm, protecting plants.

⚙ **Rime is a thick coating of ice** that forms when moisture cools well below 0°C before freezing onto surfaces.

⚙ **Hailstones can be as big as melons.** These chunks of ice can fall from thunderclouds. The biggest ones ever fell in Gopaljang, Bangladesh, in 1986 and weighed 1 kg each.

DID YOU KNOW?

There have been many reports of frogs raining down from the sky. This is probably caused by a tornado sucking up frogs from ponds and streams then dropping them from clouds like rain.

◀ A tornado starts deep inside a thundercloud, where a column of strongly rising warm air is set spinning by high winds roaring through the cloud's top. As air is sucked into this column, it corkscrews down to the ground.

Climate change

⚙ **Global warming** is the general increase in average temperatures around the world. This increase has been between 0.3°C and 0.8°C over the last 100 years.

⚙ **Most scientists** now think that global warming is caused by human activities, which have resulted in an increase in the Earth's natural greenhouse effect. Humans have added carbon dioxide gas to the air by burning coal, oil and gas at an increasing rate in the demand for electricity and car travel.

⚙ **When heat from the Sun reaches the Earth**, some of it penetrates the atmosphere and reaches the ground. Much of this heat is then reflected back into space.

⚙ **The greenhouse effect** is the way that certain gases in the air – notably carbon dioxide – trap some of the Sun's warmth like the panes of glass in the walls and roof of a greenhouse.

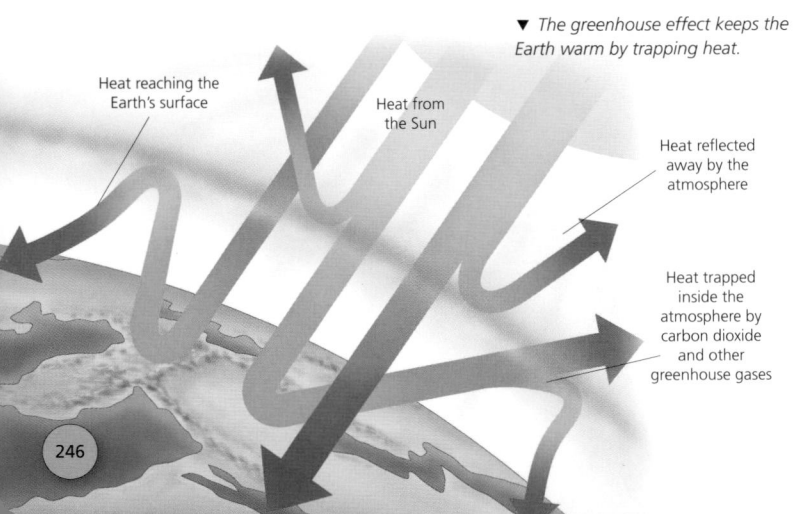

▼ *The greenhouse effect keeps the Earth warm by trapping heat.*

Heat reaching the Earth's surface

Heat from the Sun

Heat reflected away by the atmosphere

Heat trapped inside the atmosphere by carbon dioxide and other greenhouse gases

▲ *The lush vegetation of the world's rainforests absorbs carbon dioxide from the atmosphere. When the rainforest is cut down and burnt, not only does it stop absorbing, but the burning releases even more carbon dioxide to add to global warming.*

⚙ **The greenhouse effect** keeps the Earth at a reasonable temperature. Without any greenhouse effect, the average temperature would be 33°C lower and the Earth would be covered in ice.

⚙ **The gases pumped into the air** by the burning of coal and oil in factories and cars, for example, have trapped much more heat. Scientists believe that this is causing global (worldwide) warming of the climate, which could have devastating effects in the future.

⚙ **Many experts have predicted** that there will be a 4°C rise in average temperatures over the next 100 years.

⚙ **By trapping more energy** inside the atmosphere, global warming is bringing stormier weather.

⚙ **Global warming** may melt much of the polar ice caps, flooding low-lying countries, such as Bangladesh.

⚙ **Many countries have agreed** to try to reduce global warming by limiting the amount of carbon dioxide factories and cars produce.

247

Life on Earth

- **Life began on Earth** a very long time ago. The earliest fossils (remains) of life that have been found are of simple single-celled bacteria. They are about 3.8 billion years old. It is thought that these microscopic bacteria are the ancient ancestors of all life.

- **Scientists do not agree** about the way life began on Earth. Some believe that a mixture of chemicals was sparked into life by a source of energy, such as lightning. Others think that life first came to our planet from outer space, on a comet or by some similar means.

- **However life began**, it appears that early life-forms were very simple and remained so for an extremely long time. The first multi-celled creatures, such as sponges and jellyfish, did not appear until about 700 million years ago.

- **About 600 million years ago** life on Earth underwent an explosion in growth, and many new varieties of different animals and plants appeared in a relatively short time.

- **Since this explosion in growth**, animal and plant life has continued to develop and change (evolve) and has resulted in the huge variety of life that exists on our planet today.

- **Almost two million species**, or types, of animal have been identified by scientists so far. The science of grouping animals is called taxonomy.

- **To make sense** of the different types (species) of animals and plants on Earth, scientists put them into categories. They do this by looking at the physical characteristics of each creature; those that are similar are put in the same category, or group.

- **Life-forms are divided into groups or kingdoms**, which are then split into smaller groups.

- **Each species is given a Latin name** that is used by scientists all over the world, no matter what their own language. Humans belong to the species *Homo sapiens*, which means 'wise man'.

- **Life-forms** that are in the same group do not just share similar physical characteristics, such as appearance. They are also likely to be closely related to one another, and have evolved from common ancestors.

▶ The red-eyed treefrog has the scientific name Agalychinus callidryas.

Plants

The plant kingdom

- **The plant kingdom** includes more than 400,000 different kinds of plant.

- **The flowering plant group** contains more than 250,000 different species, including flowers, herbs, grasses, vegetables and trees (except conifers). Flowering plants are also known as angiosperms.

- **Conifer trees** have needle-like leaves that make their seeds in cones rather than in flowers. Conifers, cycads and gingkos are also known as gymnosperms.

- **Ferns live** in damp, shady places around the world. They are an ancient group of plants and have been found as fossils in rocks 400 million years old. Coal is made largely of fossilized ferns, horsetails and club mosses.

▶ *Plants range in size from huge conifer trees (such as the giant sequoia, which is the world's largest single living organism) down to single-celled algae.*

Broadleaved trees and bushes, flowers and herbs

Flowering plants

Ginkos

Conifers

Cycads

Ferns

Club mosses

Horsetails

Mosses

⚙️ **Horsetails** are amongst the world's most ancient plants and were common at the time of the dinosaurs. Horsetails once grew as tall as trees, but they are similar in lifestyle to mosses and ferns.

⚙️ **Cycads** are mostly short, stubby, palm-like trees. Some are thousands of years old. Cycads have fern-like leaves growing in a circle around the end of the stem. New leaves sprout each year and last for several years.

⚙️ **Mosses grow** in damp, shady places. They do not make seeds or have vessels to carry water. Mosses can survive for weeks without water, then soak it up like a sponge when it rains.

⚙️ **Algae are simple organisms** that live in oceans, lakes, rivers and damp mud. Algae vary from single-celled microscopic organisms to huge fronds of seaweed (brown algae) that can grow to over 60 m long.

⚙️ **Lichens can survive** in many places where other plants would die, such as the Arctic, on mountaintops and in deserts. Some Arctic lichens are over 4000 years old.

⚙️ **Phytoplankton** is made up of tiny floating plants, such as diatoms, which live in water.

▶ *Also known as maidenhair trees, gingkos are an ancient type of plant with fan-shaped leaves and fleshy yellow seeds.*

253

Parts of a plant

⚙ **There are four major parts** to a flowering plant: the roots, stem, leaves, and flowers. The roots, stem and leaves keep the plant alive, while the flowers make seeds from which new plants grow.

⚙ **Roots** are the parts of a plant that grow down into the soil or water, anchoring it and absorbing all the water and minerals that the plant needs to grow.

⚙ **Tiny hairs** grow along the outside of a plant's root. The hairs help the plant to absorb water and minerals from the soil.

⚙ **The stem of a plant** supports the leaves and the flowers. It also carries water, minerals and food up and down between the plant's leaves and roots.

⚙ **Trees have** one tall, thick, woody stem called a trunk. Trunks are at least 10 cm thick to help the tree stand up.

⚙ **Leaves allow plants to 'breathe'.** They also absorb sunlight, which provides the energy needed to create the plant's food.

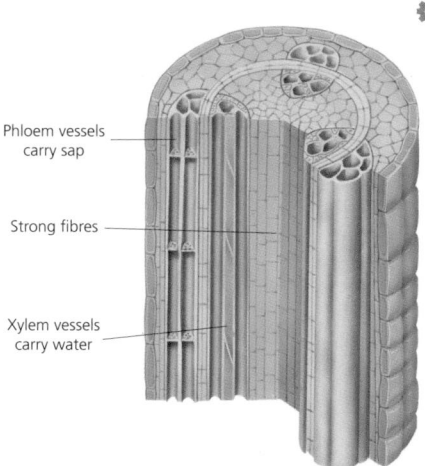

Phloem vessels carry sap

Strong fibres

Xylem vessels carry water

◀ *If you break open a celery stalk you will see fibres sticking out of the end. These fibres are from groups of tubes, called xylem vessels, which carry water through the plant.*

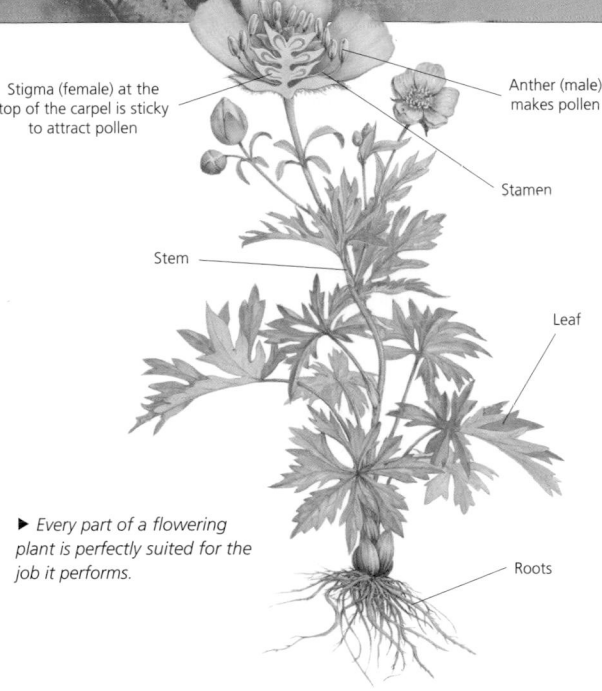

Stigma (female) at the top of the carpel is sticky to attract pollen

Anther (male) makes pollen

Stamen

Stem

Leaf

Roots

▶ *Every part of a flowering plant is perfectly suited for the job it performs.*

⚙ **Flowers contain** a plant's reproductive organs. For seeds to develop, the flower has to be pollinated.

⚙ **In gymnosperms** (conifers, cycads and gingkos) the flowers are often small and hidden. In angiosperms (flowering plants) they are usually much more obvious.

⚙ **Fruits are protective structures** that form around seeds after pollination.

⚙ **The roots, bulbs, flowering heads and leaves** of some plants are edible. Carrots and parsnips are roots. Onions are bulbs. Cauliflower and broccoli are the flowering heads of plants belonging to the cabbage family.

Food factory

⚙ **Plants** are able to make their own food. Each green plant is a remarkable chemical factory, taking in energy from the Sun and using it to combine carbon dioxide, from the air, with water to make sugary food. This process is called photosynthesis.

⚙ **Plants are made** from tiny blocks of living matter called cells. The surface of a leaf is made from flat cells that are transparent to allow sunlight through.

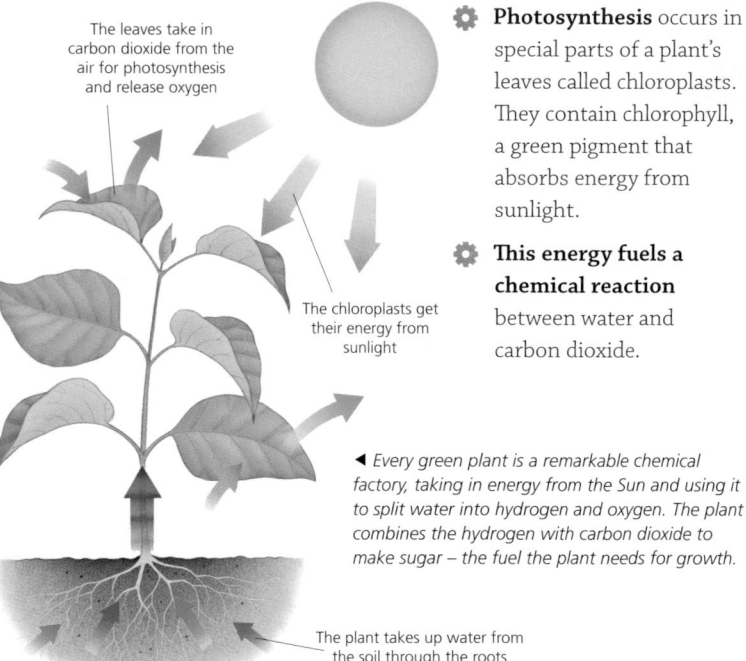

The leaves take in carbon dioxide from the air for photosynthesis and release oxygen

The chloroplasts get their energy from sunlight

⚙ **Photosynthesis** occurs in special parts of a plant's leaves called chloroplasts. They contain chlorophyll, a green pigment that absorbs energy from sunlight.

⚙ **This energy fuels a chemical reaction** between water and carbon dioxide.

◀ *Every green plant is a remarkable chemical factory, taking in energy from the Sun and using it to split water into hydrogen and oxygen. The plant combines the hydrogen with carbon dioxide to make sugar – the fuel the plant needs for growth.*

The plant takes up water from the soil through the roots

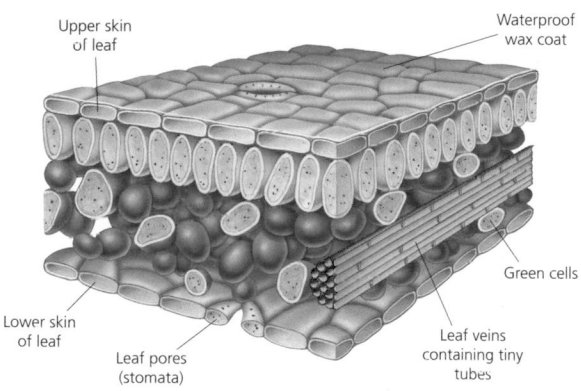

Upper skin of leaf

Waterproof wax coat

Green cells

Lower skin of leaf

Leaf pores (stomata)

Leaf veins containing tiny tubes

▲ *This is a hugely magnified slice through a leaf, showing the different layers. Leaves are thin and flat so they can catch the maximum amount of sunlight.*

⚙ **The carbon dioxide** comes from air drawn into the leaf through pores on the underside called stomata. The water is drawn up from the soil by the roots.

⚙ **The chemical reaction** produces the sugar glucose, which is then transported around the plant to where it is needed. Oxygen is produced as a waste product, and escapes into the air.

⚙ **Some of the glucose** produced by photosynthesis is burned up at once, releasing energy and leaving behind carbon dioxide and water. This process is called respiration.

⚙ **Other glucose** is combined into larger molecules called starches, which are easy for the plant to store. The plant breaks these starches down into sugars again whenever it needs extra energy.

⚙ **Together, the world's plants produce** a combined total of about 150 billion tonnes of sugar each year by photosynthesis.

How plants grow

⚙ **Inside a seed** is a tiny plant, or embryo, waiting to grow. When the seed settles in the soil, it takes in water, swells up and breaks open so that the new plant can grow out. This process of sprouting is known as germination.

1 The seed sends a root down and a shoot up

⚙ **A seed does not always sprout** as soon as it forms. It may spend some time before germination, being inactive or dormant.

⚙ **An embryo** inside a seed contains a food store (cotyledon) that is protected by the seed's tough outer casing (testa). As the growing plant increases in size the seed case breaks open.

2 The shoot bursts into the air and grows cotyledons (seed leaves)

◀ When a seed germinates, a root (radicle) grows down from it and a green shoot (plumule) grows up. The first leaves to come up are the seed leaves (cotyledons) of which there can be one or two. The cotyledons are food stores.

3 The stem and roots grow longer, and the plant soon begins to grow new leaves

🔅 **The root** is the first part to appear and it grows downwards. Later, the shoot appears and grows upwards.

🔅 **The shoot grows** towards the light, so its first leaves can make food by the process of photosynthesis.

🔅 **Only certain parts of a plant,** called meristems, can grow. These are usually the tips of shoots and roots.

🔅 **Because a plant grows** at the tips, shoots and roots mainly get longer rather than fatter. This is known as primary growth. Later in life, a plant may grow thicker or branch out.

🔅 **Spores are cells** that grow into new organisms. In seed plants, the spores develop into seeds. In plants, such as ferns and mosses, spores develop directly into a new plant called a gametophyte.

🔅 **Trees grow tall** as they compete for space and light. Branches spread out so that their leaves can reach the sunlight needed for photosynthesis.

Sapwood

Bark

Heartwood

◀ A tree's annual growth rings. These show how much the tree has grown; new rings are made beneath the bark and the oldest rings are at the centre of the trunk. Counting the rings gives the age of the tree.

259

Leaves

⚙️ **Leaves are a plant's powerhouse**, using sunlight to make sugar, the plant's fuel. Many leaves are broad and flat to catch the maximum amount of sunlight. Other shapes and styles may help to conserve water or help plants to cling to surfaces.

Tri-part leaf

⚙️ **Leaves come in many different shapes and sizes**, but there are two main types: needle-shaped leaves and broad leaves.

Heart-shaped

⚙️ **Broad leaves** are made by some trees and other woody plants in the flowering plant group. A broad leaf may be just a single leaf, such as an oak tree leaf, or be made from a group of leaflets, such as an ash tree leaf.

⚙️ **Conifers**, such as pine trees, have needle-shaped leaves.

Multiple

⚙️ **Leaves are joined to the stem** by a stalk called a petiole.

⚙️ **The flat part of the leaf** is called the blade. The leaf blade is like a sandwich, with two layers of cells holding a thick filling of green cells.

Simple

⚙️ **To cut down water loss in dry places**, leaves may be rolled-up, long and needle-like, or covered in hairs or wax.

▶ *Plants have developed many different shapes of leaf in order to survive in different conditions.*

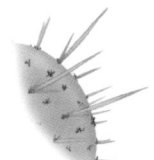

Spiky

▲ *The leaves of some trees become more colourful just before they fall, turning to shades of yellow, gold, orange and red. The colours change as the leaves lose their chlorophyll (green colouring), which allows other colours in the leaves to become visible.*

✿ **Climbing plants**, such as peas, have leaf tips that coil into stalks called tendrils. The tendrils help the plant cling to vertical surfaces.

✿ **Some plant leaves have parallel veins**, while others possess a branching network of veins, in which the veins are different sizes.

✿ **Palms have** a few large leaves called fronds. The fronds grow from the main bud at the top of a tall thin trunk. If the main bud at the top of the trunk is damaged, the tree will stop growing and die.

Flowering plants

* **There are more than 250,000 species** of flowering plant, including flowers, vegetables, grasses, trees and herbs, which are all divided into two main groups: the monocotyledons, such as grasses and bulb-plants, and the much larger group, the dicotyledons.

* **A cotyledon is a seed leaf.** Dicotyledons are plants that sprout two leaves from their seeds. Monocotyledons are plants that sprout a single leaf from their seeds.

* **There are about 50,000 species** of monocot plants – about a quarter of all flowering plants.

* **There are about 175,000 dicot species** – over three-quarters of all flowering plants.

◄ *All flowers are arranged according to a similar plan. The outer circle is made of sepals, with a circle of petals inside it.*

1 The fully formed flower is packed away inside a bud. Green flaps or sepals wrap tightly round it

2 Once the weather is warm enough, the bud begins to open. The sepals curl back to reveal the colourful petals

3 The sepals open wider and the petals grow outwards and backwards to create the flower's beautiful corolla

4 The flower opens fully to reveal its bright array of pollen sacs or anthers

▲ *At the right time of year, buds begin to open to reveal flowers' blooms so that the reproductive process can begin. Some flowers last just a day or so. Others bloom for months on end before the eggs are fertilized and grow into seeds.*

⚙ **Dicots grow slowly.** At least 50 percent have woody stems.

⚙ **Monocot stems grow** from the inside. However, dicots have a cambium, which is a layer of growing cells near the outside of the stem. Monocots rarely have a cambium.

⚙ **The flower parts of monocots**, such as petals, tend to be set in threes, or multiples of three. Dicot flowers have sets of four or five petals.

⚙ **Dicot plant leaves** usually have a network of veins, rather than the parallel veins seen in monocots.

⚙ **The biggest flowerhead** is the Puya raimondii plant from Bolivia, which can be up to 2.5 m across and have 8000 individual blooms.

⚙ **Desert plants may look dead** until the rain comes, when they suddenly burst into life, growing and flowering quickly so that the desert briefly blooms.

Non-flowering plants

- **It is difficult to imagine** just what tiny mosses and ferns could have in common with giant conifer trees, such as the redwoods of North America. But there is one key similarity – neither the mosses and ferns nor the redwoods reproduce from flowers.

- **Conifers are trees** with needle-like, typically evergreen leaves that make their seeds not in flowers but in cones.

- **With gingkos and cycads**, conifers make up the group of plants called gymnosperms, all of which make their seeds in cones.

- **All cones are green** and quite soft when they first form, then turn brown and hard as they ripen. The cone scales open to release the seeds when they are ripe.

▼ *Mosses reproduce in two stages. First, male sex cells are made on bag-like stems (antheridae) and swim to join the female eggs on cup-like stems (archegonia). Then a stalk (sporophyte) grows from the ova. On top is a capsule holding thousands of spores, which bursts, ejecting the spores. If spores land in a suitable place, male and female stems grow.*

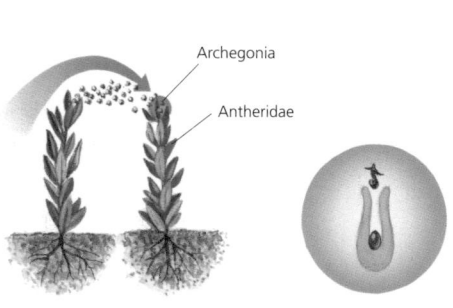
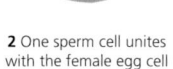

Archegonia

Antheridae

1 Male sperm cells swim to join the female egg

2 One sperm cell unites with the female egg cell

3 The fertilized egg grows into a sporophyte

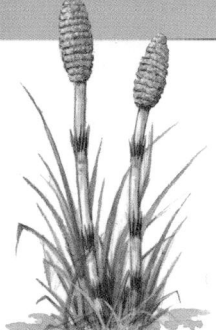

🌼 **One of the main differences between primitive plants** – including ferns, mosses, liverworts and horsetails – and more advanced plants is the way they reproduce. Primitive plants produce spores instead of seeds.

🌼 **There are about 10,000 different species of fern.** A typical fern has small roots, an underground stem (rhizome) and a spreading crown of fronds (leaves) that grows from the soil's surface. The stem creeps horizontally through the soil.

▲ Horsetails are a group of tall, fern-shaped plants that have existed on Earth for millions of years. They have leaf-like parts that resemble the spokes of a wheel, and cone-shaped reproductive parts that produce spores.

🌼 **Fern spores** are made in sacs called sporangia. These are the brown spots on the underside of the fronds. From these the spores spread out, and some settle in suitable places to grow.

🌼 **Mosses and liverworts** are low-growing plants found mostly in moist areas. They have no waterproof outer layer to protect them from drying out. They also lack a system of vessels to transport water around the plant.

🌼 **Male moss cells** can only swim to fertilize female cells when the moss is partly under water and so mosses often grow near streams.

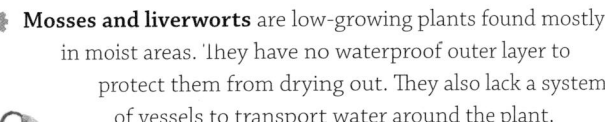

4 The sporophyte capsule bursts

5 The process begins again

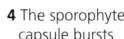

265

Pollination

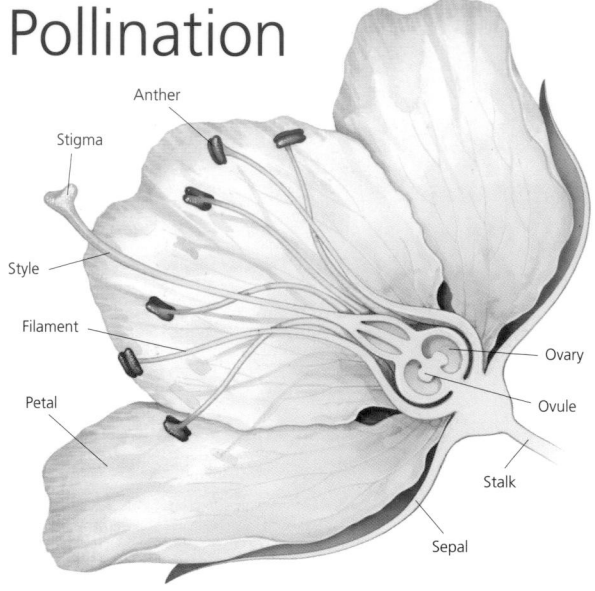

Anther

Stigma

Style

Filament

Petal

Ovary

Ovule

Stalk

Sepal

▲ *Within a flower are male parts called stamens. Each has a stalk (filament) topped by an anther, which contains the male reproductive cells. At the flower's centre are the female parts, the carpel. This has a sticky pad (stigma) on top of a long stalk (style), which widens at its base into an ovary. Inside the ovary are the female reproductive cells.*

⚙ **Before a flower can make seeds**, male pollen has to be transferred to the flower's female stigma. This is called pollination. Pollen can be carried from flower to flower by insects and other animals, and also by wind and water.

⚙ **Some flowers are self-pollinating**, meaning that pollen moves from an anther to a stigma on the same plant.

⚙ **In cross-pollinating flowers**, the pollen from the anthers must be carried to a stigma on a different plant of the same species.

- **Many flowers contain** both the male reproductive organs (stamens) and the female reproductive organs (carpel), but some plants have only one.

- **A flower can only use pollen** from the same species of plant.

- **Pollen grains** have an elaborately patterned cell wall, which prevents the pollen from drying out. The pattern of the cell wall differs in different plant species.

- **Wind-pollinated flowers**, such as grass flowers, have no need for bright colours or scents, so they are dull and have no smell. The stamens hang out of the flowers so that the wind can blow the pollen away.

- **Flowers that are pollinated by animals** make a small amount of spiky pollen. The spikes help the pollen to stick to hairs on the bodies of passing animals.

- **Many flowers have honey guides** – markings to guide the bees in. These are often invisible to humans and can only be seen in ultraviolet light, which bees and some other insects can see.

▲ To attract male bees, the bee orchid has a lip that looks and smells just like a female bee.

267

Seeds

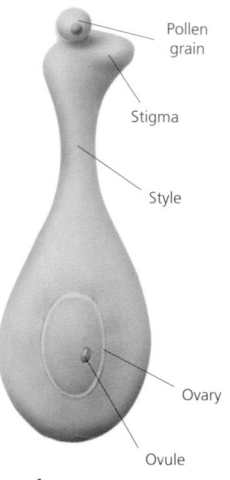

Pollen grain

Stigma

Style

Ovary

Ovule

1

🌼 **Seeds are the tiny, hard capsules** from which most new plants grow. Seeds develop from the plant's egg after it has been fertilized by pollen.

🌼 **All 250,000 flowering plants** produce 'enclosed' seeds. These are seeds that grow inside sacs called ovaries, which turn into a fruit around the seed.

🌼 **The 800 or so conifers,** cycads and gingkos produce 'naked' seeds, which means there is no fruit around them.

◀▼ **1** *When a pollen grain lands on the stigma of a flower, it grows a tube down the style and into the ovary.* **2** *The tip of the pollen tube then breaks open, releasing a male nucleus, which joins with the female nucleus of the ovule.* **3** *This joining together is called fertilization, and the new cell that forms is the start of a seed.*

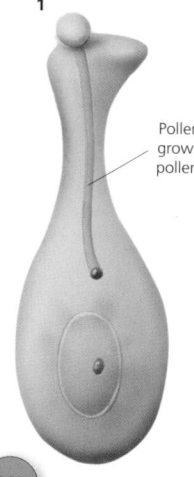

Pollen tube grows from pollen grain

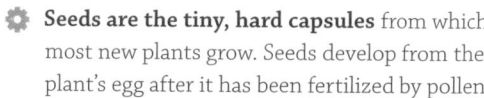

2

Female ovule

Male pollen nucleus

3

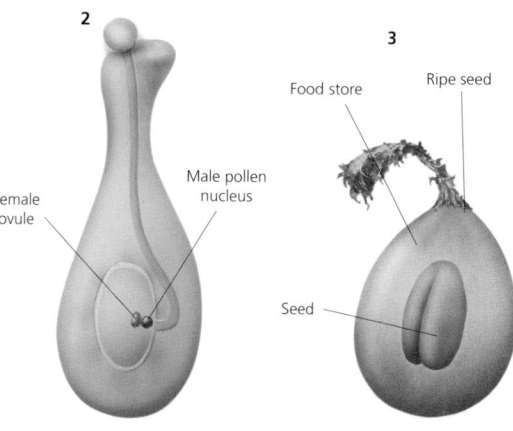

Food store

Ripe seed

Seed

- **Scientists define a fruit** as the ovary of a plant after the eggs have been pollinated and grown into seeds. Fleshy fruits, such as oranges, have soft, juicy flesh. In other fruits, such as hazelnuts and almonds, the flesh turns to a hard, dry shell.

▲ As well as eating seeds, squirrels bury them so that they have food for winter. Sometimes these buried food stores are forgotten, and the seeds sprout into plants.

- **Many seeds are light** enough to be blown by the wind. The feathery seed cases of some grasses are so light that they can be blown several kilometres.

- **Fruits are often eaten** by animals. The seeds get dispersed when they are passed out in the animal's body waste.

- **Some seeds stick to animal fur.** They have burrs (tiny barbs) that hook on to the fur, or even a sticky coating. Fruits such as geraniums and lupins explode, showering seeds in all directions.

- **The fruits of the elm**, ash, lime and hornbeam are fitted with 'aerofoils' or 'wings', which enable them to glide very long distances.

- **The largest seed** in the world comes from the giant fan palm, or coco-de-mer, which grows on the Seychelles Islands of the Indian Ocean. One seed can weigh 20 kg.

DID YOU KNOW?
Some lotus seeds have sprouted after being in a dormant (resting) state for 400 years.

269

Dryland plants

Red oat grass
African savanna

🌼 **Grassland forms** where there is not enough rain for trees to grow. In grassland habitats, there is usually a long dry season and a short rainy season.

🌼 **During the brief rainy season**, grasses and herbs grow quickly. The land becomes green with new growth, and brightly coloured flowers blanket the ground. The flowers create seeds rapidly, but dry out and die once the rains stop.

🌼 **Grasslands cover** nearly a quarter of the Earth's land surface. Temperate grasslands include the prairies of North America, the pampas of South America and the steppes of Eurasia. The tropical grassland of Africa is known as savanna.

Dallas grass
South American pampas

🌼 **Africa's grasslands** are home to vast herds of grazing animals. The animals eat the grass, but the grass also benefits, since the animals produce huge amounts of droppings that enrich the soil with nutrients.

🌼 **On Africa's savanna grasslands**, elephant grasses can grow up to 4 m in height.

Blue gramma grass
North American prairies

◀ *Many grasses reproduce by sending out underground stems or long shoots from which a new plant grows. If the top of the grass is cut, eaten or burnt new grass then grows from underground shoots.*

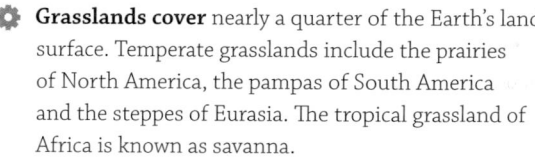

⚙ **When grasslands are destroyed by farming**, the soil can be blown away by the wind. This is what turned the Great Plains region of North America into a 'dust bowl' in the 1930s.

⚙ **Desert plants** have special adaptations to stop water evaporating from their leaves. Most have small, hard, tough-coated leaves. The reduced surface area means there is less leaf exposed to hot sunlight, which makes the plant's water evaporate.

⚙ **Some flowering desert plants** are visible for only a few days. Their seeds lie dormant (inactive) in the soil, perhaps for years, until a the rains come. Then the plants germinate and bloom quickly. These quick-growing flowers are called ephemerals.

⚙ **Huge saguaro cacti** from Arizona and California in the USA and also Mexico may live for over 200 years. They do not usually grow 'arms' until they are 75 years old.

⚙ **The pleats in the stem** expand like a concertina as the cactus soaks up water. Up to 90 percent of the weight of a cactus comes from the water stored in its fleshy stem.

Saguaro cactus

Joshua cactus

Prickly pear cactus

▶ The largest plants in most deserts are called succulents. Their thick, fleshy stems or leaves store water to help the plant survive dry periods.

271

Water plants

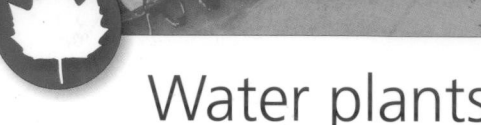

A plant is over 90 percent water, so it is not surprising that plants manage to live in water perfectly well, provided that they are able to obtain enough sunlight. Some plants float on the surface, while others root in the bottom of ponds or streams.

DID YOU KNOW?
Water hyacinths grow so quickly that they may double in number every ten days.

Many grass-like plants grow in water, including reeds, mace, irises and rushes, such as bulrushes and cattails.

Reeds are tall grasses with round stems, flat leaves and purplish flowers. They grow in dense beds in open water.

▼ *Swamp, or bald, cypress trees grow in swampy areas of North America. Their trunks are wide at the base, which helps to support them in the shifting mud. Their roots grow cone-shaped 'knees' above the water to take in air, since waterlogged mud does not contain much oxygen.*

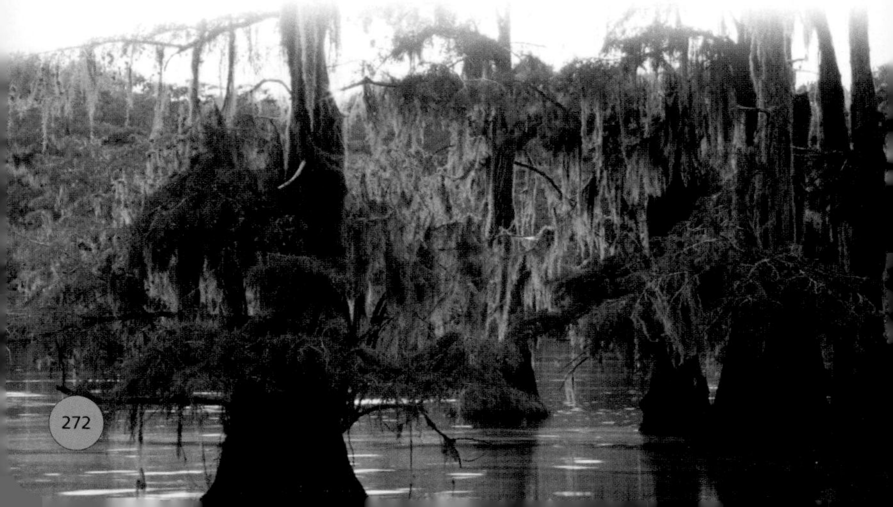

- ⚙ **Huge numbers of wildfowl**, including great crested grebes, spend winter in reedbeds. In many parts of the world, reeds are cut and used as roofing materials.

- ⚙ **Papyrus is a tall**, grass-like water plant that grows in Africa's River Nile. Stems were rolled flat by the ancient Egyptians to write on. The word 'paper' comes from papyrus.

▲ *Water hyacinths are purple American water flowers. They grow quickly, and can clog up slow streams.*

- ⚙ **Free-floating plants**, such as duckweed and frogbit, are common in marshes. In rivers, they would be washed away.

- ⚙ **Seaweeds are red**, green or brown algae. Red seaweeds grow 30–60 m down in tropical seas. Brown seaweeds, such as giant kelp, grow down to depths of about 20 m, mostly in cold water. Green seaweeds are found in rockpools and coastal rocks in temperate and tropical regions.

- ⚙ **Seaweeds grow** mainly on rocky shores, or underwater close to the coast. They hold on to the rocks to prevent being washed away. The part that attaches the seaweed to a rock is called a holdfast, and it resembles a root. It grips the rock tightly like a sucker.

- ⚙ **Seaweeds have tough**, leathery fronds (leaves) to stand up to the pounding of the waves. Their bodies are flexible, so that they can move in the water currents without breaking.

- ⚙ **Some seaweeds**, such as the bladderwrack, have gas pockets to help their fronds (leaves) float.

Coniferous forest

⚙ **The evergreen conifer forests** of the cool regions that border the Arctic Circle – such as the north of Asia, northern Europe and North America – are called boreal forests. The word boreal means 'northern'.

⚙ **For nine months of the year** boreal forests are cold and dark, but they spring to life in the brief warmth of the three-month summer.

⚙ **In Russia and Siberia**, boreal forest is called taiga, which is a Russian word meaning 'little sticks'.

▼ *Conifers come in many shapes and sizes, and grow in most parts of the world.*

Italian cypress	Stone pine	Phoenician juniper	Cedar of Lebanon	Coast redwood	Norway spruce	Silver fir
50 m	20 m	10 m	40 m	112 m	40 m	50 m

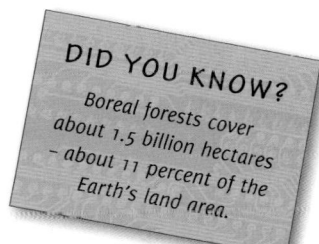

DID YOU KNOW?

Boreal forests cover about 1.5 billion hectares – about 11 percent of the Earth's land area.

- 🟢 **Many conifers are cone-shaped**, which helps them to shed snow from their branches in winter.

- 🟢 **The needle-like shape** and waxy coating of conifer leaves helps the tree to save water.

- 🟢 **Christmas trees** are usually spruce or fir trees. The modern Christmas tree tradition began in Germany, but the use of evergreen trees as a symbol of eternal life was an ancient custom of the Egyptians, Chinese and Hebrews.

- 🟢 **As trees in coniferous forests grow** very close together and keep their leaves all year round, little light reaches the forest floor, so only mosses, lichens, and other small plants can grow there.

- 🟢 **Boreal forest trees** are good at recovering after fire. Indeed, jack pine and black spruce cones only open to release their seeds after a fire.

- 🟢 **Softwood is timber** that comes from coniferous trees such as pine, larch, fir and spruce. Between 75 and 80 percent of the natural forests of northern Asia, Europe and the USA is made up of softwood trees.

- 🟢 **Pines grow fast and straight**, reaching their full height in less than 20 years – which is why they provide 75 percent of the world's timber.

Broadleaf forest

▶ *Plenty of light can filter down through deciduous trees, so that all kinds of bushes and flowers grow in the woods, often blooming in spring before the trees develop their leaves.*

- **Forests of broadleaved, deciduous** trees grow in temperate regions such as North America, western Europe and eastern Asia, where there are warm, wet summers and cold winters.

- **Very few woodlands** in Europe are entirely natural; most are 'secondary' woods, growing on land once cleared for farms.

Bluebell

- **In moist western Europe**, beech trees dominate woods on well-drained, shallow soils, especially chalk soils; oak trees prefer deep clay soils. Alders grow in waterlogged places.

- **In drier eastern Europe**, beeches are replaced by durmast oak and hornbeam, and in Russia by lindens.

- **In North American woods**, beech and linden are rarer than in Europe, but oaks, hickories and maples are more common.

- **Plenty of light** can filter down through decidious trees, so that all kinds of bushes and flowers grow in the woods, often blooming in spring before the trees develop their leaves.

- **A wide range of shrubs** grow under the trees in broadleaved woods including dogwood, holly and magnolia, as well as woodland flowers.

⚙ **Losing their leaves** in autumn helps trees to save water as they 'shut down' their food-gathering system for winter. Food pipes inside the tree branches are sealed, and as the leaves are cut off from their food supply, they die.

⚙ **The chlorophyll** that keeps the leaves green breaks down, and the leaves turn red, yellow and brown before falling to the ground. Enough food is stored within the tree to ensure that buds can grow in spring.

⚙ **Maple syrup** comes from several North American maple trees, including the sugar maple and the black maple. The syrup is 'sweet-water' sap. It is different from ordinary sap, and flows from wounds during thaws, when there is no growth.

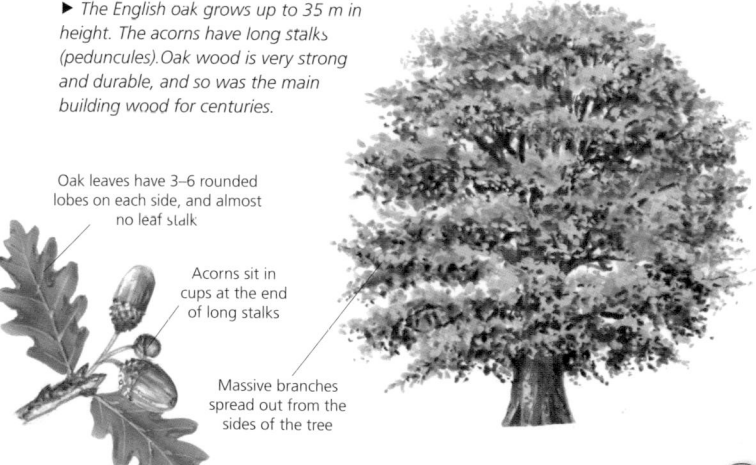

▶ *The English oak grows up to 35 m in height. The acorns have long stalks (peduncules). Oak wood is very strong and durable, and so was the main building wood for centuries.*

Oak leaves have 3–6 rounded lobes on each side, and almost no leaf stalk

Acorns sit in cups at the end of long stalks

Massive branches spread out from the sides of the tree

Rainforest

Emergent layer

🌀 **With over 2000 mm of rain** per year and average temperatures in excess of 20°C, tropical rainforests are warm and wet. These conditions make them the world's richest plant habitats.

🌀 **Most rainforest trees** are broadleaved and evergreen.

🌀 **Covering much of northern South America**, the Amazon rainforest is home to more species of plants and animals than any other place on Earth.

Canopy

🌀 **Trees of the Amazon rainforest** include rosewood, Brazil nut, rubber, myrtle, and laurel, as well as palms.

🌀 **Trees in the African rainforest** include mahogany, ebony, limba, wenge, agba, iroko and sapele.

Understorey

◀ *The leaves of the tallest trees form the top level of the rainforest, the emergent layer. Sunlight passing between these trees allows a lower, denser layer to grow – the main canopy. This layer blocks out most of the remaining sunlight, so the forest floor has few plants.*

Forest floor

⚙️ **Some tropical forests** blanket the sides of mountains. The trees here are shorter, and more plants grow on or near the ground.

⚙️ **The highest mountain rainforests** are called 'cloud' forests, because much of the forest is covered in low clouds, providing moisture for all kinds of mosses, ferns and herbs.

⚙️ **In order to attract birds** and insects in the gloom, many rainforest plants have big, bright flowers. Flowers pollinated by birds are often red, those by night-flying moths white or pink, and those by day-flying insects yellow or orange.

⚙️ **Many rainforest plants** need large seeds to store enough food while they grow. They produce fragrant fruits that attract animals. The animals eat the fruits and spread the seeds via their droppings. Fruit bats, for example, are drawn to mangoes.

⚙️ **A number of rainforest plants** are parasitic. This means that they feed on other plants. Parasitic plants include mistletoes and rafflesia.

▶ Rainforest trees are covered with epiphytes – plants with roots that do not reach the soil, but which take water and minerals from rainwater and plant debris that falls on them.

DID YOU KNOW?
Half the world's remaining rainforest will be gone by 2020 if it continues to be cut down at the current rate.

Cereals

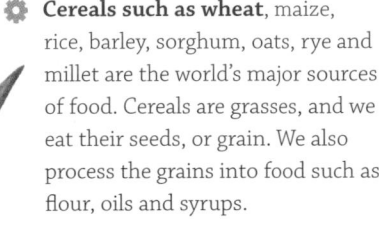

🌼 **Cereals such as wheat**, maize, rice, barley, sorghum, oats, rye and millet are the world's major sources of food. Cereals are grasses, and we eat their seeds, or grain. We also process the grains into food such as flour, oils and syrups.

🌼 **In the developed world** – that is, regions such as North America and Europe – wheat is the most important food crop.

🌼 **For half the world's population**, including most people in Southeast Asia and China, rice is the staple food.

🌼 **Maize, or corn, is the USA's main crop**, and the second most important crop around the world after wheat. Rice is the third key crop.

▲ *The ear, or head, of a corn plant is called a cob. It is covered with tightly packed yellow or white kernels of seeds. The kernels are the part of the plant that is eaten.*

🌼 **Wheat was one of the first crops** ever grown. It was planted by the earliest farmers at least 10,000 years ago.

🌼 **Pasta is made** from durum (hard-grain) wheat. Italians have been using it in their cooking since the 13th century, but now pasta dishes are popular worldwide.

🌼 **When grain is ripe** it is cut from its stalks. This is called reaping. After reaping, the grain must be separated from the stalks and chaff (waste). This is called threshing. After threshing, the grain must be cleaned and separated from the husks. This is called winnowing.

🌼 **Rice has been cultivated** since about 3000 BC, Rice seeds are first sown in drier soil, but when the young plants (seedlings) are about two months old, they are planted in paddy fields that are flooded with up to 10 cm of water.

🌼 **Brown rice** is rice grain with the husk ground away. White rice is rice grain with the inner bran layer ground away as well, and is far less nutritious.

🌼 **A lot of wheat is fed** to livestock, but 95 percent of all rice is eaten by people. Rice provides more than 20 percent of the calories consumed by humans.

▶ A combine harvester is an agricultural machine that reaps the grain, threshes it, cleans it and then pours it into bags, or reservoirs.

Fruit and vegetables

⚙️ **Vegetables** are basically any part of a plant eaten cooked or raw, except for the fruit. People also eat a wide variety of fruits, and a healthy diet includes at least five different fruits and vegetables every day.

⚙️ **Green vegetables** are the edible green parts of plants, including the leaves of plants such as cabbages and lettuces.

⚙️ **The leaves** of green vegetables are rich in many essential vitamins, including vitamin A, vitamin E and folic acid.

⚙️ **Vitamin C** (ascorbic acid) is found in many fresh fruits and vegetables, especially citrus fruits. Vitamin C is important for the growth of bones, teeth and blood vessels, and it aids the healing of wounds.

⚙️ **Citrus fruits** are a group of juicy, soft fruits covered with a very thick, waxy, evenly coloured skin in yellow, orange or green. Citrus fruits include lemons, limes, oranges and grapefruits.

⚙️ **The main temperate fruits** are apples, pears, plums, apricots, peaches, grapes and cherries.

⚙️ **The best-known tropical** fruits are bananas and pineapples. Others include guavas, breadfruit, lychees, melons and mangoes.

⚙️ **Berries are fleshy fruits** that contain lots of seeds. Many plants produce berries, including tomatoes, grape vines and bananas.

⚙️ **Strawberries, raspberries and blackberries** are not true berries. They are called 'aggregate' fruits, because they are made up of groups of tiny fruits, each containing one seed.

⚙️ **Grapes are found** all round the world, in places where there are warm summers and mild winters.

◀ Grapes are juicy, smooth-skinned berries that grow in tight clusters on woody plants called vines.

▲ A pea pod forms from the ovary of a pea plant. Only fertilized pea ovules can grow as seeds. When the pod is opened, it may contain some seeds that have failed to grow.

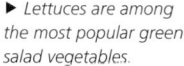

▶ Lettuces are among the most popular green salad vegetables.

◀ Root vegetables are parts of plants that grow underground. Carrots are root vegetables that are a rich source of vitamin A.

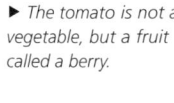

▶ The tomato is not a vegetable, but a fruit called a berry.

◀ The grapefruit is a typical citrus fruit. The juice of citrus fruits contains high levels of citric acid, which gives them their sharp flavour.

Fungi and lichens

🌼 **Fungi are not plants**, because they have no chlorophyll to make their food. So scientists put them in a group or kingdom of their own. Lichens are a remarkable partnership between algae and fungi.

🌼 **A huge group** of 50,000 species, fungi include mushrooms, toadstools, moulds, mildews and yeasts.

🌼 **Fungi were once thought** to be simple plants with no leaves. We now know that there are many differences between fungi and true plants. Some of these differences are linked to the types of chemicals that make up fungi, which are different from those of even the simplest true plants.

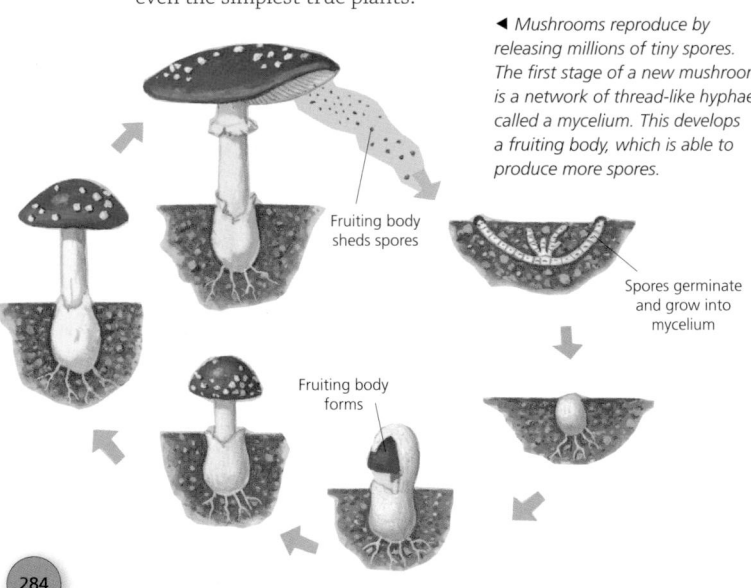

◀ Mushrooms reproduce by releasing millions of tiny spores. The first stage of a new mushroom is a network of thread-like hyphae called a mycelium. This develops a fruiting body, which is able to produce more spores.

Fruiting body sheds spores

Spores germinate and grow into mycelium

Fruiting body forms

⚙ **Because fungi cannot make their own food**, they must live off other plants and animals (their 'hosts') – sometimes as partners, sometimes as parasites.

⚙ **Fungi feed by releasing chemicals** called enzymes to break down chemicals in their host. The fungi then use the chemicals as food.

⚙ **Parasitic fungi feed** off living organisms; fungi that live off dead plants and animals are called saprophytic fungi.

⚙ *Penicillium* **moulds** are common fungi that grow on rotten fruit. One species, *Penicillium notatum*, produces a chemical that kills bacteria. It is used in the antibiotic drug penicillin, which is a treatment for bacterial infections.

⚙ **Lichens are able to survive** in some of the most difficult conditions on Earth – in poor soils, on rocks and in some of the coldest regions, including the Arctic and Antarctic, and high mountains.

▼ The algae in lichens are tiny green balls that make food and sunlight to feed the fungi. The fungi make a protective layer around the algae and hold water.

⚙ **There are 20,000 species** of lichen. Some grow on soil, but most grow on rocks or tree bark.

⚙ **Lichens are tolerant** of salty conditions, and are often found on seashore rocks.

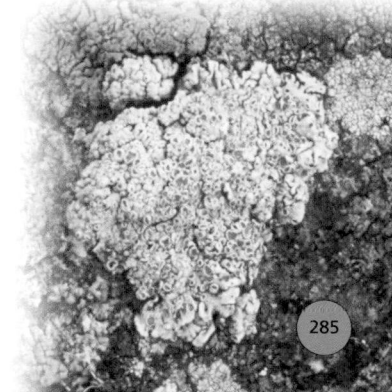

285

Animals

Animal kingdom

⚙ **There are millions of different species of animal**, which range in size from microscopic single-celled creatures, to giants that dwarf a human being. The animal kingdom is divided into a series of nested groups according to shared characteristics.

⚙ **In descending order** of numbers of species within each group, the subdivisions are: phylum (plural phyla), sub-phylum, class, order, sub-order, family, and genus (plural genera). Not all sub-divisions are used in all branches of the animal kingdom.

⚙ **Human beings**, for example, are the species *Homo sapiens* – phylum Chordate; subphylum Vertebrate; class: Mammal; order: Primate; family: Hominid; genus: *Homo*.

⚙ **The main split in the animal kingdom** is between vertebrates, which have a backbone, and invertebrates, which don't.

⚙ **The vertebrate animals** are: mammals, birds, reptiles, amphibians and fish. All other animals are invertebrates.

⚙ **The sub-division** with by far the greatest number of species is the Arthropod phylum, which includes all invertebrates that have jointed legs. The main arthropod subgroups are insects, myriapods (centipedes and millipedes), arachnids (spiders and scorpions), and crustaceans (crabs and shrimp).

⚙ **Scientists estimate** that arthropods make up at least 90 percent of all animal species. There are over one million insect species.

⚙ **Animal bodies** vary enormously – vertebrates have an internal skeleton, arthropods generally have an exoskeleton (external skeleton), while worms use the pressure of internal fluids to keep their bodies in shape.

⚙ **Animals also have widely differing lifecycles.** Some, such as mammals and birds, are born as miniature versions of the adult. Most insects, and many other invertebrates, go through an intermediate larval stage before becoming adults.

▼ *The science of grouping animals is called taxonomy. It is important in many ways, for example when making a decision about which creatures today are the closest relatives of the long-dead dinosaurs.*

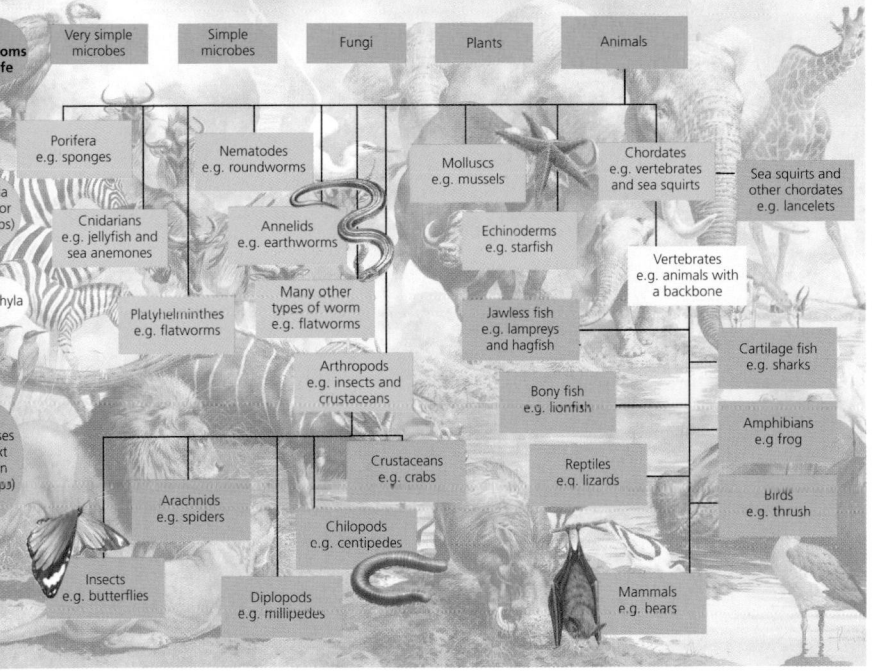

Very simple microbes

Simple microbes

Fungi

Plants

Animals

Porifera e.g. sponges

Nematodes e.g. roundworms

Molluscs e.g. mussels

Chordates e.g. vertebrates and sea squirts

Sea squirts and other chordates e.g. lancelets

Cnidarians e.g. jellyfish and sea anemones

Annelids e.g. earthworms

Echinoderms e.g. starfish

Vertebrates e.g. animals with a backbone

Platyhelminthes e.g. flatworms

Many other types of worm e.g. flatworms

Jawless fish e.g. lampreys and hagfish

Cartilage fish e.g. sharks

Arthropods e.g. insects and crustaceans

Bony fish e.g. lionfish

Amphibians e.g frog

Crustaceans e.g. crabs

Reptiles e.g. lizards

Birds e.g. thrush

Arachnids e.g. spiders

Chilopods e.g. centipedes

Insects e.g. butterflies

Diplopods e.g. millipedes

Mammals e.g. bears

How animals feed

🔩 **Carnivores** are animals that mainly eat other animals. Some are active predators that hunt down prey, while others use stealth or ambush methods. More than three-quarters of all animals in the world are herbivores (plant eaters).

🔩 **In any habitat**, there are always more herbivores than carnivores, as the carnivores must feed on the plant eaters. Plant eaters range from elephants and hippopotamuses to many kinds of bugs, beetles, moths and caterpillars.

🔩 **Deer, most gazelles, giraffes** and the black rhino are browsers, eating leaves from trees and shrubs. Zebras, cattle and the white rhino are grazers, eating leaves or grasses from the ground.

🔩 **Wild horses and ponies** can graze for up to 16 hours daily on grass, flowers, fruits and berries.

▼ *The leopard has a varied diet that ranges from dung beetles to large mammals, such as this gazelle. Leopards drag their prey up into trees out of the reach of other hungry predators and scavengers.*

▶ *The giraffe feeds by using its very long, black, powerful tongue to grasp twigfuls of leaves, pulling them into its mouth.*

⚙ **Foods, such as flesh, blood and eggs**, contain large amounts of nourishment and energy compared to plant foods, so carnivores can spend much less time eating than herbivores do.

⚙ **Meat eaters** range from killer whales and sharks in the sea, big cats and wild dogs on land, and eagles and hawks in the air, to much smaller shrews, bats, frogs, dragonflies, spiders and even sea anemones.

⚙ **Some animals** that may not seem to be carnivores actually are. A starfish might prey on a shellfish that is clamped to a rock, and spend most of a day prising it off and devouring the flesh.

⚙ **Rodents**, such as rats, mice and squirrels, use their long, continuously growing front teeth to crack open the toughest nuts.

⚙ **As darkness falls**, birds of prey, such as hawks, rest while owls come out of tree holds, cliff crevices or quiet buildings. These nocturnal hunters catch a range of prey from beetles and mice to young rabbits and squirrels.

⚙ **The open ocean** contains billions of microscopic animals and plants, called plankton. Plankton is eaten by whales and fish, and also by tiny animals, such as copepods, that are then eaten by larger animals.

291

How animals move

- **Most land animals**, from bugs to bears, use their legs for moving, or locomotion. Others fly, crawl on their bellies, wriggle, swing, slide, swim or slither.

- **Muscles get shorter**, or contract, and pull different body parts to allow movement. In vertebrates the muscles are joined to bones, which make up the skeleton.

▲ The earthworm wriggles between soil grains. The stiff hairs along its body help to grip the sides of the burrow, so the worm can thrust its front end forwards to move onwards.

- **Cheetahs are the world's fastest** land animal. Within two seconds of starting, a cheetah can reach speeds of 75 km/h, reaching a top speed of about 105 km/h.

- **Fastest of all animals** is the peregrine falcon, which has been recorded travelling at 270 km/h when it dives or 'stoops' to catch its prey.

- **Monkeys move through trees** by swinging from their arms. A gibbon's arms are twice as long as its legs and it has hook-shaped hands to hang from the branches.

- **Hummingbirds and nectar-sipping bats** flap their short, broad wings quickly, almost 100 times a second, so they can hover.

- **The African fringe-toed lizard** has to dance across the hot sand in the desert to keep its feet cool.

- **Water is very dense** so streamlining (a smooth body shape) enables fish, dolphins, seals and other sea creatures to easily move through it.

- **One of the most adaptable movers** has no limbs at all. The golden tree snake can slither fast, swim well, burrow, climb trees and even launch itself from a branch, and flatten its body, to glide for many metres.

- **Jellyfish float** about freely, moving by squeezing water out from beneath their bodies. When a jellyfish stops squeezing, it sinks.

▶ Cheetahs' spines are so bendy that they can bring their hind legs forward between their front paws when they run.

293

Animal communication

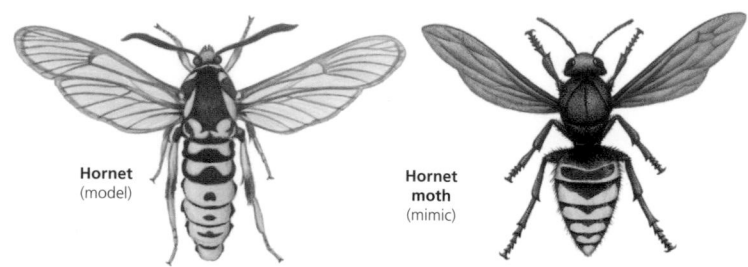

Hornet
(model)

Hornet moth
(mimic)

▲ *The hornet has a painful sting and few creatures dare to try and eat it. The hornet moth mimics the hornet. It is harmless but few creatures try to eat it either.*

⚙ **Communication means** passing on messages and information. Animals use sound, sight and movement to communicate, as well as a range of methods including scent, taste, touch and the emitting of electrical signals.

⚙ **Some messages** are understood only by an animal's own kind. Other messages can be understood by a wide variety of creatures – these are often about matters of life and death.

⚙ **Female glow worms** communicate with males through a series of flashes.

⚙ **Yellow-and-black** is one of the most common colour combinations to be used as a warning. It tells predators that an animal is venomous or tastes foul. Spiders, wasps, frogs and snakes all use this code.

⚙ **Sudden danger** needs a short, sharp message to warn others in the group. Rabbits thump the ground and many birds make a loud 'seep' or 'tic' noise. Meerkats will give a shrill shriek, while the first beaver to notice a predator will slap its tail hard on the water.

⚙ **Lemurs have different calls** to warn members of their troop whether danger is coming from above, along the ground, or is hidden in the undergrowth.

⚙ **Wolves are intelligent** animals that communicate with body language. They use facial expressions and howl at each other. The howls of a hunting pack of wolves can be heard for about 10 km, telling other wolves to keep their distance.

⚙ **Honeybees indicate** to each other the site of a rich food source, such as nectar-laden flowers, by 'dancing'. The bee flies in a figure of eight and shakes its body to indicate the direction of the food source.

⚙ **Many insects communicate** using the smell of chemicals called pheromones, which are released from special glands. The tropical tree ant uses ten different pheromones, combining them with different movements to send 50 different kinds of message.

⚙ **Crows use** at least 300 different croaks to communicate with each other. Crows from one area, though, cannot understand those from another.

▶ *One method of communication is rearing or puffing up to make oneself appear bigger. This threatening behaviour makes other animals think twice before attacking. Cobras raise their head, spread their hood and hiss at an attacker.*

What is a mammal?

⚙ **Mammals have bony skeletons**, are usually covered in fur or hair, and feed their young with milk. Amazingly adaptable, mammals can be found in a large variety of habitats, from arid deserts to the icy Arctic. They are warm-blooded and are able to keep their bodies at a constant temperature.

⚙ **There are about 4500 types**, or species, of mammal, ranging in size from the giant blue whale to tiny shrews and bats.

⚙ **Most mammals have good senses** of sight, smell and hearing, which help them to find food and detect predators.

⚙ **All mammals have three small bones** in their ears, collectively known as the ossicles. They transfer sound from the ear drum to the inner ear, from where nerves carry the signals to the brain.

⚙ **Many mammals live** a nocturnal way of life; this means that they are most active at night and have excellent night vision.

⚙ **Most mammals move on four legs**, but not all: sea-living mammals have streamlined bodies that are well-suited to moving through water. Bats are the only flying mammals.

⚙ **Fur and fat protect** mammals from the cold. When they do get cold, mammals curl up, seek shelter or shiver.

⚙ **Some mammals save energy** in winter by resting, or hibernating. Mammals are also able to cool their bodies down – by sweating, panting or resting.

⚙ **Larger mammals**, such as elephants, usually produce just one offspring (baby) and care for it over several years. Smaller mammals, such as rats, may have ten or more babies that grow quickly and are independent in just a few weeks.

DID YOU KNOW?

The speediest mammal in the water is the killer whale, moving at around 55 km/h, sometimes in groups of 30 or more.

▶ *Like all mammals, these piglets will feed exclusively on their mother's milk during the first weeks of life.*

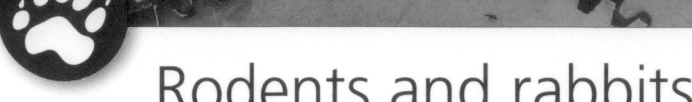

Rodents and rabbits

⚙ **There are more than 1700 types**, or species, of rodent and they make up the largest group of mammals.

⚙ **Rodents are usually small**, four-legged creatures with long tails and sharp senses. They have four long incisor teeth, which keep growing throughout the animal's life. Rodents are often intelligent, agile and adaptable, and can be found living all over the world, in almost every habitat.

⚙ **The capybara** is the largest-living rodent and measures about 1.3 m long. It lives around ponds, lakes and rivers in South America.

⚙ **Voles are mouse-like rodents.** They normally eat plant matter and often live in meadows and on farmland.

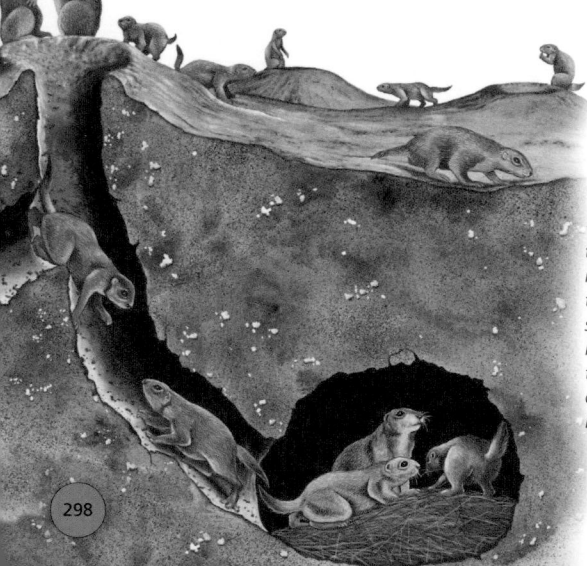

◀ Prairie dogs are some of the best burrowers of the mammal world. Despite their name they are ground squirrels. Families live together in groups called coteries and their underground warrens can extend for hundreds of kilometres.

▶ *Flying squirrels are gliders rather than true flyers. They have a hairy membrane between their limbs that acts like a parachute. They use their tails like a rudder, to direct them in the air.*

⚙ **Rats and mice** are often regarded as pests as many of them live with or near humans. They eat stores of grain and will invade cupboards and kitchens, given the opportunity.

⚙ **Rabbits, hares and pikas** belong to a group of mammals called lagomorphs. They are similar to rodents, and like them have large incisor teeth that grow continuously. They have superb senses of hearing and sight, and strong, muscular legs that help them to move at great speed.

⚙ **The common rabbit** originally came from Spain and North Africa, but it has travelled to many other countries where it has pushed native animals out of their habitats and eaten local plants in huge quantities.

DID YOU KNOW?
There are more than 270 different types of squirrel.

⚙ **Rabbits dig burrows**, but hares do not. The burrows may connect to make a huge underground labyrinth, or warren. Each burrow is wide enough for one rabbit to pass at a time, and may end in chambers where females give birth.

⚙ **Baby rabbits** are called kittens, adult males are called bucks and adult females are called does. Baby hares are called leverets.

Small carnivores

🔧 **Shrews, hedgehogs, moles** and similar animals are known as insectivores. This name means 'insect eaters', but many of these small, busy, active, darting mammals feed on a variety of tiny prey, including worms, snails, slugs and spiders. There are about 345 species of insectivore around the world.

🔧 **Most insectivores** have long, pointed, whiskery noses, little eyes and ears and very sharp teeth. They are mainly active at night and they use their keen senses of smell and touch, rather than sight, to catch prey.

🔧 **Pygmy shrews** are the smallest of all land mammals, weighing only 2 g and measuring hardly 6 cm long – including the tail. They rely on their quick reactions to hunt and catch creatures larger than themselves, including beetles and grasshoppers.

🔧 **A mole** spends most of its life in its large burrow network, feeding on worms, grubs and other creatures found in the soil. Moles are virtually blind. The mole's front feet are like shovels and are used to push aside earth. Molehills are loose soil that the mole thrusts up from its tunnels – which can stretch for up to 150 m.

◀ *It is believed that water shrews have toxin, or poison, in their saliva, which helps them to kill their prey.*

▲ *The American badger is smaller than its Eurasian cousin and, also unlike the Eurasian badger, it lives and hunts alone rather than in a group, or colony, with other badgers.*

🌼 **Otters, stoats, weasels and badgers** all belong to the mammal group of mustelids. They are long-bodied, short-legged, sharp-toothed hunters. They are active, flexible, fast-moving and often race into holes or burrows after their prey.

🌼 **The mustelid group** of mammals contains a wide variety of animals living in different habitats. Martens, for example, live in trees, badgers live in a burrow, and minks live on the water's edge.

🌼 **Badgers are very strong**, powerful animals that come out at night. They live in family groups in huge networks of underground chambers and tunnels, called setts. Badgers eat a variety of foods, including worms, insects, frogs, lizards, birds and fruit.

🌼 **Weasels are among the smallest** animals in the mustelid group, although the males are often twice the size of females and eat different prey. They hunt on mice, which they can pursue down burrows thanks to their narrow skulls and thin bodies.

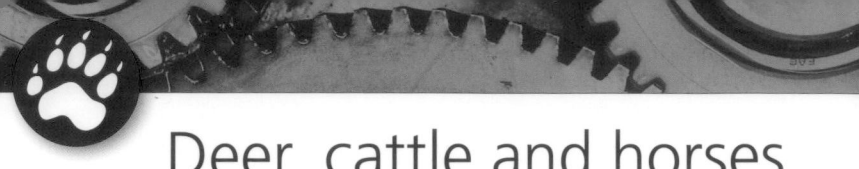

Deer, cattle and horses

⚙ **Horses, ponies, zebras and asses** all belong to the same mammal group – the equids. Equids have manes of long hair on their head and neck, and a thick, tufted tail. Their long legs, deep chest and powerful muscles allow them to run a long way, at great speed, without becoming tired.

⚙ **Equids are highly social** animals and prefer to live in family groups, called herds. The herd is usually led by a mare and contains only one adult male. If startled, horses can run away quickly. The mares stay close to their youngsters to protect them.

⚙ **Camels, deer and giraffes** all belong to a large group of hoofed mammals called artiodactyls. They are placed in this group because they have an even number of toes in their hooves (the toes may not be visible, but the bones are still there).

Deer are characterized by their antlers. These growths emerge directly from the animal's skull and are covered in thin skin, called velvet. The velvet has disappeared by the mating, or rutting, season, when the antlers are used by males to fight one another. Antlers fall off when the mating season is over.

> **DID YOU KNOW?**
> The very first horse-like animal is thought to have lived about 50 million years ago. It is called hyracotherium or eophippus.

A giraffe's neck may be more than 2 m long, but it has only seven bones in it. That is the same number as is found in a human neck.

Alpacas and llamas are close relatives of camels. They live at great heights in the South American Andes and are prized for their wool.

Cattle and their relatives belong to a mammal group called bovids. They have horns that, unlike deer horns, are almost never lost, and their hooves are divided into two. Bovids are a large group of mammals – there are about 140 species. Although they are found throughout the world, Africa has the biggest range of bovids. The family includes cows, bison, goats, sheep and antelope.

◀ *Zebras have startling patterns of black-and-white stripes. They live in Africa, where they inhabit the savanna. There are three types of zebra: Grevy's, Burchell's and the Mountain zebra.*

Elephants, rhinos and hippos

🐾 **The three kinds of elephant** are the largest land animals in the world. A large African elephant male stands more than 3 m tall, has a head and body nearly 7 m long and weighs over 5 tonnes.

🐾 **The elephant's trunk**, which is really its very long nose and upper lip, is like a multipurpose fifth limb. It can grasp and pull leaves and similar food into its mouth for chewing. The trunk sucks up water and squirts it into the mouth when the elephant drinks.

🐾 **Rhinoceroses are massive**, hoofed creatures with extremely thick skin, bulky, strong bodies and at least one horn on the nose. Tapirs resemble pigs, and have changed little in the last 25 million years.

🐾 **The largest of all rhinos**, the white rhino, reaches a length of 4.2 m, with a shoulder height of 1.9 m and a weight of 3.5 tonnes. The 'white' of its name does not refer to the beast's colour, which is grey, but means 'wide' from the rhino's broad snout.

🐾 **Black rhinos**, which are actually grey-brown, range widely across Africa. The black rhino's long, flexible upper lip can grasp leaves and shoots as it browses.

🐾 **There are only four species of tapir**: South American tapir, Mountain tapir, Baird's tapir and Malayan tapir. They have slender pig-like bodies and long snouts. Their sense of smell is excellent and they also have good hearing.

> **DID YOU KNOW?**
> A male hippo can grow to 4 m in length and can weigh well over 3 tonnes.

⚙ **Hippopotamuses** spend most of their time under, or near, water and it is now believed that they are more closely related to whales than any other of the world's hoofed mammals.

⚙ **Hippos lie in water** with just their nostrils, eyes and ears visible at the surface. Each hippo herd occupies a stretch, or territory, of river. Male hippos sometimes fight each other for territory or for females at breeding time. They can inflict fatal wounds on one another, using their enormous canine teeth.

⚙ **Hippos come out of water at night** and graze on the shore of the river. Their diet is mostly grass, although they have been known to eat small animals or nibble at other plants.

◄► *The African elephant (on the left) is the largest of the three elephant species. The Asian elephant (on the right) has smaller ears than its close relative, and the tusks are either short, or (in females) absent altogether.*

Dogs and bears

- **All dogs,** whether they are domestic or wild, are members of the mammal group, canids. There are 36 species of canids, including wolves, foxes, coyotes and jackals.

- **Wild dogs inhabit** almost all regions of the world, except the African island of Madagascar, and New Zealand. Many species of wild dog are in danger of extinction because they are hunted, or their habitats are being destroyed.

- **Coyotes are very fast runners** and can reach speeds of 65 km/h when chasing rabbits. These wolf-like wild dogs live in North and Central America, and at night their howling can be heard across mountains and plains.

- **A well-known member of the dog family,** the red fox is found all over Europe, Asia, America and Australia. Like other foxes, red foxes dig burrows below ground where they can protect their cubs.

- **There are eight species of bear.** They tend to be very large, strong and aggressive mammals. While bears have an excellent sense of hearing, their eyesight and sense of smell are poor. Most bears have thick brown, black or white coats and strong paws that are equipped with dagger-like claws.

◀ *African wild dogs are extremely social animals that live in packs of 30 or more.*

▲ *Female polar bears may go without eating for up to eight months, surviving only on their body fat, while over-wintering and feeding their newborn young.*

⚙ **Bears generally live** in woodlands and forests. They inhabit areas of Europe, Asia and North America, and are found in smaller numbers in South America and parts of Africa.

⚙ **Bears that live** in cool or cold climates sleep, or become dormant, for much of the winter in a specially prepared den to conserve energy. They survive on stores of body fat, but their body temperatures do not drop. Cubs are often born at this time.

⚙ **The yellow-white fur** of the polar bear blends with the snow and ice of its Arctic home, allowing it to creep up on its prey of seals. Polar bears also hunt fish and swim well; they are the only species of bear that exists almost entirely on a diet of meat.

Cats

- **Cats belong to a group** of mammals called felidae. Big cats are the most fearsome hunters in the animal world. They stalk in silence, pounce, and slaughter their victims using razor-sharp teeth and claws. Like the smaller cats, they are carnivores with keen senses, quick reactions and great agility.

- **Most cats are loners** and inhabit a territory, which they defend against intruders. Youngsters normally stay with their mothers until they are between one and three years old.

> **DID YOU KNOW?**
> An adult male lion can eat up to 30 kg of meat in one go, and will not need to eat again for several days.

▼ Lions usually live in prides of four to six adults and their cubs.

⚙️ **All cats have rough tongues** – a scratchy surface is ideal for scraping meat off bones. Cats can turn their tongues into a scoop shape, which enables them to lap up large quantities of water.

⚙️ **The tiger** is not only the biggest of the cats, it is also one of the largest carnivores living on land. Siberian tigers are the largest of the five surviving varieties of tiger, and may weigh as much as 350 kg and measure up to 3 m in length. A tiger's stripes help to camouflage it as it hides in tall grass and thick vegetation.

⚙️ **Cheetahs are the world's fastest** land animals. They live in the grasslands and deserts of Africa, the Middle East and western Asia. Although a female may have between four and six cubs in each litter, only one in 20 cubs survives to adulthood.

⚙️ **Pumas inhabit** a wide range of habitats, from the southern tip of South America all the way northward to Alaska. They are often regarded as the most graceful species of big cat.

⚙️ **Of all the big cats, jaguars** are the most water-loving. They live in swampy areas in Central America and in the Amazon basin.

⚙️ **Leopards are probably the most common** of all big cats. They hunt at night and will hunt and eat almost anything that comes along, including dung beetles.

⚙️ **There are around 37 species of cat** in the world, and 300 breeds of domestic (pet) cat. Most of the big cats are in danger of extinction.

Bats

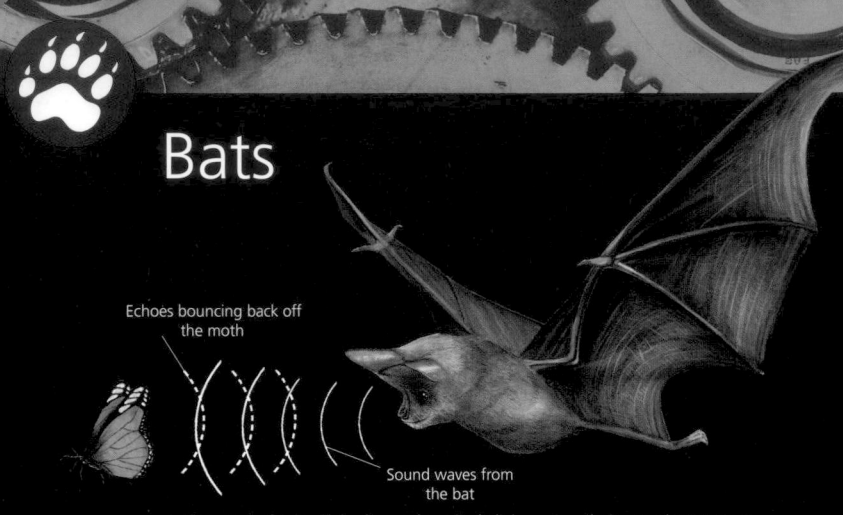

Echoes bouncing back off the moth

Sound waves from the bat

▲ *Bats make high–pitched sounds, called clicks, using their mouths or noses. The sound hits an insect and bounces back to the bat's ears. The reflected sound gives the bat information about the location and size of the insect.*

⚙ **Few people see bats** because they usually fly at night, often in dense forest or woodland habitats. Yet of all the species of mammal, about one in five is a bat. They are found in all but the coldest places on Earth. Most bats are small and feed on other flying creatures, such as moths.

⚙ **Bats are divided** into two main groups. The largest group, the microchiropterans, are night-flyers and use echolocation to find their prey.

⚙ **Bats have hook-like leg claws** with which they grip branches or rock ledges when they roost. They usually roost in groups for warmth and safety. Each bat wraps its wings around its body for extra protection and to preserve its body heat.

⚙ **Most bats sleep** during the day in sheltered places, such as tree holes or caves. A few sleep out in the open, on tree branches or on cliff faces. They rely on keeping still or camouflage for safety from predators.

- **Bats' wings** are formed from special layers of skin that make up a membrane, called a patagium, which extends beyond their limbs.

- **Fruit bats**, which belong to the megachiropteran group of bats, have long snouts and their faces resemble dogs or foxes – giving them the common name of flying fox. Most types roost in trees by day and flap their wings to keep cool.

- **Many tropical nectar- and pollen-eating bats** are important pollinators of plants, including some trees. They transfer the pollen from one plant to another as they feed inside the trees.

- **Mexican free-tailed bats** form the largest colonies of any bat (and of almost any animal). As many as 10 million may cluster together in a single cave.

- **There are more than 130 types** of fruit bat across Africa, Asia and Australia. The body of the Wallace's fruit bat is about 20 cm long and it has a wingspan of 40–45 cm.

- **Microchiropteran bats** have large ears and small eyes. They often have a strangely shaped nose, called a nose leaf, which plays a vital role in the use of echolocation.

▶ *The vampire bat feeds on blood. At night it seeks a victim and crawls up its leg onto its body. The bat uses its sharp teeth to shave away a small area of flesh and uses its tongue to lap up the blood that oozes from the wound.*

Primates

🔧 **Apes are close cousins** of monkeys and our closest living relatives. They have large heads and brains, relative to body size, forward-facing eyes, front limbs that are longer than the hind limbs and no tail.

🔧 **Apes are divided into two groups**: great apes (gorillas, chimps and orang-utans) and lesser apes (gibbons).

🔧 **Like other apes, chimps** eat a largely vegetarian diet, but they also eat termites, ants and caterpillars. Groups of males sometimes band together to hunt for other animals, such as small deer or birds.

🔧 **Gibbons have the longest arms** relative to body size, of all primates and can hang by just one arm. They are more closely related to orang-utans than to chimps and gorillas.

🔧 **Busy, active, inquisitive creatures**, monkeys live in groups, leap about in trees and make various whooping and screeching noises. Most kinds of monkey live in social groups, often led by one dominant and powerful male. Monkeys are intelligent, quick learners with good memories.

◀ *Dusky titi monkeys eat grubs, fruits and other plant matter. They live in the Amazon Basin region of South America.*

▶ High up in the forest canopy, black–handed spider monkeys hang by a hand, foot or tail and swing at speed between branches.

⚙ **Monkeys are divided into two groups**: Old World and New World. Old World monkeys (from Africa and Asia) are more closely related to apes and usually have flatter faces. New World monkeys (from the Americas) have long, grasping tails and longer muzzles.

⚙ **Monkeys normally move** using four limbs, but they can sit on their rumps, or even walk on two feet. This frees their front limbs for picking food, grooming and holding their young.

⚙ **Lemurs, lorises and aye-ayes** are more primitive than monkeys and apes and are placed in their own group, the prosimians. These mammals have snouts and a highly developed sense of smell.

⚙ **All lemurs live** on the island of Madagascar where they evolved in isolation, separated from the African mainland by the 300-km wide Mozambique Channel. Lemurs were able to evolve into their many species on Madagascar mainly because they had no competition from monkeys or other primates.

Marine mammals

- **Seals, sea lions and walruses** all belong to a mammalian family called pinnipeds. Their bodies are shaped like bullets and perfectly suited to movement in water.

- **These mammals are covered** in fine, waterproof hair, and have thick layers of blubber, or fat. Blubber keeps them warm and acts as an energy store for times when food is scarce.

▲ *Common, or harbour, seals are the most widespread and numerous of all seals.*

- **Although pinnipeds** spend much of their lives in water, they stay on land during mating and breeding times. The females return to the sea, and come back to land when it is time for them to give birth, between eight and 15 months later.

- **The walrus** is the largest member of the pinniped family. It lives along Arctic coasts and swims with its flipper-like limbs. The tusks of the walrus are very long canines and can be up to 1 m in length.

- **When a seal dives deep**, its heartbeat slows from 55 to 120 beats a minute to just four to 15 beats a minute. By breathing more slowly, the seal needs less oxygen, and can stay longer underwater.

1 The sperm whale surfaces and breathes in and out powerfully several times

2 It then straightens out its body and may disappear beneath the surface

3 The whale then reappears and begins to arch its back

DID YOU KNOW?
The world's largest mammal herd consists of up to 1.5 million northern fur seals, which breed on two islands in the Pacific.

🔹 **Whales, dolphins and porpoises** all belong to the family of mammals called cetacea, and they are known as cetaceans. They may look very different from mammals that live on land, but they all have mammalian features, such as breathing air, giving birth, and feeding their young with milk.

🔹 **Some whales communicate** with a range of sounds that humans cannot hear, and male humpbacks sing elaborate 'songs' lasting 20 minutes or so, perhaps to woo females.

🔹 **Most dolphins live** in the oceans or seas but some are adapted to life in freshwater. These river dolphins are shy and little is known about them.

🔹 **Some whales and dolphins** can find and catch their prey using echolocation. They send out sounds, and use the echoes to work out where the prey is.

🔹 **Killer whales**, or orcas, are big deep-sea predators. They are actually a type of dolphin and can reach 9 m in length.

▼ *The sperm whale is one of the greatest diving whales and may perform this sequence each time it dives to the cold, dark depths of the ocean.*

4 By arching its back and tipping its head downwards, the whale prepares to dive

5 Its tail is lifted out of the water as it begins to dive

6 The sperm whale dives deep into the darkness of the ocean

315

Marsupials and monotremes

▶ When they are first born, kangaroos are naked and just a few centimetres long. Straight away they have to haul themselves up through the fur on their mother's belly and into her pouch. Here the baby kangaroo grows for 6 to 8 months.

🌼 **The strangest mammals** are monotremes and marsupials. Monotremes are egg-laying mammals, of which there are only three types: the duck-billed platypus and two echidnas. Marsupials are born in a tiny, undeveloped form. There are nearly 300 species of marsupial, including kangaroos and opossums.

🌼 **Most marsupials develop** inside their mother's pouch, where they remain attached to a teat, sucking milk. Small marsupials, including some opossums, do not have pouches.

🌼 **A koala baby** spends six months inside its mother's pouch, and another six months riding on her back. Adult koalas spend up to 18 hours a day sleeping. When they are not sleeping, they are likely to be eating leaves from eucalyptus trees.

🌼 **The wombat's pouch** faces backwards, so the young are protected from flying earth when the mother is digging. Wombats are heavily built with muscular bodies that suit their burrowing way of life. They can dig tunnels that measure up to 200 m.

⚙️ **Tasmania, a small island** off the southern coast of Australia, is home to the largest marsupial carnivore: the Tasmanian devil. This nocturnal creature hunts at night and eats almost any meat, dead or alive, including insects, opossums and wallabies.

⚙️ **There are more than 60 species** of opossum and they all live in the Americas. Most opossums are the size of a domestic cat, or smaller. They can eat many types of food, including fruit, insects and eggs.

⚙️ **Duck-billed platypuses** have webbed feet and spend much of their time in water. The females lay eggs in a burrow by a river bank, and when the young hatch they lick the milk that oozes out over the fur of their mother's belly.

⚙️ **Echidnas are also known as spiny anteaters** because they are covered in spines and eat ants, termites, worms and grubs. They live in a wide range of habitats including woods, deserts, mountains, and grasslands in Australia and New Guinea.

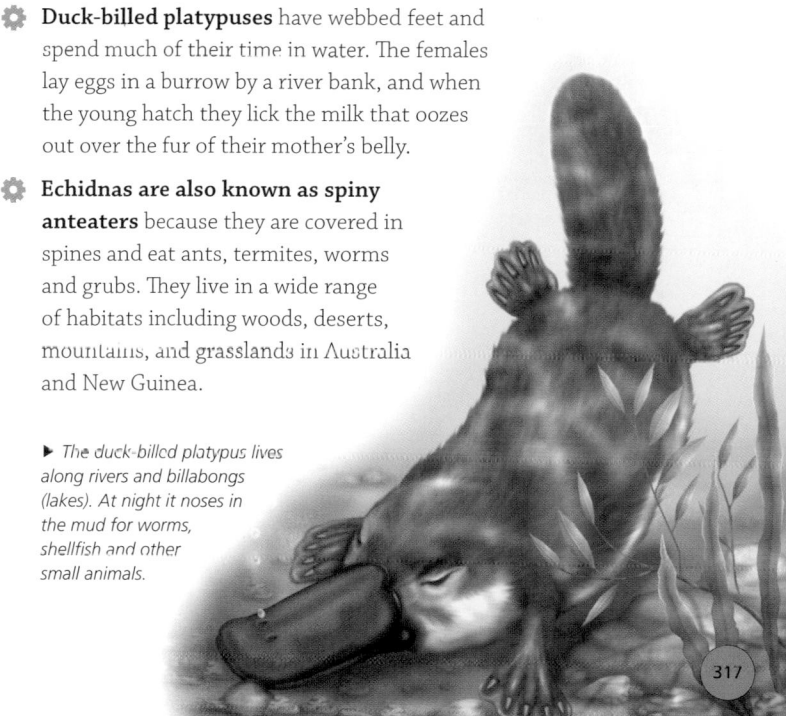

▶ *The duck-billed platypus lives along rivers and billabongs (lakes). At night it noses in the mud for worms, shellfish and other small animals.*

317

What is a bird?

- **Birds are warm-blooded vertebrates** (animals with backbones). Their feathers keep them warm and help them to fly. They walk on two back legs, while their front limbs have become wings. All birds lay eggs.

- **The 9000 bird species** are organized into about 180 families. Species in a family share characteristics, such as body shape.

- **Birds have a body temperature** of 40°C to 44°C – higher than other warm-blooded animals.

- **A bird's bones** have a honeycomb structure. The bones are so light that they account for only about 5 percent of the bird's total weight.

- **A bird's muscles** make up 30–60 percent of their total weight. The biggest are the flight and leg muscles.

- **The skeleton of a bird's wings** has a similar structure to the human arm, but the wrist bones are joined. Also, a bird has only three fingers, not five fingers like a human.

◀ *This grey heron has caught a fish, which it will swallow whole, after flipping it round so it slides head-first down the bird's throat.*

⚙ **No bird has more than four toes**, but some have three, and the ostrich has only two. Four-toed birds have different arrangements of toes: in swifts, all four point forwards; in most perching birds, three point forwards and one backwards; and in parrots, two point forwards and two backwards.

⚙ **A beak is made up** of a bird's projecting jaw bones, covered in a hard horny material.

⚙ **Most birds make sounds** using a specialized voice box called a syrinx in the neck. Calls are usually short and harsh to warn of danger. Songs are longer and more tuneful. Birds have an in-built ability to sing and mimic other birds.

⚙ **Ravens and pigeons** can work out simple counting sums. Parrots, budgerigars and mynahs can mimic human speech (though that is not the same as talking), and some parrots can name and count objects.

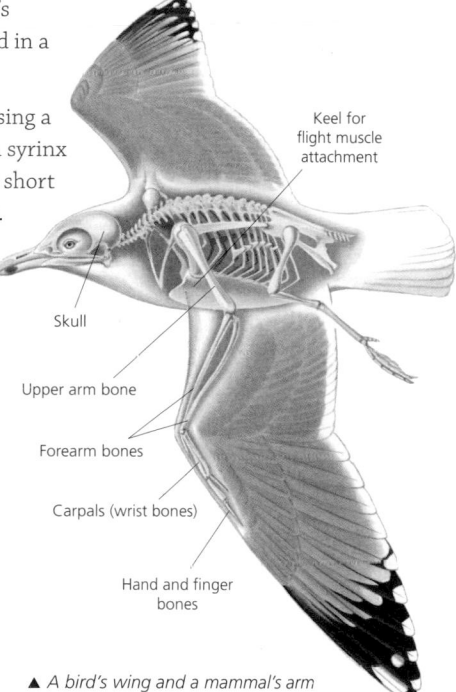

Keel for flight muscle attachment

Skull

Upper arm bone

Forearm bones

Carpals (wrist bones)

Hand and finger bones

▲ *A bird's wing and a mammal's arm evolved from the same limb. Wing bones form a system of levers worked by muscles.*

Songbirds

⚙️ **Nearly half of all living bird species** are songbirds, including sparrows, thrushes, warblers, tits, swallows and crows. Male songbirds usually sing complex songs when courting or defending their territory. Songbirds have grasping feet with four toes; the big toe points backwards.

⚙️ **A bird usually sings** to tell other birds to stay away from the territory where it lives and often feeds.

⚙️ **The blackbird** is an enthusiastic visitor to the bird-table. It is one of the earliest members of the dawn chorus, and likes to sit high on a tree or roof-top to sing its melodious, fluting song.

⚙️ **The willow warbler** is full of nervous energy, and is forever on the move, flicking its wings as it busily forages for insects. A fine singer, the warbler sings its song from trees and bushes while moving through foliage in search of food.

⚙️ **Manakins are small song birds** that live in Central and South America. There are about 57 species.

⚙️ **The chaffinch** is the commonest of Europe's finches. It has a cheerful, attractive song.

◀ *The male northern oriole, also known as the Baltimore oriole, has vibrant orange and black plumage.*

▲ *The song thrush makes its nest from dried stems lined with mud and rotting wood, bound with saliva to make a dry hard cup. The female lays 4–5 pale-blue, speckled eggs inside the nest.*

⚙ **The mistle thrush** is the largest British thrush. It sings from the treetops in stormy weather.

⚙ **In the USA** there may now be as many as 150 million house sparrows.

⚙ **Skylarks make special, fluttering flights** accompanied by a distinctive song.

⚙ **The 43 species of vireo** live in North, Central and South America. These songbirds range in size from 10–16 cm.

321

Tropical birds

▼ The tropical rainforest is home to more species of bird than any other type of habitat. Many of the birds in the canopy (the upper forest layer) are amazingly colourful. Game birds and small insect-eating species patrol the forest floor.

1	*Harpy eagle*
2	*Quetzal*
3	*Scarlet macaw*
4	*Jungle fowl*

- **Rainforests contain** a greater variety of birds than any other habitat. The weather is warm all year round, and the trees and other plants provide plenty of food and safe nesting places. The birds live at different levels in the trees, to avoid competing for the same resources.

- **Parrots are** among the most lively, inquisitive and intelligent of all birds. A typical parrot has colourful feathers, a large head, big eyes and a strong, hooked beak to crush even the hardest seeds.

- **There are about 350 species** in the parrot group, including birds such as macaws, budgerigars, lories and cockatoos. They live in Central and South America, Africa, southern Asia and Australasia.

- **The pattern of feathers** on each side of the red-and-green macaw's face is unique – no two birds look identical.

- **Cockatoos have a distinctive crest** of feathers on their head, which they raise when they are alarmed or excited.

- **The colourful, long-tailed quetzal** lives in Central America. It was sacred to the ancient Maya and Aztec civilizations, and it is the national bird of Guatemala.

- **The scarlet macaw** is one of the largest parrots in the world. It moves in flocks of 20 or so that screech loudly as they fly from tree to tree feeding on fruit and leaves.

- **Like the other 41 species** in the bird of paradise group, the king bird of paradise lives mainly in rainforest. During his mating display the male holds out his wings and vibrates them like a fast-shaking fan.

Waterbirds

🌼 **A wide variety of birds live** in wetland habitats, from herons, storks and pelicans to grebes, kingfishers and ducks. There is plenty of food in the water, and the reedbeds and riverbanks provide safe nesting places.

🌼 **Like most herons**, the grey heron feeds on fish and frogs, which it catches with swift stabs of its beak.

🌼 **The greater flamingo** lives in huge flocks around lakes and deltas in Europe, Asia, parts of Africa, the Caribbean and Central America.

🌼 **Kingfishers make their nests** in tunnels along riverbanks. Using their strong beaks, a male and female pair excavate a tunnel up to 60 cm long, and then make a nesting chamber at the end.

🌼 **There are more than 100 duck species**, living all over the world, except in Antarctica.

🌼 **Torrent ducks live** by fast-flowing streams in South America's Andes Mountains. When young ducklings hatch from their eggs, they leap straight into the swirling waters.

▲ The long legs of a flamingo enable it to wade into salty water without damaging its plumage. Flamingos use their feet to stir up mud so that they can feed on bottom-dwelling animals.

Most swans are white, but Australian black swans are not. Because of their unusual colour, they have been taken to lakes and ponds around the world as a dark, contrasting addition to the local white swans.

Many birds hunt for food in the oceans but rest and breed along the shore. Seabirds have waterproofed feathers, webbed feet and sharp bills to catch fish. Nesting in colonies on cliffs keeps the young birds safe from predators.

The auk family includes 22 species of diving birds, including auks, guillemots, puffins and razorbills. They live in and around the North Pacific, Atlantic and Arctic Oceans.

The gannet makes an amazing dive from a height of up to 30 m above the sea to catch fish. This seabird spots its prey as it soars above the ocean. Then with wings swept back and neck and beak held straight out in front, the gannet plunges like a dive-bomber.

◄ Puffins nest in burrows. While many other birds jostle for space on high cliff ledges, puffins dig a burrow on the clifftop. Here, they lay a single egg. Both parents feed the chick for the first six weeks.

Birds of prey

- **Some of the largest** and fiercest birds are raptors, or birds of prey. They have powerful toes with sharp claws called talons to seize prey, and a pointed, hooked beak to tear off lumps of flesh. Most birds of prey have large eyes and hunt by sight.

▲ Kestrels feed on small mammals (especially voles), beetles, worms and small birds. They have extraordinary eyesight and can spot a beetle 50 m away.

- **One of the most powerful** of all birds, Steller's sea eagle has a wingspan of 2.4 m and a massive beak to rip the flesh from fish, dead seals and beached whales.

- **Eleonora's falcon** specializes in hunting small birds. It breeds unusually late in the summer, in colonies on rocky islands in the Mediterranean Sea.

- **The sparrowhawk preys** mostly on other birds, ranging in size from tits to pheasants.

- **The jackal buzzard** hunts mainly in mountainous country. It can be seen hovering on air currents, searching for small mammals, birds and snakes to eat.

- **The Egyptian vulture** steals birds' eggs. It cracks the eggs by dropping them on the ground or by throwing stones at them.

🌼 **Bald eagles eat carrion** (dead animals) and prey such as small birds and fish. They steal meals from other birds of prey and fight among themselves over food.

🌼 **The 150 or so species of owl** are found in most parts of the world, with the exception of the far north, New Zealand and Antarctica. About 80 species of owl hunt mostly at night.

🌼 **An owl's eyes are large** and forward-facing to enable it to judge distances accurately when flying and hunting prey.

🌼 **Huge eyes** give the owl good night vision, but its hearing is even better – four times more sensitive than the ears of a cat.

▶ The Philippine eagle has a wingspan of more than 2 m and is a formidable predator, catching prey such as flying lemurs in mid–flight.

Fish

⚙ **Fish are cold-blooded** vertebrates that breathe through gills, and their bodies are usually covered in scales. There are more than 21,000 species of fish.

⚙ **Freshwater fish live** in freshwater (lakes and rivers), while marine fish live in the salty water of the seas and oceans.

⚙ **Nearly 75 percent** of all fish live in the seas and oceans. The biggest and fastest fish, such as swordfish, live near the ocean surface, far from land.

⚙ **Speedy fish**, such as marlin, tuna and wahoo, have long, slim bodies that narrow to a point. Thrust (the force to move forwards) comes from the tail, which is pulled from side to side by huge blocks of muscles along either side of the body.

⚙ **Muscles make up** approximately 70 percent of a fish's weight. A fish uses its fins for steering – the tail fin, for example, acts as a rudder.

⚙ **Most fish have several fins** that help them to swim and cut through the water. On the back are the dorsal fins. Pectoral fins are on the lower sides near the front, and pelvic fins on the lower sides near the tail. The anal fin is on the underside just in front of the tail. The tail itself is called the caudal fin.

◀ *Measuring the top speed of big, fast ocean fish is very difficult. But the sailfish can probably reach speeds of about 100 km/h.*

🌼 **Not all fish are the same shape**, and their shape often determines how they move. Flatfish have flat bodies, shaped for lying on the seabed rather than swimming. Eels are long and thin and swim mainly by wriggling – just like a snake – rather than using fins, and by reversing the wriggle they can swim backwards.

🌼 **Gills are like 'inside-out' lungs**. They have the same branching, frilly structure, but they are outside the body, in contact with the water. In fish, water flows in through the fish's mouth and over the feathery, thin-walled, blood-filled gills. Oxygen passes from the water to the blood that flows through the gills enabling the fish to 'breathe'. Stripped of oxygen, the water then flows out through the gill slits on either side at the rear of the fish's head.

▶ *The conger eel grows to 3 m long. Eels have no separate tail fin but one, long 'wraparound' fin along the back, rear-end and underside. They are not strong swimmers and spend much time hiding in cracks and caves.*

329

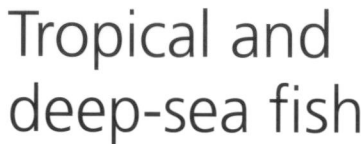

Tropical and deep-sea fish

- **Coral reefs are found in warm** and shallow waters, usually within 30° north and south of the Equator. They are home to a great variety of brightly coloured fish and many other marine animals such as molluscs, crustaceans, anenomes and sponges.

- **The fine, silvery sand** of coral reefs is actually from fish droppings. It comes from the crunched-up food of fish, such as parrotfish, which scrape off and swallow bits of rocky coral.

- **Clownfish live** a sheltered life among the tentacles of sea anemones. The anemone protects the fish from predators, and the fish returns the favour by keeping its host's tentacles clean.

- **Gobies from tropical waters** tend to have brighter colours than those in colder waters so that they can be noticed among the corals.

- **Cleaner wrasse are little fish** that are 'paid' for cleaning. The wrasse nibble parasites from around the eyes and gills of larger fish such as groupers and moray eels.

⚙ **On the bottom of the deep sea** there is almost no light at all. Some creatures here have huge eyes to peer in the gloom. Others find food mainly by smell and touch, and also by sensing weak pulses of electricity given off in the water by the active muscles of their swimming prey.

⚙ **Prey is scarce** in the vast blackness of the deep ocean, so fish like the gulper have large mouths to grab whatever they can. This eel is a relative giant of the depths at 60 cm long.

⚙ **About 1500 different deep-sea fish** give off light. As well as tempting prey, light also confuses predators.

⚙ **The lantern fish's whole body glows**, while the dragonfish has light organs dotted along its sides and belly. The belly of the cookiecutter shark gives off a ghostly glow.

⚙ **The tripod fish** is one of the deepest-dwelling of all fish, found more than 6000 m below the surface. It 'walks' along the soft mud of the seabed on the long spines of its two lower side fins (pelvics) and lower tail. It probably eats small shrimp and similar shellfish.

▼ Tropical coral reefs are the habitat of an amazing range of marine plants and creatures.

DID YOU KNOW?

As well as glowing fish in the deep sea, there are also glowing sea urchins, starfish, worms, octopuses and many other types of glowing creature.

Sharks and rays

⚙ **Sharks and rays belong** to the cartilaginous group of fish. There are more than 400 species in oceans across the world. Some sharks, like the bull shark, can also survive in freshwater.

⚙ **Most sharks have torpedo-shaped bodies**, which make them streamlined and so very good swimmers. They also have large tail fins that give them most of the power for swimming.

⚙ **A shark's skin** is not covered with smooth scales like bony fish. Instead, a shark's skin is covered with tiny, tooth-like structures called dermal denticles that give the skin a sandpaper-like quality.

⚙ **Sharks are the primary predators**, or hunters, of the ocean. They have special abilities to locate prey. The great white shark, the most feared predator of all, can smell a single drop of blood in 100 litres of water.

⚙ **Most sharks have a very good sense of smell.** It is believed that almost a third of the shark's brain is devoted to detecting smell.

▼ A shark has a skeleton, including a skull, ribs and spinal column (backbone) like other fish. This skeleton is made not of bone, but from cartilage or 'gristle', which is strong, light and slightly bendy.

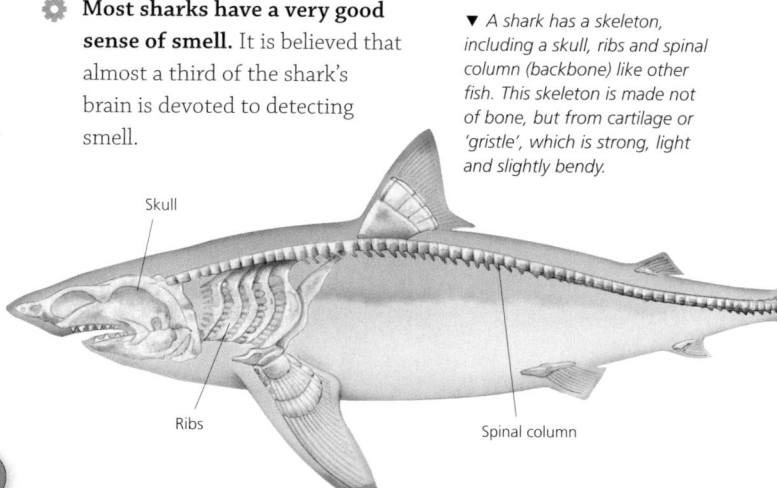

Skull

Ribs

Spinal column

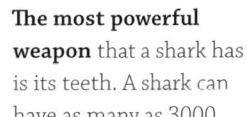

▶ Rays, like the stingray, swim by rippling their side 'wings', which are really their fleshy pectoral fins.

🌸 **The most powerful weapon** that a shark has is its teeth. A shark can have as many as 3000 teeth set in three rows. The fish relies on the first row of teeth to strike the initial blow, which often injures or kills the prey.

🌸 **Sharks do not have** external ear flaps. Instead, their ears are on the insides of their head, on either side of the brain case. Each ear leads to a small sensory pore on the skin of the shark's head. It is believed that sharks can hear over a distance of 250 m.

🌸 **A pair of fluid-filled canals** runs down either side of the shark's body, from its head to its tail. This is the lateral line and helps the fish sense minute vibrations in the water.

🌸 **The world's biggest** predatory, or hunting, fish is the great white shark. It is certainly large – at 6 m in length and weighing more than 1 tonne. They have a fearsome reputation and have been known to attack humans.

🌸 **Whale sharks** are the largest fish in the world. The average length is about 14 m. However, some are said to have grown to over 18 m in length.

DID YOU KNOW?

The smallest shark is the dwarf lanternshark, at just 20 cm long. It is so small that it could lie curled up in your hand.

What is a reptile?

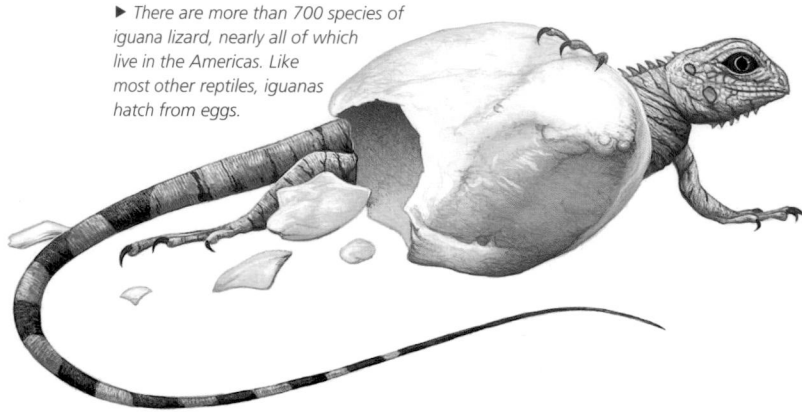

▶ There are more than 700 species of iguana lizard, nearly all of which live in the Americas. Like most other reptiles, iguanas hatch from eggs.

⚙ **Reptiles include lizards**, crocodilians, chelonians, tuataras and snakes. A reptile's skin looks slimy, but it is in fact quite dry. It retains moisture so well that reptiles are a dominant animal group in deserts.

⚙ **Reptile skin consists of scales** made of keratin – the same sort of material that forms human fingernails and toenails.

⚙ **A reptile's scales** may be rough or smooth, and they can form very thick, horny plates called scutes. In some species, the skin contains bony plates called osteoderms.

⚙ **All reptiles shed** their outer skin to replace their scales. Snakes shed their skin in one piece. In lizards, crocodilians, chelonians and tuataras, the old skin comes away in flakes or chunks.

⚙ **Unlike the limbs of mammals** and birds, a reptile's legs support its body from the side. This gives it a sprawling gait when it moves.

- **Lizards, snakes and chelonians** have a depression in the roof of the mouth called the Jacobson's organ, which allows them to 'taste' the air.

- **Geckos and iguanas** cannot blink. Instead of having movable eyelids, they have a fixed transparent scale over each eye called a brille.

- **Many lizards**, including iguanas, can see in colour. This is important, because it enables them to distinguish between the sexes. Iguanas communicate using their colourful crests, head ornaments and throat fans.

- **You can usually tell** whether a reptile is active by day or night from its eyes. If the pupil is a slit that closes almost completely in sunlight, the animal is nocturnal. A wide, round pupil means a reptile is active by day.

- **The tuatara is the only survivor** of a group of animals that became extinct 60 million years ago. No one knows why the tuatara survived and the others died out. The two tuatara species live on about 30 offshore islands in New Zealand.

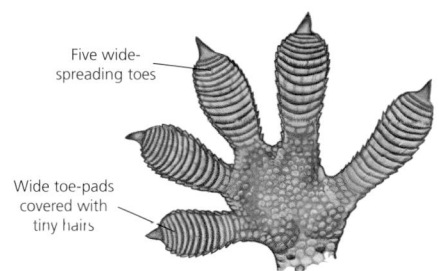

▶ Each gecko foot has about 500,000 tiny hairs, and each hair tip has thousands of microscopic 'stickers', creating a powerful adhesive. This enables the gecko to walk on any surface, including vertical ones.

Five wide-spreading toes

Wide toe-pads covered with tiny hairs

Tortoises and turtles

- **Land-living chelonians** are known as tortoises. All chelonians have four limbs, a shell, and a horny, toothless beak. There are two parts to the shell: the shield on the reptile's back is known as a carapace, while the flat belly section is called the plastron. Tortoises have a high, domed shell that is difficult for predators to bite or crush.

- **The shell is made up of two layers**: an inner layer of bone covered by an outer layer of horny plates called scutes, which are made of keratin.

- **A chelonian's ribs** are fused to its shell, so the ribs cannot move to draw air into the lungs. Instead, special muscles at the tops of the legs pump air into the lungs so that the reptile can breathe.

- **Most tortoises are primarily herbivorous**, feeding on plant leaves and fruits, but they will also eat tiny animals such as caterpillars.

- **The Galapagos giant tortoise**, the world's largest tortoise, grows to 1.2 m in length. The size and shell shape of this tortoise vary according to which of the individual Galapagos islands the animal originates from.

◀ *The shell of a baby sea turtle is fairly soft and provides little protection from predators.*

High, rounded upper shell

Clawed feet

Sturdy, club-shaped legs

▲ *Tortoises are placid and very slow moving, with an average walking speed of 0.2–0.5 km/h.*

⚙ **In many chelonian species**, the scutes on the shell have 'growth rings' that show how much they have grown each year. Counting the growth rings can help to determine the chelonian's age.

⚙ **Sometimes called terrapins**, freshwater turtles have webbed, clawed feet that make them well-equipped for both moving on land and swimming in water.

⚙ **Some freshwater turtles** have soft, flexible shells that enable them to squeeze under rocks or into nooks and crannies to evade predators.

⚙ **Sea turtles feed**, mate, and even sleep at sea. Females come ashore only once each year to lay their eggs. They use their flippers to drag themselves up the beach so that they can deposit their eggs in the sand.

⚙ **The leatherback sea turtle** is the world's heaviest chelonian. Adults typically weigh at least 450 kg. One leatherback washed up on a beach in Wales, UK, in 1988 weighed 961 kg.

Crocodilians

- **Crocodilians are large reptiles** with powerful bodies, thick skin and snapping jaws. These semi-aquatic predators inhabit lakes, rivers and lagoons. Some species will journey out to sea. This reptile group includes crocodiles, alligators, caimans and gharials.

- **Most crocodiles** have eyes and nostrils at the top of their heads, which enable them to drift along just under the surface of the water unnoticed.

- **Crocodilians can stay underwater** for many minutes or even hours. They sometimes store prey underwater so that the victim's body starts to rot and is easier to dismember.

- **A Nile crocodile** can shut its jaws with a devastating force of up to 2000 kg per sq cm. However, the muscles used to open the crocodile's mouth are weak. Incredibly, its jaws can apparently be held shut with a thick rubber band.

- **On muddy river banks**, crocodiles usually slither along on their belly, with their legs splayed out to the side. On dry land, they can walk at 2–4 km/h on all fours, with their body raised off the ground. They can even make short gallops with their tail held up in the air, reaching speeds of up to 18 km/h.

- **The saltwater, or estuarine, crocodile** ranges through the tropical regions of Asia and the Pacific. At up to 7 m long and with a maximum recorded weight of more than 1 tonne long, it is the largest reptile in the world.

- **Crocodilians show** an unusually high level of parental care compared to most reptiles. A mother crocodile will carry her newly hatched babies to safety in her open mouth.

⚙ **Alligators have broader snouts** than crocodiles. When the mouth is shut, the fourth tooth on the lower jaw is visible in a crocodile, but not in an alligator.

⚙ **Crocodilians communicate** by slapping their heads on the water's surface or snapping their jaws together. Male American alligators roar loudly during the breeding season.

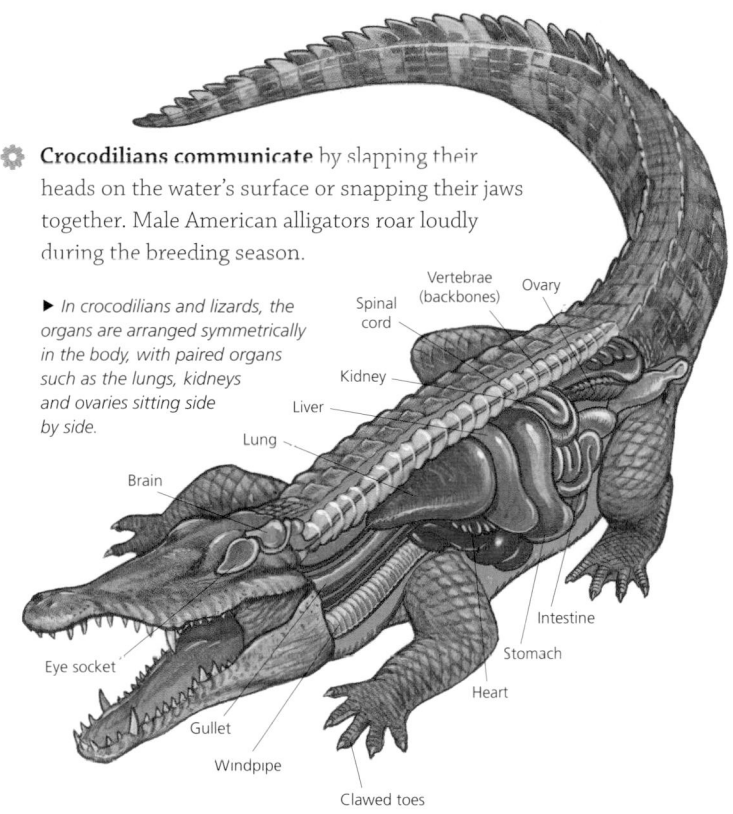

▶ In crocodilians and lizards, the organs are arranged symmetrically in the body, with paired organs such as the lungs, kidneys and ovaries sitting side by side.

Vertebrae (backbones)

Ovary

Spinal cord

Kidney

Liver

Lung

Brain

Eye socket

Gullet

Windpipe

Clawed toes

Intestine

Stomach

Heart

339

Snakes

⚙ **Snakes are** about 3000 species of legless reptile with long, slender, muscular bodies. Despite having no legs or claws, snakes are superb hunters that can move swiftly and tackle every type of terrain. They are expert climbers and many species can swim well.

⚙ **A snake moves** by gripping the ground or a branch with its scaly skin and pushing itself forwards with muscles attached to its ribs.

⚙ **A snake has to swallow** its prey whole, because it has no large back teeth for crushing its victims and cannot chew. The snake's jaw bones can separate to allow it to eat huge eggs or animals that are much larger than its head. A large snake can swallow an entire pig or deer.

⚙ **Snakes are generally solitary**, usually coming together only to mate. However, some snake species congregate in large numbers to hibernate in communal dens. A den of common garter snakes, for example, may contain hundreds or even thousands of individuals.

⚙ **Constrictors include boas**, pythons, anacondas, ratsnakes and kingsnakes. A constrictor kills its victims by squeezing them to death. It winds itself around the prey and gradually tightens its coils. Each time the animal breathes out, the snake applies a little more pressure, and the prey eventually suffocates.

⚙ **Boas and anacondas** are the large constrictors of South America. Boas capture their prey by lying in wait, hiding motionless under trees and waiting for victims to pass by. In common with other snakes, boas can go for weeks without eating.

Venomous snakes use modified teeth called fangs to inject venom into their prey. Venom is a cocktail of harmful chemicals that either subdues or kills the victim. Of nearly 700 species of venomous snake, only about 50 have a bite that is potentially lethal to humans.

DID YOU KNOW?

Fer-de-lance (lancehead) snakes have 60 to 80 babies, each of which can give a dangerous bite.

▶ This young tree python will gradually acquire a distinctive green colouration as it grows older.

Amphibians

⚙ **The word amphibian** comes from the Greek *amphibios*, which means 'double life'. It refers to the fact that these animals can live both on land and in water. Frogs, toads, newts, salamanders and caecilians are all amphibians.

⚙ **Amphibians have bare skin**, with no hairs or scales. They possess poison glands in their skin. These produce secretions that are distasteful or even toxic (poisonous) to predators.

⚙ **Oxygen can pass easily through** the skin, which is important because most adult amphibians breathe through their skin as well as through their lungs.

1 Frog spawn floats on top of freshwater

2 Tadpoles hatch from the eggs

4 The froglet loses its tail and grows into an adult frog

3 Tadpoles grow legs and change into froglets

⚙ **Some salamanders** have no lungs. They can absorb oxygen only through their skin and the lining of their mouth. If the skin dries out, oxygen is no longer able to pass through it, and the salamander dies.

⚙ **Amphibian larvae** breathe through feathery external gills. Some species retain these gills into adulthood, but in most the gills are lost during metamorphosis.

◀ *Female frogs usually lay between 1000 and 20,000 eggs in a mass of jelly, in or near a pond or stream. This large cluster of eggs is called spawn. Like many amphibians, frogs go through different stages, called metamorphosis, before becoming adults.*

Toads hibernate on land during the winter

Newts swim by lashing their tails

⚙ **Frogs and toads** generally lay between 1000 and 20,000 eggs. In salamanders and newts, the number of eggs laid varies from four or five to about 5000.

⚙ **There are about 4400 species** of frog and toad. The difference between frogs and toads is not clear cut. However, most frogs live in damp places and tend to have strongly webbed feet, long back legs and smooth skin. Toads generally spend their time on dry land. They don't have webbed feet and their skin is warty and quite dry.

⚙ **Frogs are mostly smaller** and better jumpers than toads. Toads are bigger, with wartier skins that hold on to moisture better, allowing them to live on land for longer.

⚙ **Newts and salamanders** are amphibians with tails. They are not so common as frogs and toads but they can be found in tropical forests as well as lakes and forests in cooler climates.

⚙ **With patterns and colours** that enable them to hide, newts and salamanders tend to be well camouflaged. However, some species are brightly coloured, often to warn predators that they are toxic.

Insects

Insects are by far the most common type of animal. More than nine out of ten living species are insects. They flourish in nearly every part of the world, except under the sea and in the very coldest places. Insects are so successful because of their powerful exoskeletons, their ability to fly and their small size.

The segmented body of an insect is divided into three parts: head, thorax (middle section) and abdomen (rear section). All insects have six legs that are joined to the thorax. They usually have either one or two pairs of wings, also joined to the thorax.

Insects have an open circulatory system without lots of tubes for carrying blood. The heart of an insect is a simple tube that pumps greenish-yellow blood all over the body.

Insects breathe through special openings on the sides of the body known as spiracles.

Most insects walk by moving three of their six legs at a time. The front and back legs on one side and the middle leg on the other side stay put, forming a stable tripod shape. The other three legs move forwards.

A flea can leap 30 cm high, which is more than 100 times its body length. It has rubbery pads at the base of its hind legs. These are kept compressed, like coiled springs, until they are released by a trigger mechanism, catapulting the flea into the air.

◀ *Firebugs are easy to spot because of the interesting red-and-black pattern on their backs. They mostly eat seeds, but they can also attack and eat small insects.*

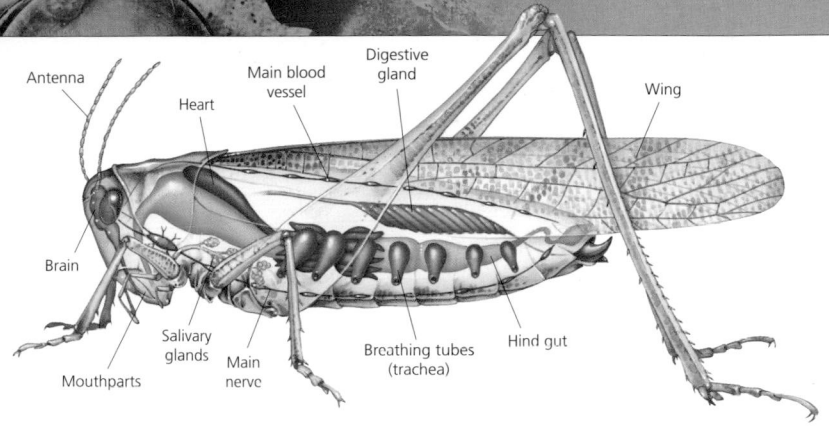

Antenna · Heart · Main blood vessel · Digestive gland · Wing · Brain · Salivary glands · Main nerve · Mouthparts · Breathing tubes (trachea) · Hind gut

▲ *A grasshopper has the body parts of a typical insect. Insects breathe through a network of tubes (trachea) that lead from small holes (spiracles) along the body.*

Most insects have evolved two pairs of wings, which help them to fly. They are membrane-like structures with veins and nerves running across them, through which blood and oxygen are circulated. The wing edge is usually thicker and sturdier than the main part of the wing. This helps the wing to slice through the air more easily during flight.

In insects, such as beetles, the front pair of wings is hard and protects the hind wings, which are more delicate. In flies, the hind wings are reduced to knob-like structures called halteres, which help the insect to balance itself in the air.

To moult, insects expand their body by swallowing air or water, or by raising their blood pressure. The exoskeleton splits, and the insect wriggles free. Moulting takes a long time, and the insect is vulnerable to attack during this period, so most insects moult in secluded places.

Ants, bees and wasps

🔧 **Ants are** among the most successful insects on Earth. There are more than 9000 different species. Ants are social insects that live in huge colonies. These colonies consist of the queen ant, female workers and male ants.

🔧 **Ants use their powerful jaws**, called mandibles, to dig holes, as well as to bite and carry food. The size of the mandibles varies between ant species.

🔧 **An ant has two stomachs**. One stomach carries the ant's own food, while the other carries food that will be shared with other ants. This secondary stomach is called the crop.

🔧 **Wasps are related** to bees and ants. They have four transparent wings, two large compound eyes and sharp cutting jaws with jagged edges. Wasps are solitary as well as social insects. Social wasps live in huge colonies, while solitary wasps live alone. There are about 17,000 species of wasp, but only about 1500 are social.

🔧 **Wasp nests** can be simple or complex. Some nests are just burrows in the ground, while others are built with mud and twigs and may contain many cells and tunnels.

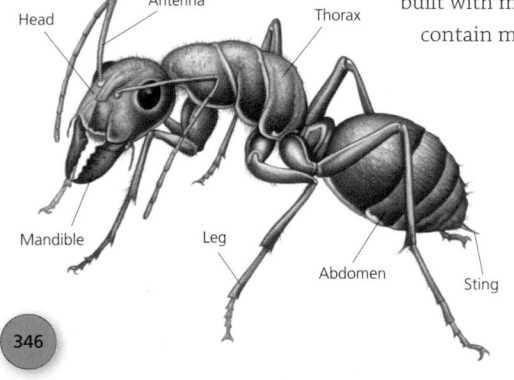

Head
Antenna
Thorax
Mandible
Leg
Abdomen
Sting

◀ *The body of an ant is divided into three distinct parts – head, thorax and abdomen. There is a sting at the end of the abdomen.*

- **Adult wasps feed** on nectar, and fruit and plant sap, while wasp larvae feed on insects.

- **Hornets are huge**, robust, social wasps, up to 30 mm long. Apart from their larger size, hornets can be distinguished from other wasps by their deeper yellow colouration.

▲ Honeybee workers crowd around their queen. The workers lick and stroke her to pick up powerful scents called pheromones, which pass on information about the queen and tell the workers how to behave.

- **There are approximately 20,000 species** of bee. Many bees live alone, but over 500 species are social and live in colonies. Bees look like wasps, but they have more hair and thicker, more robust bodies. Unlike wasps, bees have specialized organs for carrying pollen.

- **Worker bees perform** various tasks, such as cleaning the nest, producing wax and collecting food for the colony. They also guard and feed the larvae and keep them warm.

- **The honeybees** that you see on flowers are female workers. Like bumblebees, honeybees have a pollen basket, or corbiculum, on the outside of each hind leg. The pollen baskets are made up of long, stiff bristles.

▶ The sugars in ripe fruit provide wasps with a source of high-energy food.

347

Butterflies and moths

1 Female butterfly lays tiny eggs, usually under leaves

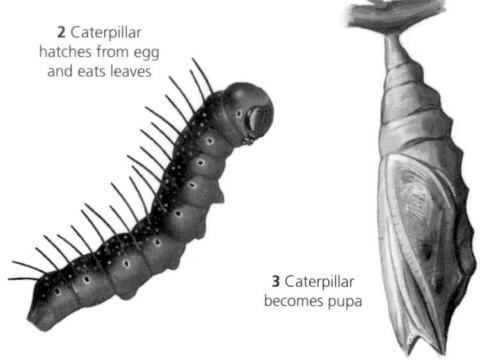

2 Caterpillar hatches from egg and eats leaves

3 Caterpillar becomes pupa

⚙ **There are more than** 165,000 species of butterfly and moth. There is no scientific distinction between butterflies and moths, but butterflies tend to be brightly coloured and fly by day, while most moths are active after sunset and have a duller colouration.

⚙ **The wings** of butterflies and moths are covered with millions of microscopic scales, which overlap each other like roof tiles.

⚙ **Butterflies and moths** pass through four different stages of development during their life-cycle. They begin life as an egg laid on a plant. The egg hatches into a larva called a caterpillar. The caterpillar then develops into a pupa or chrysalis. Finally, the pupa matures into a butterfly or moth.

⚙ **Caterpillars usually eat leaves.** They have jaws with overlapping edges and grinding plates for slicing up and chewing their food.

⚙ **In some species**, the caterpillars are armed with stinging hairs containing poisons. These hairs cause irritation or pain when touched.

◄▼ This diagram shows complete metamorphosis in a butterfly. The larvae of butterflies and moths are called caterpillars.

4 Pupa's case splits open

5 Adult butterfly emerges

⚙ **Most moth caterpillars** weave a structure around themselves for pupation. This is called a cocoon and is made of silk, leaves or soil. Most butterflies do not weave such cocoons and the pupae are naked.

⚙ **Adult butterflies and moths** only consume liquid food, such as flower nectar and liquids from rotten fruits or vines. Some butterflies and moths even feed on liquid animal waste.

⚙ **Butterflies and moths have** a long, straw-like structure called a proboscis under their head, which helps them to suck nectar and other juices.

⚙ **The painted lady butterfly** occurs in temperate regions across Asia, Europe and North America, especially around flowery meadows and fields. Its caterpillar feeds mainly on thistle plants.

⚙ **Atlas moths** are among the largest moths, with a wingspan of up to 25 cm. When they fly, these moths are often mistaken for birds.

Spiders and scorpions

◀ The wolf spider lies in wait, still and silent, ready for an insect or spider to pass by. As it's prey approaches, such as this cricket, the wolf spider pounces.

🔧 **There are about 75,500 species** of arachnid. Arachnids include a variety of creatures, including spiders, scorpions, ticks, mites, harvestmen and pseudoscorpions.

🔧 **Arachnids range** from just a few millimetres to more than 20 cm in length. Their hard, segmented body casing, or exoskeleton, protects them from enemies. The exoskeleton is made of carbohydrates and calcium.

🔧 **Arachnids have eight legs.** They also have two pairs of appendages (the chelicerae and the pedipalps) at the front of the body, which are used to grasp and hold prey.

🔧 **An arachnid's body** is divided into two parts: the cephalothorax (joint head and thorax) and the abdomen. The cephalothorax has sensory organs, mouthparts, stomach and limbs, while the abdomen contains the heart, lungs and gut.

⚙ **Arachnids do not have teeth** and jaws to chew their food, and most cannot digest solid food. This is why they suck fluids from their prey's body.

⚙ **Scorpions are easily identified** by the venomous sting at the end of their tail and their lobster-like pincers.

⚙ **Scorpions grab their prey** with their pincers, or pedipalps. Then they use their sting to inject venom, which paralyzes their victim.

⚙ **Famous for their web-spinning** activities, spiders are predatory arachnids that use fangs to inject venom into their prey. There are about 40,000 spider species.

⚙ **Most spiders have** six or eight eyes. Spider eyes are 'simple', meaning that they do not have multiple lenses like the compound eyes of many insects.

⚙ **All spiders can make** very fine threads called silk. Spiders spin their silk for many reasons. About 20,000 different kinds of spider make webs or nets to catch prey. Some spiders wrap up their living victims in silk to stop them escaping, so the spider can have its meal later.

▶ *Few animals are more deadly than the fat-tailed scorpion of north Africa. Its lethal venom, which is as toxic as a cobra's, can kill an adult human in a few hours if the victim is not treated with anti-venom.*

Crustaceans

⚙ **Crustaceans are animals** such as crabs, lobsters, prawns, shrimps, krill and barnacles, with a hard outer-body casing and several pairs of jointed legs. There are more than 40,000 species of crustacean.

⚙ **Most crabs live** in the sea, but a few species can be found in freshwater. The common shore crab can live in both salty and fresh water. It can even stay out of water for a few hours.

⚙ **Crabs have five pairs of limbs.** One pair of large, claw-like limbs, called pincers, is used for grabbing prey. The rest of the limbs are used to move around. The rear part of the crab, called the abdomen, is very small and can be tucked under its shell.

⚙ **Unlike other crustaceans**, crabs can move sideways. Owing to their peculiar body shape, it is easier for crabs to escape into their burrows this way.

◄ The ghost crab is so-called because it is white or light grey in colour. It hides in a burrow in the mud when the tide goes out.

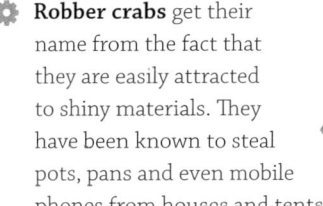

Robber crabs get their name from the fact that they are easily attracted to shiny materials. They have been known to steal pots, pans and even mobile phones from houses and tents.

▲ *The mantis shrimp uses its claws to smash crab shells and crack them open. Its movement is one of the fastest in the animal world – far too quick for us to see.*

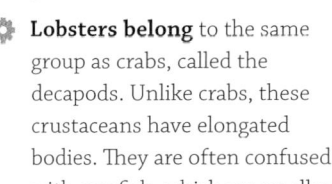

Lobsters belong to the same group as crabs, called the decapods. Unlike crabs, these crustaceans have elongated bodies. They are often confused with crayfish, which are smaller and mainly freshwater.

Most lobsters live on the ocean floor, where they can hide by slipping into the spaces between rocks. They mostly feed on the remains of dead creatures. Lobsters also eat clams, snails, worms and sea urchins.

Shrimps and prawns are very similar in appearance. Both look like miniature lobsters. A hardened shell also covers their bodies, but this shell is not as thick or hard as that of lobsters.

Shrimps have bodies that are flattened from top to bottom, while the body of a prawn is flattened from either side. Shrimps crawl around the seabed, while prawns swim using five pairs of paddle-like limbs, which are located on their abdomen.

Barnacles are small crustaceans found in oceans, seas and lakes across the world. The body of a barnacle is covered with a hard shell made up of plate-like structures.

Molluscs

⚙ **Sea snails and shellfish,** along with octopus and squid, belong to the huge animal group called the molluscs. Most smaller molluscs have a hard, outer shell to protect the soft, fleshy body inside.

⚙ **There are more than 50,000** kinds of snail, including whelks, spire shells, limpets, top shells, winkles, cowries and cone shells.

▲ *A pearl is formed when a foreign object lodges itself inside the shell of an oyster, clam or mussel. These creatures coat the object with a substance called nacre, which creates a pearl.*

⚙ **Snails belong** to the class gastropoda, which means 'belly-footed animals'. Some sea snails live along the coast, in rock pools and shallow water, while others live on the deep ocean floor. Unlike land snails, some sea snails are very colourful.

⚙ **Like sea snails, sea slugs** are molluscs and have a soft and slimy body. However, their body is not enclosed in a hard shell. Some feed on poisonous sponges and take in the poisons, which go into their own tentacles.

⚙ **Several species** of freshwater and marine mussels are found around the world. They are usually wedge-shaped or pear-shaped and are 5–15 cm long. Mussels are known as bivalve molluscs, because they have two shell parts (valves) enclosing their soft bodies. Others in this group include oysters, clams, scallops and cockles.

⚙ **Mussels breathe** with the help of their gills. The gills have hair-like filaments, called cilia, over which water passes. The cilia are also used to capture food. Mussels are filter-feeders that feed on planktonic plants and animals.

⚙ **Most mussels have** a strong and muscular tongue-shaped foot that extends from their body and sometimes remains outside their shells. They use this foot to dig.

⚙ **Squid, octopus and cuttlefish** are soft-bodied animals. They belong to a group of molluscs called cephalopods. All of them are fierce predators.

⚙ **Octopuses have soft**, sack-like bodies and large eyes that can distinguish between different colours. The most striking feature of the octopus is its eight arms, or tentacles. Each tentacle has two rows of suckers, which help the octopus not only to hold its prey, but also to climb rocks.

⚙ **All squid have ten tentacles**, or arms, two of which are long and slender. All the tentacles have suckers at the ends. They are used to grab prey. These creatures can swim very fast. They move by releasing jets of water through a fleshy tube called a siphon, located near the head.

▶ *A squid has two side fins at its rear end, which help it to change direction and prevent it from spinning like a corkscrew as it jets along.*

Simple animals

⚙ **Invertebrates are animals** that do not possess a backbone. This group makes up about 97 percent of all known animal species. They include arthropods, molluscs, worms and echinoderms.

⚙ **Cold-blooded animals**, invertebrates depend on their surroundings to maintain their body temperature.

⚙ **Myriapods are land-dwelling** arthropods with long, tube-like bodies and many legs. They live in soil and leaf litter. Myriapods include centipedes and millipedes.

⚙ **Worms are slender**, soft-bodied creatures. The three most important groups are roundworms, flatworms and segmented worms. Garden earthworms are a type of segmented worm.

⚙ **Some invertebrates are parasitic**, meaning that they live on or in the bodies of other animals, which are referred to as hosts. Ticks and leeches are external parasites. Some flatworms and roundworms, including tapeworms and flukes, are internal parasites.

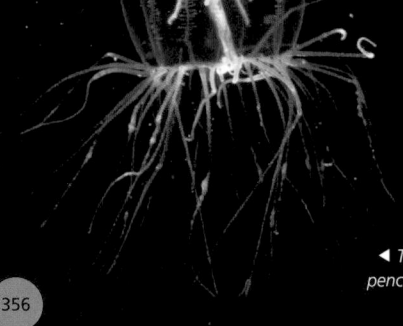

⚙ **Other invertebrates feed** on the remains of dead plants and animals. Known as 'decomposers', these animals perform a valuable role in breaking down and recycling the natural world's waste material.

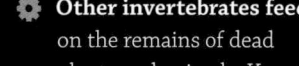
◀ *The see-through bodies of jellyfish, like this pencillate jellyfish, show their insides.*

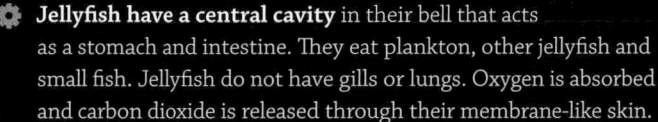

▶ *Round, or nematode, worms are among the most common animals. They inhabit virtually every type of environment. Parasitic roundworms are a major cause of human and animal disease.*

⚙ **Jellyfish, sea anemones and coral polyps** are all members of the cnidarian group, containing almost 10,000 different species. Most live in the sea and have a jelly-like body or stalk, and a ring of tentacles that sting their prey.

⚙ **Jellyfish have a central cavity** in their bell that acts as a stomach and intestine. They eat plankton, other jellyfish and small fish. Jellyfish do not have gills or lungs. Oxygen is absorbed and carbon dioxide is released through their membrane-like skin.

⚙ **All echinoderms live** in the sea. Their name means 'spiny-skinned' and they include starfish and urchins, most of which have sharp spines, sometimes poisonous. Other types of echinoderm include sea cucumbers, which are usually sausage-shaped and sort through seabed mud for food particles. Sea lilies are also echinoderms.

DID YOU KNOW?

A species of earthworm found in Asia is known to climb trees to save itself from drowning after a heavy downpour.

⚙ **Most starfish** have five arms, but some species have seven or even up to 40 arms. Starfish have developed a unique way of moving. They have hundreds of tiny, tube-like feet.

357

Glossary and Index

Glossary

abyssal plain The flat, featureless, mud-covered seabed that extends under most of the world's oceans at a depth of about 5000 m.

acceleration Any change in the velocity of an object, more specifically the rate of change of velocity.

acid A chemical solution that contains positively charged hydrogen ions. The strength of acids is measured using the pH scale, and strong acids can cause severe burns.

acoustics (1) The study of how sounds are created, transmitted and received. (2) The sound properties of a room or building.

air Earth's atmosphere – this consists of a mixture of gases (mainly nitrogen and oxygen), dust and moisture.

alkali A solution that contains negatively charged ions, often of hydrogen and oxygen. The strength of alkalis is measured using the pH scale.

alloy A stable combination of two or more metals.

alternating current (AC) Electrical current that changes direction many times per second. Mains electricity is alternating current.

angular momentum The momentum of a spinning object.

annual In botany, a flowering plant that completes its life cycle in a year or less.

atmosphere A blanket of gases surrounding a planet or moon.

atom One of the tiny particles that make up all substances; the smallest possible amount of a pure chemical element.

atomic number Each element has a different atomic number, which is the number of protons in the nucleus of its atom.

biennial In botany, a flowering plant that takes two years to complete its lifecycle.

binary code A numerical system consisting of just two digits (0 and 1) that is used by computers, which read ones and zeros as 'on' and 'off' commands for their electronic circuits.

biology The study of living things.

black hole An object with so much mass that its extremely strong gravity pulls in anything near it. Even light waves cannot escape; meaning it has disappeared from the visible Universe.

boiling point The temperature at which a liquid substance becomes a gas. The boiling point of water is 100°C.

botany The scientific study of plants.

buoyancy The ability of an object to float.

byte The basic unit of computer data, consisting of eight digits of binary code.

candela (Cd) The unit for measuring the brightness of a light source.

carbohydrates Compounds that contain carbon, hydrogen and oxygen. Carbohydrates, such as sugars and starches, are a major source of energy for animals.

carbon dioxide A gas that is found in small quantities in Earth's atmosphere, but which has a major role in the greenhouse effect.

carnivore An animal that feeds on the flesh of other animals.

catalyst A substance that speeds up a chemical reaction or enables it to occur.

cathode ray tube (CRT) A device widely used in televisions and computer monitors to produce an image on a screen.

cell In biology, a cell is the basic building block of all living organisms.

Most plant and animal bodies contain different types of cell that perform different functions.

central processing unit (CPU) The 'brain' at the heart of a computer where data is processed according to instructions from the user.

chemical formula The abbreviated expression of the number and type of atoms in one molecule of a substance. The chemical formula for water is H_2O, which indicates two hydrogen atoms bonded to one oxygen atom.

chemical reaction The process by which two or more elements or compounds interact chemically to change the bonds between atoms.

chemistry The study of the properties of substances and how they react with other substances.

chlorophyll A substance found in the green parts of plants that enables them to convert air and water into food through the process of photosynthesis.

climate The long-term pattern of weather in a particular place, usually described in terms of average temperature and annual rainfall.

clone An organism that is an exact replica of its 'parent' and has identical DNA.

compound A substance made when the atoms of two or more different elements join together to form a molecule.

condensation The process by which molecules of a gas cool sufficiently to become a liquid.

conduction The transfer of heat or electricity between objects that are in direct contact.

conductor A substance that will permit electrical energy or heat to travel through it.

conifer A non-flowering plant that produces its seeds inside cones.

continental drift The process by which the continents gradually move across the Earth's surface over millions of years.

convection The circulation of heat within a fluid.

covalent bond A bond between atoms in which electrons are shared.

crater A roughly circular depression in the Earth's surface caused either by a volcanic eruption or the impact of a meteorite or asteroid.

crust The solid outer layer of the Earth, which varies in thickness from 5–80 km.

crystal A solid substance that has its atoms arranged in a regular geometric lattice (network).

current In physics, the flow of electricity around a circuit. The rate at which current flows is measured in amps.

decibel (dB) The unit used to measure the loudness of sounds.

deciduous Describes trees that lose their leaves in winter.

delta A flat piece of land formed from mud and other sediment deposited by a river where it flows into the sea.

density The ratio of the mass of a substance to its volume.

digital Describes any type of information that has been translated into binary code, or a device that makes use of such information.

direct current (DC) Electrical current that flows in one direction only. Batteries produce direct current.

distillation A process that separates a mixture of liquids through the controlled heating and collection of vapour given off at different temperatures.

DNA (deoxyribonucleic acid) A molecule found in the cells of all living organisms, which contains the coded information (in the form of genes) as to how the organism is to grow and function.

earthquake A brief, localized and often violent shaking of the Earth's crust, which is usually caused by the sudden movement of a tectonic plate.

elasticity The degree to which an object returns to its original size and shape after being stretched or squeezed.

electricity A form of energy that will flow along wires made of a conducting substance.

electromagnet A device that only becomes magnetic when an electrical current flows through it.

electromagnetic spectrum The range of wavelengths of electromagnetic energy that travels in the form of photons.

electron Subatomic particles that orbit around the nucleus of an atom and have a negative electric charge.

electron shell One of the distinct layers in which electrons orbit the nucleus of an atom.

electronic Describes any device that makes use of electrical circuits containing transistors.

element A pure chemical substance that contains only one sort of atom. There are 92 elements that occur naturally on Earth, and scientists have created over 20 artificial ones.

energy The capacity to do work.

engine A machine that converts fuel into movement.

enzyme A molecule that speeds up chemical reactions.

epicentre The place on the Earth's surface directly above an earthquake's centre, where most damage occurs.

Equator An imaginary line running east-west around the middle of the Earth at 0° latitude.

erosion The gradual wearing away of the landscape by the action of wind, rain, ice, rivers and waves.

evaporation The process by which molecules of a liquid substance absorb enough heat to be released as atoms of vapour (gas).

evergreen Describes plants that keep their leaves throughout the year.

evolution The gradual process by which plants and animals adapt to changing environmental conditions through natural selection.

exoskeleton The tough outer casing of some invertebrates, such as insects and crustaceans, which provides both support and protection for their bodies.

fault A vertical or near vertical fracture in rock, where one block of rock is able to slide against another.

fertilization The process by which a male sex cell (e.g. sperm, pollen) and a female sex cell (e.g. egg, ovule) join together.

fluid A non-solid substance – a liquid or gas.

force A push or pull, something that causes an object to move.

freezing point The temperature at which a liquid substance becomes a solid. The freezing point of water is 0°C.

friction A force that acts to oppose the motion of two objects in contact with each other.

fuel cell A device that produces electricity by combining hydrogen and oxygen.

fundamental forces Four fundamental forces operate throughout the Universe: gravity, electromagnetic force (electricity and magnetism), and two nuclear forces that operate within atoms.

fundamental particles Sub-atomic particles that cannot be broken down into smaller components. There are three groups of fundamental particles: quarks, leptons (such as the electron) and bosons ('messenger' particles that carry forces at the sub-atomic level).

gas A state of matter in which the individual atoms or molecules are not bound to each other.

gene The basic unit of biological inheritance, consisting of a sequence of chemical code in the DNA molecule.

genetic engineering (genetic modification) Altering the DNA of an organism in a laboratory in order to produce a particular result.

germination The process by which a seed begins to grow and produces a plant seedling.

gills Breathing organs used by fish and some other water-dwelling animals to extract oxygen from water.

glaciation A severe form of widespread erosion caused by the action of glaciers upon the landscape.

glass A solid inorganic substance that lacks a regular crystalline structure.

global warming The long-term and gradual increase in the average temperature of the Earth's atmosphere and oceans.

gravity An attractive force between objects that is a basic property of matter. The more mass an object has, the greater the force of gravity it produces.

greenhouse effect The insulating effect of certain gases in the atmosphere that increase the amount of heat that is trapped near the Earth's surface.

heat A form of energy that results from the movement and vibration of atoms and molecules.

herbivore An animal that feeds exclusively on plants.

hertz (Hz) The unit for measuring the frequency of a wavelength in cycles per second.

hologram A three-dimensional photograph produced using one or more lasers.

hydrocarbon A compound that consists of hydrogen and carbon atoms.

hydrogen The element with the simplest atomic structure; an atom of hydrogen has one proton and one electron. At normal temperatures, hydrogen is a gas.

igneous rock Rock that was produced by the gradual cooling of magma from the Earth's interior.

incandescent Describes any substance that has been heated to a temperature at which it emits light.

inertia The tendency of an object to resist any change in its velocity caused by a force. Inertia is a basic property of matter.

inorganic In chemistry, describes any compound that does not contain the element carbon.

integrated circuit A thin slice of silicon that is covered with thousands of microscopically small transistors arranged in circuits.

Internet A global network that connects millions of computers around the world.

invertebrate An animal that does not have an internal skeleton with a backbone.

ion An atom that has gained or lost electrons.

ionic bond A bond between atoms in which electrons are exchanged.

iridescence Shimmering rainbow colours that appear on the surface of some substances.

isotope A form of element that has a different number of neutrons in the nucleus of its atoms than other forms of the same element.

joint A place on a skeleton or exoskeleton where two parts fit together in such a way as to permit movement.

laser A device that produces a coherent beam of light, which has a single wavelength with all the waves in the same phase (their peaks and troughs aligned).

latitude Distance north or south of the Equator measured in degrees; lines of latitude are imaginary lines that are parallel to the Equator.

lava The hot molten rock that is ejected by volcanoes.

liquid A state of matter in which the atoms or molecules are loosely bound and can vibrate and slide past each other.

liquid crystal A substance that can flow like a liquid but that has the regular arrangement of atoms found in solid crystals.

longitude Distance east or west of the Greenwich Meridian – an imaginary line that runs from pole to pole at right angles to the Equator, and which passes through Greenwich in Britain. Like latitude, longitude is measured in degrees.

magma The liquid and semi-solid rock that forms the Earth's mantle.

magnetic field The area around a magnet inside which magnetic force can be detected.

magnetism The property of some substances to attract metals such as iron and nickel.

mantle The thick layer of hot liquid and semi-solid rock that lies beneath the Earth's crust.

mass The amount of matter in an object.

metal A substance that does not crystallize when it cools from a liquid to a solid, but forms a massive structure in which electrons can move about freely. Metals are good conductors of electricity.

metamorphic rock Sedimentary rock that has been altered by the effect of the heat and pressure resulting from volcanic eruptions.

microchip A popular term for an integrated circuit.

microwaves A portion of the electromagnetic spectrum that is used in both cooking appliances and radar equipment.

mineral A non-living substance that occurs naturally in the Earth's crust. Most rock contains a variety of different minerals.

molecule Two or more atoms bonded together to form a unique substance. A water molecule, for example, consists of two hydrogen atoms bonded to one oxygen atom.

momentum The mass of an object multiplied by its velocity.

monsoon The heavy seasonal rainfall that dominates the climate of southern Asia.

nanotechnology The design and study of extremely small machines.

neutron One of the subatomic particles that form the nucleus of an atom, neutrons have a neutral electrical charge.

newton (N) The unit for measuring force. 1 N is the force required to accelerate a mass of 1 kg by 1 m per second every second.

noble gas One of the gases in the Periodic Table that are highly non-reactive and rarely form compounds with other elements.

nuclear energy Energy released by changes in the nucleus of atoms, either when a nucleus splits (fission) or two nuclei join (fusion).

nuclear power Electricity produced by harnessing nuclear energy in a reactor.

nucleus (1) The central part of an atom, which is surrounded by one or more orbiting electrons. (2) The central part of a complex living cell. Simple single-celled organisms, such as bacteria, lack a nucleus.

optical fibre Thin strands of glass that carry information in the form of pulses of laser light.

organ A structure within an animal's body, such as the heart or stomach, which performs a particular function.

organic In chemistry, describes any compound that contains the element carbon.

oxidation A chemical reaction in which oxygen combines with other substances. Burning and rusting are both examples of oxidation.

oxygen A highly reactive element that is extremely abundant on Earth where it occurs naturally as a gas in the atmosphere, as well as forming many chemical compounds with other elements. Oxygen gas is essential to almost all living things.

particle accelerator A large device that accelerates sub-atomic particles to velocities approaching the speed of light so that scientists can study what happens when these particles collide with each other.

perennial In botany, a plant that has a life cycle that lasts more than two years.

Periodic Table An arrangement of the elements that places them in ascending order of the number of protons in the atomic nucleus, and groups together elements with similar chemical properties.

pH scale A scale used to measure the comparative strength of acids and alkalis. On the pH scale, pure water is pH 7, the strongest acid is pH 1, and the strongest alkali is pH 14.

photon A particle of energy.

photosynthesis The process by which plants use the energy of sunlight to convert air and water into food in the form of sugars.

plankton Tiny plants and animals (less than 1 cm in length) that live in water and are eaten by many larger animals.

plasma A state of matter that consists of an ionized gas that will conduct electricity and is affected by magnetism.

plastic Synthetic material that is easily shaped and moulded. Most plastics are made from hydrocarbons extracted from crude oil and natural gas.

pollen Male sex cells that are produced by most plants.

pollination The process by which pollen is transferred to the female parts of a plant.

pollution The unnatural presence of any harmful or potentially harmful substance in an environment.

polymer A substance that consists of long chains of organic molecules.

predator An animal that catches and eats other animals.

pressure Force applied to a surface.

prey An animal that is caught and eaten by other animals.

primary colour Of light, one of the three basic colours (red, blue, green), which can be combined to produce all other colours.

proton One of the subatomic particles that forms the nucleus of an atom, protons have a positive electrical charge.

quantum physics The branch of sub-atomic physics that studies how electrons emit energy.

quarks The fundamental particles that make up protons, neutrons and some other rare sub-atomic particles.

radiation The transfer of energy across empty space.

radioactivity Harmful energy and sub-atomic particles produced by the decay of some atoms.

RAM (random access memory) The components in a computer that receive new data and user instructions.

reactants The substances involved in a chemical reaction.

reactor A device for converting nuclear energy into heat energy that can be used to drive machines.

reduction A chemical reaction in which a substance loses oxygen.

refraction The slight change in the direction of light waves when they pass from one transparent substance to another.

relativity The idea that distance, speed and time are not absolutes, but are relative to each other as stated in Albert Einstein's two theories of relativity.

reproduction The process by which living things create offspring.

resistance The degree to which the materials forming an electrical circuit impede the flow of current. Resistance is measured in ohms.

respiration (1) The transfer of gases between an organism and its environment, i.e. breathing. (2) The breaking down of food inside cells to release energy.

robot A machine that can perform an automated task that it has been programmed to do.

ROM (read-only memory) The components in a computer that contain data that a user can access but cannot alter.

saturated solution A solution in which no more solids will dissolve.

scalar quantities Quantities that have magnitude but no direction, such as temperature, mass and density.

sediment The tiny particles of sand and clay that are carried along by fast-flowing water and deposited when the water slows down as it enters a lake or sea.

sedimentary rock Rock that is composed from compressed layers of sediment once carried by rivers, or from wind-blown dust and sand.

seed A capsule containing a fertilized plant ovule and an initial store of food.

semiconductor A substance that can change its ability to conduct electricity.

shell (1) The hard, non-living structure that some animals produce to protect their bodies. (2) *See* electron shell.

solid A state of matter in which the atoms are locked rigidly together so that they can vibrate but not move.

solute The solids in a solution.

solution A liquid that has a solid dissolved within it.

solvent A liquid that will dissolve solids.

space-time Einstein's view of the Universe with time as the fourth dimension.

species The basic unit for the classification of living things. A species consists of all the individuals who share the same characteristics and can interbreed.

spectrum A range of wavelengths, for example, the rainbow of colours that make up white light.

spore A tiny capsule produced by non-flowering plants, such as mosses and ferns, which contains a piece of the parent that will grow into a new plant.

stalactite A column of rock hanging from the roof of an underground cavern.

stalagmite A column of rock rising from the floor of an underground cavern.

stomata Small holes in the leaves of plants that allow respiration to take place.

strata The layers of rock that compose the uppermost part of the Earth's crust. Rock strata are usually roughly horizontal to the surface, but may have become tilted or bent by earth movements.

stress A force that misshapes something.

subatomic particle One of the extremely small particles that combine to make an atom.

surfactants Substances that can remove dirt and grease from surfaces.

synthetic Artificial, man-made.

tectonic plate One of the huge plates of rock that fit together like a jigsaw puzzle to form the Earth's crust.

temperature The measurement of how hot or cold something is.

transistor An electronic device that automatically controls the flow of electricity in a circuit.

tributary A stream or river that flows into a larger river.

tropics The warmest part of the Earth's surface, extending about 22° north and south of the Equator.

tsunami A fast moving wave on the ocean surface caused by an undersea earthquake. In open water the wave may only be about 1 m high, but when it reaches shallow coastal water a tsunami can be 20 m in height.

vector An arrow diagram that shows the direction and strength of a force.

vector quantities Quantities that have both magnitude (size) and direction, such as velocity, force and acceleration.

velocity The rate at which an object moves in a particular direction.

vertebrate An animal that has an internal skeleton with a backbone and spinal cord.

visible light The small portion of the electromagnetic spectrum that the human eye is sensitive to.

voltage The potential difference between the two ends of an electrical circuit, which is measured in volts.

weight The apparent downwards force that results from gravity acting upon an object.

white light Sunlight, which can be split into its component colours by a glass prism.

work The force applied to an object multiplied by the distance the object is moved.

World Wide Web The public part of the Internet, which is accessed by a computer program known as a browser.

wormhole A theoretical link across the Universe between two black holes.

X-rays High energy light that is invisible to the human eye and can shine through some solid objects.

Index

Page numbers in **bold** refer to main subject entries; page numbers in *italics* refer to illustrations.

Acknowledgements

All artwork from the Miles Kelly Artwork Bank

The publishers would like to thank the following sources for the use of their photographs:

Front cover Laguna Design/Science Photo Library

Back cover (t) David Evison/Shutterstock.com, (c) Dreamstime.com, (b) Sascha Burkard/Shutterstock.com

Corbis 72 Wang Song/Xinhua Press

Dreamstime 75 Nolexa; 76 Sebcz, Gary718; 77 Shariffc; 92 wjphoto; 94 Taranova; 100 K.walkow; 107 Zoom-zoom; 129 Artoncanvas; 138 Dklimke; 139 Adam1975; 140 Paha_l; 148 Silverstore; 162(t) Michael Brown;169 Tamarwhite; 191Ichip

Fotolia.com 51 Canakris; 54 Olga Lyubkina; 63 Anatoliy Samara; 86 Ruta Saulyte; 111 Roman Sigaev; 147 Dole; 155 (inset, second from bottom) Andres Rodriguez; 198 photlook; 202 Markku Vitikainen; 203 Julydfg

iStockphoto.com 55 ariusz; 74 toaphoto; 154 Photobuff; 162(b) LDF; 173 Elerium

NASA 208 NASA Marshall Space Flight Center (NASA-MSFC)

Photolibrary 178 George Kelvin

Science Photo Library 14 Russell Kightley; 24 Tony McConnell; 60 US Navy; 61 Martin Bond; 66 Russell Kightley; 68 Prof. K Seddon & J Van Den Berg/Queen's University, Belfast; 80 Russell Kightley; 87 TRL ltd.; 93 GustoImages; 137 Patrick Landmann; 157 Brian Bell; 163 Andrew Brookes, National Physical Laboratory; 170 Pascal Goetgheluck; 185 Makoto Iwafuji/Eurelios; 186 Volker Steger; 187 Nasa; 194 Peter Menzel; 197 Lawrence Livermore Laboratory; 201 DEEP LIGHT PRODUCTIONS; 209 Antoine Rosset

All other photographs are from: Corel, digitalSTOCK, digitalvision, fotolia.com, John Foxx, istockphoto.com, NASA, PhotoAlto, PhotoDisc, PhotoEssentials, PhotoPro, Stockbyte

Every effort has been made to acknowledge the source and copyright holder of each picture. Miles Kelly Publishing apologizes for any unintentional errors or omissions.